Henry Jones Ford

The Rise and Growth of American Politics

A Sketch of Constitutional Development

Henry Jones Ford

The Rise and Growth of American Politics
A Sketch of Constitutional Development

ISBN/EAN: 9783337076955

Printed in Europe, USA, Canada, Australia, Japan

Cover: Foto ©Suzi / pixelio.de

More available books at **www.hansebooks.com**

THE RISE AND GROWTH OF
AMERICAN POLITICS

THE RISE AND GROWTH OF AMERICAN POLITICS

A Sketch of Constitutional Development

BY

HENRY JONES FORD

New York

THE MACMILLAN COMPANY

LONDON: MACMILLAN & CO., Ltd.

1898

Norwood Press
J. S. Cushing & Co. — Berwick & Smith
Norwood, Mass. U.S.A.

PREFACE

THE purpose of this work is to tell the story of our politics so as to explain their nature and interpret their characteristics. Consideration of questions of public policy or of party issues does not enter into the plan, and they are referred to only as they have affected the formation of political structure ; but in this respect their influence has been so continuous that the work presents a view of our political history from colonial times to the present day. The object, however, has been to give an explanation of causes rather than a narrative of events, so that the reader may understand the actual system of government under which we live.

Our politics do not become intelligible until they are viewed as an offshoot from English politics, and the growth of the variety is studied with regard to the characteristics of the stock. This is the method pursued in the present work, with results which, I hope, will show the operation of principles of order and progress.

H. J. F.

PITTSBURGH, PENN.

CONTENTS

PART I

ORIGINS OF AMERICAN POLITICS

PART II

POLITICAL DEVELOPMENT

vii

PART III

THE ORGANS OF GOVERNMENT

PART IV

TENDENCIES AND PROSPECTS OF AMERICAN POLITICS

APPENDIX

THE RISE AND GROWTH OF AMERICAN POLITICS

———•———

PART I

ORIGINS OF AMERICAN POLITICS

———•———

CHAPTER I

COLONIAL METHODS

ENGLISH colonies at the present day do not afford a parallel to the political conditions of the American colonies at the time of the outbreak of the Revolution. The imperial sovereignty is now a protectorate which does not interfere with colonial independence in domestic affairs, and party divisions in the colonies take place on issues quite distinct from those which agitate English constituencies. But before the Revolution of 1776, England exercised its jurisdiction whenever it saw fit, action being generally for the purpose of binding American trade to suit English interests. The colonies had to keep agents at Westminster to

look after their interests.   In such a capacity
Benjamin Franklin began his illustrious diplomatic career.   American politics were merged into
the general movement of English politics.   Colonists were Whigs or Tories as hotly as in England.
John Adams tells us : "In every colony divisions
have always prevailed.   In New York, Pennsylvania, Massachusetts, and all the rest, a court and
country party has always contended.   Whig and
Tory disputed sharply before the Revolution and in
every step during the Revolution." [1]

There was, however, very little community of
sentiment between the people of the various
colonies.   The facilities of travel and intercourse
which now give a national fluidity to opinion and
apply a steady corrective to local prejudice, were
then unknown.   Intense antipathies were cherished by people in one locality against those of
another.   When the colonies assumed the powers
of states, these prejudices acquired great importance.   They had to be reckoned with at almost
every step taken by the Continental Congress.
With the very beginning of federal government,
sectional antipathies infused into national politics
a rancor, some of whose bitterness still remains.
In a letter written in 1815, when sectional hatred
had reached a maddening pitch, John Adams said :
"It sprang from the little intercourse and less
knowledge which the people of the then British

[1] Adams' Works, Vol. X., p. 23.

provinces possessed of each other antecedently of the American Revolution, and instead of being dissipated by an event so honorable to them all, has been cherished and perpetuated for political party purposes."

Colonial society was a copy of English society of the same period, a little caricatured. The caste spirit was rather more pronounced, for it had more to contend with, and hence was disposed to emphasize visible distinctions. People were expected to dress according to their rank and keep their proper place. At the inn, the parlor and club-room were reserved for the gentry; the tradesman and his wife went to the tap-room or the kitchen. A man's seat in church was expected to correspond with his social position. Even in New England, whose levelling tendencies were one source of the prejudice felt against that section in other colonies, it was the practice to "dignify the congregation" in the assignment of sittings. Common people wore leather and homespun; gentlemen put flounces of lace on their linen, adorned their coats and waistcoats with gold and silver braid, wore silks and satins, even in such colors as red and blue, and crowned the ornate edifice of their attire by removing the natural thatch of their heads to give place to the crisp volutes and frizzed convexities devised by the art of the perruquier. When men could dress in such fashion, imagine to what monstrosities of elegance the ladies were pushed to maintain the superiority of their sex! Brissot de Warville, a French traveller, who visited this country soon after the Revolutionary War, was astonished at the luxurious fashions and costly dress of the ladies, and thought some gowns he saw at a party given by Cyrus Griffin, president of Congress, were scandalously indecent. Simplicity of dress did not come in until after the French Revolution.

Politics, the organic activity of society in its civic character, bore a like aristocratic stamp. As in England at the same period, the laws bore hardly on the poor and tended to perpetuate distinctions between patricians and plebeians. Poor Richard's saying, that the borrower is servant to the lender, had special point to it in the days of imprisonment for debt. The humane reforms, which in every civilized country have swept away the ancient barbarities of the penal code, were yet to be begun. The jails were sinks of filth and depravity; and the whipping-post, the stocks, and the pillory were in active employment. The suffrage was closely restricted by property qualifications, and when it came to holding office these were raised to a point at which only men of wealth were eligible. Drinking was the inevitable accompaniment of the transaction of public business of almost every kind and at election times liquor flowed in abundance. In New England, the town-meeting system produced peculiar political methods which bore the stamp of Puritan church procedure, but in most of the colonies electioneering was carried on as in England. Candidates announced themselves in flourishing addresses to electors and were expected to maintain lavish hospitality. Among the items of a bill of election expenses incurred by Washington in 1757 are one hogshead and one barrel of punch, thirty-five gallons of wine, and forty-three gallons of hard cider.

Early in the history of the colonies variations from English methods began which eventually came to be regarded as American characteristics; but Americanisms in politics, like Americanisms in speech, are apt to be Anglicisms which died out in England but survived in the new world. The American practice of requiring that representatives should be inhabitants of their districts, was an old idea of English politics. Anciently the king's writ, expressly confirmed by a statute of Parliament, required that none but resident burgesses should be elected to Parliament. The law was disregarded and became dead letter in England; transplanted to America it lived and flourished.

The early introduction of the ballot in America was likewise the fruition of ideas which in England fell upon stony ground, but which found a fair field in the new world. Among the reform projects with which the political theorists of the seventeenth century busied themselves, the ballot occupied a prominent place. A political tract, published in the time of William and Mary, refers to the use of the ballot as being then an old established custom in the borough of Limmington, Hampshire; but this was an exception which passed away, and the ballot was not established in England until the Australian system was adopted in 1872. In the colonies, however, the ballot system took root at an early period. It is prominent in the philosophic constitutions prepared for the proprietary colonies of South Carolina, West Jersey, and Pennsylvania. Theoretic considerations had probably, however, much less to do with the growth of the ballot system than the circumstances of colonial life. Before the formal introduction of the ballot anywhere, a practice had sprung up in Virginia, in the New England colonies, and perhaps elsewhere, of sending votes in writing to avoid the trouble of personal attendance at elections. This practice was suppressed in Virginia at an early date, but was methodized into a regular system throughout New England, where elections came to be known as "proxings" because the votes of the freemen were given by proxy by means of voting papers. At the time of the Revolution, New Jersey and North Carolina, which had at one time used the ballot, had adopted the English system of *viva-voce* voting, which also prevailed in New York, New Jersey, Maryland, Virginia, and Georgia. Voting papers or ballots were in use throughout New England and in Pennsylvania, Delaware, and South Carolina.[1] The ballot, in the modern sense of a party ticket put into the hands of voters, is a comparatively late development. In 1794, John Adams extenuated "a very unwarranted and indecent attempt . . . upon the freedom of elections" committed by his own party, on the ground that "the opposite party . . . practise arts nearly as unwarrantable in secret, and by sending agents with printed votes."[2]

Party organization, whose astonishing development since the adoption of the constitution causes it to be regarded as peculiar to the politics of the republic, is a growth from colonial politics, and its beginnings were common to England and America. In 1769, during the excitement over the famous Middlesex election, the holding of mass meetings first became a political practice in England, and many reform associations were organized. To keep up communication with one another they appointed committees on correspondence. The American Whigs were in hearty sympathy with these movements. Before the year was out the South Carolina assembly had an angry contention with the provincial council, because the latter refused to concur in a grant of

[1] Bishop's Colonial Elections, Chap. III.
[2] Adams' Works, Vol. I., p. 474.

10,500 pounds currency (equal to about 1500 pounds sterling) as a contribution to the funds of the English Constitutional Society. In 1771, Samuel Adams wrote to Arthur Lee, of Virginia, — then in London and active in politics there as a supporter of the famous demagogue John Wilkes, — proposing that committees should be formed in the colonies to correspond with "the Society of the Supporters of the Bill of Rights" in England.[1] Towards the close of the following year, the Boston town meeting took the lead in banding together the Massachusetts town meetings by means of such committees of correspondence. Soon after, intercolonial committees of correspondence were organized under the lead of the Virginia House of Burgesses. These committees are the lineal predecessors of our state central committees.

Another feature of modern political methods which was derived from colonial politics is the caucus. It made its appearance in the politics of New England long before the Revolution. The historian William Gordon, writing in 1774, says the system was in operation fifty years before that time. An entry of February, 1773, in John Adams' diary, presents a picture whose traits are curiously modern. He writes: "This day I learned that the caucus club meets at certain times in the garret of Tom Dawes, the adjutant

[1] Hosmer's "Samuel Adams," Johns Hopkins University Studies.

of the Boston regiment. He has a large house, and he has a movable partition in his garret, which he takes down, and the whole club meets in one room. There they smoke tobacco till you cannot see from one end of the room to the other. There they drink flip, I suppose, and there they choose a moderator who puts questions to the vote regularly; and selectmen, assessors, collectors, firewards, and representatives are regularly chosen before they are chosen in the town." [1]

In the Middle and Southern colonies, the position of control held by the New England caucus was occupied by groups of leading men, the nature of whose association was as much social as political. Their influence was exercised in connection with the proceedings of the provincial assemblies, whose sessions brought on the gay season in the world of society. More closely resembling in their composition and demeanor the caucus club described by John Adams, were the committees of safety which sprang up during the Revolution, but for lack of such an instrument to work with as the town meeting, they had less direct political influence and were prone to mere rowdyism. Some did such work as Thomas Paine referred to in the second of his " Crisis " series of pamphlets, when he spoke of the shame felt by all sensible men at the tarring, feathering, and carting through the streets, of suspected loyalists.

[1] Adams' Works, Vol. X., p. 110.

During the Revolutionary period, constitutional means of popular participation in the conduct of government were so undeveloped that party as an agency of political control denoted little more than a connection of interest among the gentry. Even in caucus-ruled Boston, John Adams says that three rich merchants, Thomas Hancock, Charles Apthorp, and Thomas Green, when united could carry any election almost unanimously. He remarks that "half a dozen or at most a dozen families had always controlled Connecticut."[1] The course of New York politics was determined by the attitude of the great families — the Livingstons, the Schuylers and the Clintons. In the South, political power depended almost wholly on social influence and family connection. Democratic activities gave the Revolutionary movement explosive violence in Boston, and caused ferments in other centres of population which hastened the progress of events towards independence; but the urban population was small — not one-thirtieth of the whole. There were but four cities in the country with over 10,000 inhabitants. Boston had a population of about 18,000. The chief city was Philadelphia, with 42,000 population. One-fifth of the total population of the country was embraced within the bounds of Virginia, a colony which had no large towns. The mass of the people were outside the area of democratic influence.

[1] Adams' Works, Vol. VI., pp. 506, 530.

There are still to be found isolated districts, particularly in the South, which exhibit to a notable extent the prevailing social conditions of the Revolutionary period. One finds among the people in a locality of this sort an abundance of political prejudice combined with very little knowledge. When one seeks the basis of an opinion it is discovered to consist of popular confidence in the local magnate from which it was derived, and thus being really an article of faith between man and man it is held with peculiar fervor. This relationship is finely illustrated by an anecdote recorded by the Marquis de Chastellux, who visited America in 1780–1782. Governor Benjamin Harrison, of Virginia, said that when he was setting out with Jefferson and Lee to attend the first session of the Continental Congress, his anxiety over the crisis was increased by the fact that a number of the plain people of the neighborhood waited on him and said, "You assert that there is a fixed intention to invade our rights and privileges; we own that we do not see this clearly, but since you assure us that it is so, we believe the fact." They expressed their confidence that he would do what was right, and returned to their homes to abide the issue whatever it might be, while he went on his way with a heavy consciousness of the trust reposed in him.[1]

Such deference by the people must not be taken

[1] Chastellux's Travels, Vol. II., p. 157.

to imply any subserviency of disposition. It was a necessary consequence of the fact that agencies for the creation of an intelligent public opinion were not in existence. There were only thirty-seven newspapers in the entire country in 1775, and they had no regular sources of intelligence. Leading men in different localities kept one another informed of political movements by correspondence. The political conditions were such that as a rule only those in social relations with the governing class — that is to say, the gentry — were in a position to obtain the information, and arrange the concert of action, necessary to the execution of political designs. The men who organized the Continental Congress and gave a national character to the Revolutionary struggle, who bombarded king and Parliament with constitutional arguments, and who finally declared their independence of the British crown, were men of the same breed as those who upset the throne of James II. The English revolutionists of 1688 called in William of Orange to depose James II. The American revolutionists of 1776 called in the French power to depose George III from his colonial dominion.

The scheme of taxing the colonies did not originate as a party measure. The great increase of imperial expenditure on account of the American civil and military establishment, caused by the French and Indian War, was likely to suggest it to any economical administration. The idea of imposing taxes was broached as early as 1739 when the Whig leader, Walpole, was at the head of affairs, but was rejected by that prudent states-man. The angry contention in Massachusetts over the issue of general search warrants for the discovery of smuggled goods, in which James Otis distinguished himself, and which John Adams re-garded as the first step towards revolution, began while the elder Pitt was still prime minister. The passage in 1765 of the first stamp act met with little opposition in Parliament and was almost un-noticed in England. The violent outburst of re-sentment in America took English statesmen by surprise.

Although the stamp act was repealed by the short-lived Whig ministry of 1765–1766, the right of Parliament to tax the colonies was strongly affirmed ; but moderation and considerateness were such habitual characteristics of Whig policy that had the Whigs remained in power, means might have been found to satisfy imperial needs without outraging colonial sentiment. The real issue was one of home rule. The colonies had become too big to remain in tutelage to English politicians. A profound change in their relations to the home government would have been required in any event to make room for the growing spirit of self-reliance and incipient nationality. No class of men were less fitted to deal with such a delicate

matter than the Tories under Lord North, whom
George III raised to power in 1770 as the instrument of his personal will, and for whom he provided a parliamentary majority by the exercise of
every influence which the crown could bring to
bear.   Their sole idea of dealing with American
affairs was to meet colonial resistance with stubborn determination.

The burning interest with which party leaders
in our own times follow the fortunes of a decisive
campaign in an important state, affords as good
an idea as different political conditions will allow,
of the kind of feeling with which the English
Whig leaders regarded the struggle of the American Whigs, but can give no idea of its depth or
intensity.   They believed their party existence —
nay, the very life of the English constitution —
was staked on the issue.   At the time the American discontents broke out in open insurrection, the
Whig party in England was in a dispirited state.
The spirit of resistance to crown encroachments
which had flamed so audaciously in the letters
of Junius and in the diatribes of Wilkes seemed
to have died out altogether.   "England," wrote
Chatham, "is no more like old England or England forty years ago than the Monsignori of modern Rome are like the Decii, the Gracchi, or the
Catos."   Burke declared : " The people have fallen
into a total indifference to any matters of public
concern.   I do not suppose that there was ever

anything like this torpor in any period of our history." Junius wrote to his publisher that it would be folly for him to write anything more, since the cause had become hopeless. The only effective resistance to the designs of the court was that which came from the colonies. If that was broken down, it was the belief of the Whig leaders that the ruin of English liberties would follow. The Duke of Richmond took steps to provide himself with a suitable asylum in France, in case American defeat should be the signal of proscription in England.[1] The Whig leaders compared the Continental troops to the army of deliverance led by William of Orange, in 1688, and with good reason. The surrender of Cornwallis gave the death-blow to the system of personal rule which the king had laboriously erected, and ended a long crisis by definitely setting the course of English constitutional development in the ways of parliamentary government. A still more pregnant consequence was the establishment of American independence, leaving the American Whigs with separate political interests to administer in profoundly altered circumstances which soon caused changes of vast importance to human destiny.

The event was a victory for the Whigs on both sides of the water, and was treated as such. Terms of separation were arranged without rancor. Nominally, the American interests were in charge of

[1] Lecky's History of England, Vol. III., pp. 590, 591.

France ; but the American commissioners, by direct negotiation with the Whig ministry then in power, obtained greater concessions than France had intended, as it was not her policy to favor the rise of a great power in America.   Her intention was that the sole navigation of the Mississippi, and dominion over the unoccupied Western country, should be the compensation which Spain would receive for entering the alliance against England.   On her own account, France was opposed to giving so great a share in the Newfoundland fisheries as was claimed by the American commissioners.   Yet, by the aid of their Whig friends, the American commissioners were successful at every point.   The young nation was accorded liberal fishery rights, and territorial claims were conceded which provided a continental area in which to expand.[1]   It was a generous settlement of the family quarrel.

[1] Lecky's History of England, Vol. IV., pp. 278–284.

CHAPTER II

THE POLITICAL IDEAS OF THE FATHERS

THE writings of the statesmen of the Revolutionary period show that they regarded political institutions with prepossessions of another character than those which now influence men's minds. The world was very different then, and a different set of traditions guided opinion. Such conceptions as self-government, the sovereignty of the people, the rights of nationality, whose validity is now generally regarded as obvious, were then innovating ideas which had yet to make their way. Rousseau's "Social Contract," which developed the doctrine of the sovereignty of the people to extreme lengths, exerted marked influence upon French thought in the last quarter of the eighteenth century, but it had no visible effect upon English or American politics. The colonists did not trouble themselves about speculative conceptions of popular rights. It took practical grievances to move them, and in their remonstrances they had recourse to the laws and constitution of the realm. Only when they came to actual separation did they fall back upon the abstract principles of liberty which are set forth in the Declaration of

Independence. That was a manifesto for a particular occasion, and history shows that only slowly and by degrees did it come to be regarded as an embodiment of principles of government.

Among the things which make Mr. Bryce's great work on "The Holy Roman Empire" a good preparation for the study of American history, is the fact that it brings vividly to the mind the recent origin of the cardinal ideas of our times. It exhibits to us a period when the ideas of nationality, which gradually emerged in Europe after the migrations of peoples had ceased, were opposed by venerable traditions of legality and civilization. To the jurists and reformers of the thirteenth and fourteenth centuries, the development of nationality seemed to be a baleful disintegration of the Holy Roman Empire. The emperor was the Lord's Anointed, to whom kings and peoples owed their obedience. Dante did not see how freedom could be possible except under the government of an universal monarch, who, having no rival to fear and no further ambition to gratify, could have no motive save to rule in wisdom and in equity. To Petrarch, the existence of an imperial jurisdiction, coextensive with Christendom, was as obvious a necessity as that a body should have a head. In language, which reads like a bitter satire upon the condition of Europe at the present day, he remarks what a hideous portent would be a creature of many heads, biting and fighting one another.

The sublime ideal of universal peace and justice under the wise providence of a supreme magistrate, elevated above the reach of temptation, was never held more fervently than during the incessant war and political chaos of the Middle Ages. It was never absolutely renounced, but its hopelessness as a practicable design gradually removed it from serious consideration. Its vitality as a political principle was shown even during the present century in an astonishing way, by Napoleon Bonaparte's efforts to convert the kingdoms of Europe into dependencies of his empire. "There will be no repose in Europe," he said, "until it is under one head, under an emperor whose officers would be kings."[1]

At the time of the American Revolution, the Holy Roman Empire still preserved a nominal existence. In the Federalist, the term "the Emperor" is used as an unique, distinctive title; but the old conception of the Emperor as the supreme magistrate of Christendom was extinct, and in its place the idea of a balance of power in Europe had been developed as a practical expedient for the control of international relations, while as a basis of social order royal authority was solidly fixed in public confidence. Political ideas take their stamp from impressions received during the unfolding of race destiny. During the Middle Ages, no other political institution rendered such

[1] Taine's Modern Régime, Vol. I., note to p. 36.

service to the public welfare as kingship. It was
the upholder of justice, the redresser of grievances,
the guardian of the commonwealth, the conservator
of the public peace; it was the shelter of the people
against the arrogance of the nobles. The substitution of hereditary succession for election strengthened these functions by placing the crown beyond
the reach of bargain and intrigue. The change
established a self-perpetuating national magistracy
of indefeasible tenure. In the instinctive effort to
raise up an authority strong enough to counteract
the disintegrating influences of feudalism, it was
for centuries the great aim of European jurisprudence to develop regalian rights so as to confer
upon royal authority the omnipotence with which
the Roman law vested the head of the state.
Sanctions of divine right were attached to kingship
which were originally attributed to imperial authority alone. Monarchy came to be regarded as a
part of the natural order of things, the likeness in
human affairs of God's providence in the universe.
Popular dislike of individual kings weakened this
sentiment no more than dislike for a president of
the United States weakens respect for the constitution. Revolts at particular acts of royal authority
might take place, but the principle of constitutional
law that royal authority should be supreme might
not be questioned. The distinction is finely illustrated, with perfect fidelity to historic truth, by
the sentiment which Dumas puts in the mouth of

one of his famous musketeers. Athos tells his son :
" Learn how to distinguish the king from royalty;
the king is but a man ; royalty is the gift of God.
Whenever you hesitate as to whom you ought to
serve, abandon the exterior, the material appearance, for the invisible principle ; for the invisible
principle is everything. Should the king prove a
tyrant — for power begets tyranny — love, respect
royalty, that divine right." [1]

Popular assemblies, institutions originally common to the barbarian peoples who parcelled Europe
among them, were so much in the way of the executive
tive power required by the militancy of the times
that they were gradually shorn of authority and
almost suppressed. The historian Taine dates the
deposit of absolute authority in the French crown
from the English invasions of the fifteenth century,
when the life of the nation depended upon the removal of every restraint upon the ability of the
king to command at will all its resources. Only in
a country naturally sheltered from invasion, as was
England, could parliamentary bodies safely retain
their authority. At the time when the disaffec-
tion of the American colonies began, the various
Continental powers seemed to enjoy conditions of
security and progress strictly in proportion to the
extent to which hindrances upon the efficiency of
executive power had been removed. The Italian
republics which sprang up during the Middle Ages

[1] Alex. Dumas' Twenty Years After, Chap. XXII.

had passed away, leaving odious memories of crime and disorder. Venice was in a state of hopeless decay. Most of the Swiss cantons had fallen under the rule of narrow oligarchies. Poland, which had preserved the principle of elective kingship originally common among European peoples, was declining into anarchy. The principle of vitality which upheld Holland amid the corruption and enfeeblement of the states general seemed to be the *quasi*-royal position obtained by the House of Orange in 1749. All the vigorous states of the continent were despotic in constitution.[1]

The extinction of means of participation in the government must not be regarded as implying a sense of oppression among the people. As a general thing they were no more aggrieved by it than the residents of the District of Columbia were in our own time by the abolition of their legislature. The Revolution of 1772 in Sweden, by which Gustavus III crushed the authority of the Parliament, was hailed with joy by his people. The abolition of serfdom, the removal of many feudal oppressions, the betterment of social conditions, and the enlargement of liberty of thought were derived from the exercise of royal power, while such extraneous organs of constituted authority as still survived were apt to be centres of resistance to reform.[2] Voltaire, the great apostle of liberalism,

---

[1] Lecky, Vol. III., pp. 241, 242.
[2] *Ibid.*, Vol. V., pp. 315-318.

wrote to D'Alembert in 1765: "Who would have thought that the cause of kings would be that of philosophers? But yet it is evident that the sages who refuse to admit two powers are the chief support of royal authority." Again he said, "There ought never to be two powers in the state." Liberal principles of government were in fashion among kings until the French Revolution caused a violent reaction.

England presented the example of a monarchy of limited prerogative and distributed authority, but for a long period before the French Revolution, the relative esteem in which France and England were held as regards stability of government was almost exactly the reverse of what it has been since. It was England that was associated with traits of levity and changefulness. Milton, in his treatise on "A Free Commonwealth" published in 1660, referred to "the fickleness which is attributed to us as we are islanders," and remarked that "good education and acquisite wisdom ought to correct the fluxible fault, if any there be, of our watery situation." In 1649, Parliament destroyed kingship, only to lose its own privileges under the autocratic rule of Cromwell. In 1660, the nation restored royalty without conditions. In 1688, the king was driven from his throne. During the eighteenth century, the turbulence of English politics was proverbial. The admixture of popular representation with royal authority in the English constitution seemed to be a source of political corruption and civic instability. Bribery was resorted to without scruple to carry the public business through Parliament. The control of the secret-service fund went by the name of the "management of the House of Commons." Wraxall, in his memoirs published in 1781, remarks that it is "a branch of administration unfortunately interwoven with, and inseparable from, the genius of the British constitution; perhaps of every form of government in which democracy or popular representation makes an essential part." The philosopher Hume, in an essay published in 1741, points out the tendency to amass authority in the House of Commons, with its accompanying prospect of a tyranny of factions, and concludes that "we shall at last, after many convulsions and civil wars, finds repose in absolute monarchy, which it would have been happier for us to have established peaceably from the beginning." The efforts of George III to create a system of personal rule, which would put the king of England on a level of authority with his fellow-monarchs of Europe, were given strength and opportunity by a widespread conviction that a vigorous exercise of prerogative was necessary to destroy the oligarchical power of party combinations and end the reign of corruption. Goldsmith, in his well-known poem "The Traveller," expressed this sentiment in the lines : —

"When I behold a factious band agree
To call it freedom when themselves are free,
Each wanton judge new penal statutes draw,
Laws grind the poor and rich men rule the law,
The wealth of climes where savage nations roam,
Pillaged from slaves to purchase slaves at home —
Fear, pity, justice, indignation, start,
Tear off reserve and bare my swelling heart;
Till, half a patriot, half a coward grown,
I fly from petty tyrants to the throne."

Persons of fastidious culture turned for relief from the coarseness of English manners to the contemplation of French order and decency. Hume's letters complain of "the rage and violence of parties" in England, and he fondly cherished the hope of being able to make his home in Paris where "the taste for literature is neither decayed nor depraved as with the barbarians who inhabit the banks of the Thames." The historian Gibbon deplored the fact that circumstances compelled him to live in England instead of among a people "who have established a freedom and ease in society unknown to antiquity and still unpractised by other nations." There is much in the Franco-mania of that period that reminds one of the Anglo-mania of the present day. The aversion which many cultivated persons have for American politics, and their admiration for English models, curiously echo a tone of sentiment in England towards France before the Revolution of 1793.

The actual vigor of representative institutions in England during this period is complete proof of the existence there of an order of political ideas counteracting the tendency to exalt royal prerogative, dominant elsewhere in Europe; but those ideas owed nothing to democratic sentiment. On nothing were men better agreed than that democracy meant licentiousness, anarchy, and oppression. The brief republican experiment begun in England in 1648 was a figment of military rule, promoted by theocratic ideas mixed with millennial dreams. Those ideas had no ancestry in common with English ideas of freedom. Calvin, whose theocratic republic at Geneva was regarded by his adherents throughout the Protestant world as an example of a Christian commonwealth, agreed with the mediæval jurists in holding both church and state of divine origin; but instead of regarding the Pope as Christ's vicegerent upon earth, exercising His jurisdiction over the souls of men, and the Emperor as His vicegerent in secular affairs, Calvin held that Christ himself was the true head of church and state, thus establishing their organic union, the function of the state being to control external conditions so as to secure the church in the maintenance of its doctrines, order, and discipline.[1] The operation of such ideas was accompanied by a disposition to discard the his-

---

[1] Osgood's "Political Ideas of the Puritans," *Political Science Quarterly*, March–June, 1891.

toric appliances of English liberty. Milton's " Ready and Easy Way to Establish a Free Commonwealth " was for the people to exhaust their rights of suffrage in one constituent act. They should choose once and for all time their ablest and wisest men to sit as a grand council for the management of public affairs. He refers to the experience of ancient and mediæval republics as proof that popular assemblies " either little availed the people, or else brought them to such a licentious and unbridled democracy as in fine ruined themselves with their own excessive power." The reason why kingship is esteemed " the more safe and durable " form of government is " because the king, and for the most part his council, is not changed during life." This stability may be given to a republic by adopting the same principle of a perpetual tenure of authority. " Safest therefore to me, it seems, and of less hazard and interruption to affairs, that none of the grand council be moved, unless by death or just conviction of some crime; for what can be expected firm or steadfast from a floating foundation." Such a government, he argued, would maintain the commonwealth in peace and prosperity, " even to the coming of our true and rightful, and only to be expected king, only worthy, as He is our only Saviour, the Messiah, the Christ."

The Cromwellian commonwealth left behind it memories of sanctimonious despotism which made hatred of republics and all their belongings one of the strongest of English prejudices. A crisis arrived when this prejudice became influential in determining the course of English constitutional development. When James II became a fugitive, the Tories were driven, by stress of their party principle of the indefeasible tenure of royal authority, into proposing that the absence of the king should be treated as if it were a case of physical disability, and that the government should be carried on in the king's name by a regent. The Whigs met this by the argument that since there was no prospect that James would fail of heirs, the nation might have to be governed perpetually by regents or protectors, and would thus approach much closer to a republic than if another king were put upon the throne. The settlement of English kingship upon a parliamentary title, making it an institution intrinsically republican, was thus promoted by the strength of anti-republican prejudice.[1]

The English tendency to restrict royal prerogative, while enthusiastically upholding it, was the result of a sort of concordat between popular attachment to representative institutions and popular

[1] A Tory argument against the establishment of the Bank of England, in 1694, affords a grotesque instance of the activity of this prejudice. The banks famous at that time were those of Venice, Genoa, Amsterdam, and Hamburg, and hence it was argued that a bank was a republican institution which it would be dangerous to introduce in a monarchy. Macaulay's History, Chap. XX.

reverence for kings. The circumstances were such that neither principle of government could exterminate the other, so they were brought into accommodation by means of a doctrine in which each found its place. Prerogative and popular rights should be so balanced as to protect the nation from tyranny on the one side and from mob rule on the other. The different estates of the realm should be so represented in the government that each should be able to check excess upon the part of another. Support for this doctrine was found in the writings of Aristotle, Polybius, Cicero, and Tacitus. Montesquieu's adherence to it in opposition to the general current of European opinion made his "Spirit of the Laws" more influential in England and America than that great work ever was in the author's own country. Blackstone exhibited this doctrine as the fundamental principle of the British constitution, with such a parade of learning as to make his conclusions seem indisputable, and with such noble resources of style that the "Commentaries" took rank as a literary classic as well as a law book. The same doctrine eventually received from Edmund Burke the most eloquent expression ever given to political ideas. It floats in the music of his grandest passages — as when he speaks of "that action and interaction which in the natural and in the political world, from the reciprocal struggles of discordant powers, draws out the harmony of the universe."

Two currents of thought may be discerned in colonial politics. One of these had received its impulse from the Puritan movement. A theocracy has really no love for democratic ideas; at a later period abundant evidence of this was furnished by New England. But it is always the disposition of theocracy, when confronted by royal authority, to encourage the assertion of popular rights, and in Massachusetts, especially, the state of popular sentiment showed an infusion of anti-monarchical prejudice. The main stream of colonial ideas was, however, that which flowed in the channels of English law, bearing with it an inveterate attachment to prerogative as an essential ingredient of a free constitution, a necessary counterpoise to representative institutions. Even so radical a thinker as Thomas Paine was forced to defer to this sentiment. In his celebrated pamphlet, "Common Sense," issued in January, 1776, after urging the people to look above to a king, "who doth not make havoc of His people like the royal brute of England," he adds: "Yet that we may not appear defective in earthly honors, let a day be solemnly set apart for proclaiming the charter; let it be brought forth, placed on the divine law, the work of God; let a crown be placed thereon, by which the world may know that so far as we approve of monarchy, in America the law is king." Prejudice against democracy is turned on the Tories by the argument that England is too far

away to give adequate protection, so that if America should neglect to provide herself with a government of her own, "some Masaniello may hereafter
arise who, laying hold of popular disquietude, may
collect together the desperate and discontented,
and by assuming to themselves the powers of
government finally sweep away the liberties of
the continent like a deluge." Paine's suggestion
is prophetic of what happened. After the adoption
of the constitution the veneration became attached
to it which was formerly felt for royalty.

Failure to appreciate the intensity of public
attachment to the principle of balanced powers
of government would leave concealed the true
cause of the Revolutionary struggle. It was the
firm conviction of thinking men that the only hope
of free institutions lay in the adjustments of the
English constitution. If these seemed to place the
liberties of the people in a dangerous strait between
the rock and the whirlpool, so much the more
reason why any deviation from the traditional
course should meet with resolute resistance. It
was not the extent of the taxation—that was triv-
ial in comparison with that which independence
made necessary ; it was not that the doctrine "no
taxation without representation " was regarded as
an essential principle of legitimate government—
it was not included in the enumeration of rights
attached to the constitution and has never been
formulated as a constitutional principle ;—not be-

cause of these things did the revolt of the colonies take place. It was because the actions of the British government assumed an absolute authority which violated the spirit of the English constitution, the fundamental compact controlling the relations between the king and his people. The deepest political instincts of the race were outraged.

This state of public sentiment explains those diverse manifestations which make the American uprising unique among revolutions : sincere professions of loyalty to the British crown in the very thick of battle with British armies ; extreme hesitancy in effecting an alliance with France even after George III had set the example of calling in a foreign power by the hire of foreign mercenaries ; great aversion to issuing a declaration of independence even after it had become a manifest necessity to enable the colonies to obtain help from abroad. The declaration of the cause of taking up arms, which repudiates any intention of separating from the British crown, was read before the troops on Prospect Hill, in July, 1775, amid such shouts that the British on Bunker Hill put themselves in array for battle.[1] It required somewhat violent methods to force a declaration of independence through Congress. · Evidently the American leaders were revolutionists, not from choice, but from compulsion. They renounced

[1] Bancroft's History, Vol. VIII., p. 47.

their allegiance to the English king without breaking their attachment to the English constitution. The traditional ideas still controlled political thought, but their expression in the government of the union was hindered by obstacles which long seemed insurmountable.

D

CHAPTER III

THE ideas of government held by the American Whigs could find no satisfaction in the Confederation. That was merely an agency of state coöperation for the management of common interests. It was not thought of as a regular government. The Articles of Confederation committed to Congress the control of the national budget, the regulation of the army and navy, the appointment of public officers, and in fine the entire management of public affairs. The concentration of authority was as great as in English parliamentary government in our own times, and was altogether incompatible with the ideas of those times, but public opinion was calmly indifferent. In 1781, Jefferson wrote, "An elective despotism was not the government we fought for; but one which should not only be founded on free principles, but in which the powers of government should be so divided and balanced among several bodies of magistracy as that no one could transcend their legal limits without being effectually checked and restrained by the others."[1] He was thinking, however, of the changes in the Virginia constitution by which the selection of

[1] Notes on Virginia, Chap. XIII.

the governor and other officers formerly appointed by the crown had been taken over by the legislature. The case of the Confederation was far more obnoxious to the principle he states, but it does not occur to him. In 1787, John Adams wrote, "If there is one certain truth to be collected from the history of all ages, it is this : that the people's rights and liberties, and the democratic mixture in a constitution, can never be preserved without a strong executive, or, in other words without separating the executive power from the legislature." This passage occurs in his "Defence of the Constitutions of Government of the United States of America," written in reply to a criticism by Turgot on American institutions. The great French publicist objected to them on the ground that they did not collect all the authority of government in one centre to represent the will of the nation.[1] It did

[1] Writing to Dr. Richard Price of London, March 22, 1778, Turgot said : " I see in the greatest number (of the American state constitutions) an unreasonable imitation of the usages of England. Instead of bringing all the authorities into one, that of the nation, they have established different bodies, — a House of Representatives, a council, a governor, — because England has a House of Commons, lords, and a king. They undertake to balance these different authorities, as if the same equilibrium of powers which has been thought necessary to balance the enormous preponderance of royalty could be of any use in republics, formed upon the equality of all citizens ; and as if every article which constitutes different bodies was not a source of divisions. By striving to escape imaginary dangers, they had created real ones." The criticism of the sagacious French statesman has not lost its point.

not occur to Adams to refute the objection by citing the Articles of Confederation, but he ransacked history from civilization's dawn unto his own times to justify the course of the American states in adopting governments of distributed powers. In his voluminous work the sole reference he makes to the body whose ambassador he then was, is this: "Congress is not a legislative assembly, nor a representative assembly, but only a diplomatic assembly."[1] He would not commit the absurdity of classing a revolutionary junto among regularly constituted governments.

People cared nothing about the principles on which the government of the Confederation was based, because they cared nothing for that government. The Congress of the Confederation, although it remained in existence fourteen years, never took root in the affection or respect of the people. Its sittings were private, and its proceedings made no appeal to public opinion. It remained in existence by sufferance only. The states flouted its authority whenever they felt disposed to do so. None of its plans to reform the government came to anything. The constitution was the result of an outside movement which Congress obeyed, but did not direct. The

[1] Adams' Works, Vol. IV., p. 379. In the constitutional convention, Edmund Randolph spoke of Congress in the same way. He said, "Elected by the legislatures who retain even a power of recall, they are a mere diplomatic body, with no will of their own."

period of the Confederation was one in which the functions of general government were in abeyance. Crown jurisdiction had been thrown off, but no succession to it had been provided. The Confederation was a makeshift, " neither fit for war or peace," as Hamilton remarked.

During the war, incapacity of government and defects of administration were remedied to a saving extent by French subsidies of money and troops, but now the stripling nation was left to its own resources. Although its success and prospects had excited some popular enthusiasm in Europe, rulers regarded it as a troublesome parvenu. It hardly retained the good will of its former ally, France. " We have never pretended," wrote the Cabinet of Versailles to its representative in America, " to make of America an useful ally ; we have had no other object than to deprive Great Britain of that vast continent. Therefore we can regard with indifference both the movements which agitate certain provinces and the fermentation which prevails in Congress." [1]

It was easy to take advantage of a nation so weak and incapable. England would not allow American goods to enter her ports unless they came on English ships. New England, the world-wide enterprise of whose seamen furnished Edmund Burke with an eloquent passage of his great speech

[1] Bancroft's History of the Constitution, Vol. II., pp. 415, 424, 438.

on American Conciliation, now found herself in a sorry plight. Spain would not allow American vessels to navigate the lower Mississippi, and the Western country was kept in a state of constant irritation by the closing of the natural outlet of its trade. Negotiations for commercial privileges were fruitless. Foreign nations would not make treaties with a nation which really had no government and was expected to go to pieces. Cyrus Griffin, President of Congress, told a correspondent: " The British courtiers are ridiculing our situation very much and tell Mr. Adams, in a sneering manner, when America shall assume some kind of government then England will speak to her." [1]

The development of internal resources was no less sorely oppressed. Enterprise could not avail itself of opportunities because of the lack of stable government and of security for investors. Creditors were kept out of their own by stay laws or were defrauded by legal tender acts. The anarchical influences set in motion by the Revolution swept so strongly over some of the states that the foundations of social order seemed to be dissolving. The situation in New England caused great anxiety. Puritanism, being an intense reaction of individualism against constituted authority, contains a political virus. The "generation of odd names and natures," which the Earl of Strafford noted among the English Roundheads, was the

[1] Bancroft's History of the Constitution, Vol. II., p. 469.

result of mental characteristics, which, strongly
infused into American society by Puritan emigration, have played a great part in our politics. The
virus which those characteristics are able to distil
has long since spent its force in the region of its
original culture, but it continues to produce typical
fevers in Western communities most deeply in-
oculated with the New England strain. The
delirious politics which ensue may afford some
idea of the situation in New England during the
period of social debility after the Revolutionary
War. The policies which commanded strong popular support excited the astonishment of observers,
and other communities were then asking, What
is the matter with New England?

The control of affairs had slipped away from the
leaders of the Revolution. Their correspondence
is marked by extreme anxiety, almost despondency.
Although Washington had refused to consider the
offer of some of the army officers to make him
king, the correspondence of prominent men
towards the close of the Confederation period
shows that they were coming to the belief that a
return to kingship was the only way out of the
troubles of the times. A British secret agent
reported to his government, "I can assure you
that where you had one friend in the last war, you
would find three now."[1] The wretched state of the
times is powerfully set forth in Number 15 of the

[1] Bancroft's History of the Constitution, Vol. II., p. 424.

Federalist. In conclusion the article asks : " What indication is there of national disorder, poverty, and insignificance that could befall a community so peculiarly blessed with natural advantages as we are, which does not form a part of the dark catalogue of our public misfortunes ? "

Meanwhile, the forces of progress were finding a natural channel in conformity with the lay of popular character. It was generally admitted that something ought to be done about the affairs of the Confederation. But something had to be done about such matters as Virginia's loss of trade because of the lower rates of duty imposed by Maryland, and the menace to Maryland's commerce contained in Virginia's claim of the right to levy tolls upon vessels passing between the capes of the Chesapeake. Complications of interest troubled New York and New Jersey with regard to the commerce of New York Bay, and New Jersey and Pennsylvania with regard to Delaware Bay. To adjust such matters joint action was required, and even during the war commercial negotiations took place between colonies.

In 1785, commissioners appointed by Maryland and Virginia to frame an agreement for the regulation of Chesapeake Bay commerce, were to meet in Alexandria. Washington invited them to his residence, Mount Vernon. That meeting was the starting-point of the movement for the establishment of a more perfect union. The proceedings afforded an opportunity which the national school of politicians adroitly seized. The ostensible object of the series of interstate negotiations which followed was to establish an uniform system of commercial regulations. The purpose of the national politicians was to prevent this while using the movement to prepare the way for the adoption of a national constitution. Their management was a masterpiece of political strategy. The commercial convention which met at Annapolis, September 11, 1786, was completely under their control.[1] An address was issued, drawn up in language whose tact and ingenuity make it the illustrious predecessor of the literary efforts of succeeding generations of politicians in concocting manifestoes for use among the people. Anxious concern was expressed as to the effect the adoption of a scheme of commercial regulation might have upon the operations of the general government, and it was recommended that every state should send commissioners to a convention to consider the subject in all its bearings.

After Madison's death there was found in his papers an account of these proceedings, which allows a glimpse into what would now be called the inside politics of the movement. He relates

---

[1] Twelve commissioners were present, representing five states. Eight of those commissioners were chosen as delegates to the constitutional convention. Among them were : Alexander Hamilton, James Madison, Edmund Randolph, and John Dickinson.

that a number of the commissioners stayed away from "a belief that the time has not yet arrived for such a political reform as might be expected from a further experience of its necessity."[1] We have, however, a full disclosure of the plans of the national leaders in a letter of October 10, 1786, from Otto, the French minister, to his chief, Count Vergennes. Otto tells him: "Although there are no nobles in America, there is a class of men denominated 'gentlemen,' who, by reason of their wealth, their talents, their education, their families, or the offices they hold, aspire to a preëminence which the people refuse to grant them; and although many of these men have betrayed the interests of their order to gain popularity, there reigns among them a connection so much the more intimate as they almost all of them dread the efforts of the people to despoil them of their possessions, and, moreover, they are creditors, and therefore interested in strengthening the government and watching over the execution of the laws. . . . The attempt, my lord, has been vain, by pamphlets and other publications, to spread notions of justice and integrity, and to deprive the people of a freedom which they have so misused. By proposing a new organization of the general government, all minds would have been revolted; circumstances ruinous to the commerce of America have happily

---

[1] Introduction to Madison's Journal.

arisen to furnish the reformers with a pretext for introducing innovations."

Otto describes the movement for a commercial convention and continues : " The authors of this proposition had no hope, nor even desire, to see the success of this assembly of commissioners, which was only intended to prepare a question much more important than that of commerce. The measures were so well taken that at the end of September no more than five states were represented at Annapolis, and the commissioners from the Northern states tarried several days at New York in order to retard their arrival. The states which assembled, after having waited nearly three weeks, separated under the pretext that they were not in sufficient numbers to enter on the business, and, to justify this dissolution, they addressed to the different legislatures and to Congress a report, the translation of which I have the honor to enclose you."

" In this paper the commissioners employ an infinity of circumlocutions and ambiguous phrases to show their constituents the impossibility of taking into consideration a general plan of commerce and the powers pertaining thereto, without at the same time touching upon other subjects closely connected with the prosperity and national importance of the United States. Without enumerating these objects, the commissioners enlarge upon the present crisis of public affairs, upon the dangers to which the Confederation is exposed, upon the want of credit of the United States abroad, and upon the necessity of uniting, under a single point of view, the interests of all the states. They close by proposing for the month of May next a new assembly of commissioners, instructed to deliberate, not only upon a general plan of commerce, but upon other matters which may concern the harmony and welfare of the states, and upon the means of rendering the federal government adequate to the exigencies of the union."

The call for the convention, which met at Philadelphia, May, 1787, provided that it should "revise the Articles of Confederation." That pretext having served its purpose, no more attention was paid to it. As soon as the delegates met, the real design of a restoration of government was taken in hand. The scheme of the national politicians was thus borne to its destination on the back of a movement for commercial regulations. It is an early specimen of "the rider," that ruse so frequently resorted to in political strategy for the control of legislation.

CHAPTER IV

THE way things had been going on since the colonies had become independent states had greatly excited among the delegates the traditional prejudice against democracy. That which they had feared all along, which had made them so reluctant to carry their resistance to parliamentary oppression to the point of declaring their independence of the British crown — the outbreak of democratic licentiousness — had come to pass, and they were aghast at the evil look of the times. They met behind closed doors, and could talk freely. Roger Sherman, a signer of the Declaration of Independence, solemnly laid down the rule that "the people should have as little to do as may be with the government."[1] George Mason thought "it would be as unnatural to refer the choice of a proper character for chief magistrate to the people, as it would be to refer a trial of colors to a blind man." Madison did not think large bodies of men had much regard for honesty. "Respect for character is always diminished in proportion to the number

[1] All the quotations from the convention debates are taken from Madison's Journal.

45

among whom the blame or praise is to be divided."
Elbridge Gerry remarked that "he did not deny
the position of Mr. Madison, that the majority will
generally violate justice when they have an interest
in doing so." The great argument in behalf of the
states' rights doctrine, to which the particular interests of the smaller states naturally impelled them,
was that its adoption would provide additional social
security, making the ship of state a compartment
vessel, as it were, so that a democratic inundation
would be limited to the vicinity of the breach, and
would not at once overwhelm the whole fabric.
Said John Dickinson, "Of remedies for the diseases of republics which have flourished for a
moment only and then vanished forever, one is the
double branch of the legislature, and the other the
accidental lucky division of this country into distinct states."

Frequent reference was made to the corruption
and incapacity of state legislatures. Madison complained that "the backwardness of the best citizens to engage in the legislative service gave too
great success to unfit characters." John Francis
Mercer of Maryland dwelt upon the need of protecting the people "against those speculating legislatures which are now plundering them throughout
the United States." But there was small hope
that a national legislature would be much better.
Mason remarked that, "notwithstanding the precautions taken in the constitution of the legislature,

it would still so much resemble that of the individual states that it must be expected frequently to pass unjust and pernicious laws." Edmund Randolph argued that "the Senate will be more likely to be corrupt than the House of Representatives, and should therefore have less to do with money matters." Hamilton remarked: "We must take man as we find him, and if we expect him to serve the public we must interest his passions in doing so." Gouverneur Morris said: "One interest must be opposed to another interest. Vices, as they exist, must be turned against each other."

But how was this to be accomplished? The model of government all had in mind was the English constitution. Many eulogistic references to it were made in the course of the debates. It was, however, admitted that American society did not afford materials from which such a constitution could be formed. There were no distinct orders in the state which could be balanced against one another like the crown, lords, and commons. The best the delegates could do was to frame a government on the principles of the English constitution. They were agreed on this, but there were sharp differences as to the application of those principles under the conditions set by the political situation. In addition, they had to consider above all things the practical question: How were the states to be brought into subordination again? Since their approval was necessary to give effect to any plan of union, some way had to be found to reconcile their conflicting pretensions. Under the Articles of Confederation the states, large or small, met as equals in Congress. Consent to that had been easy, since in practice each state might decide for itself whether it would abide by what was done. The case was very different when it was proposed to establish a government of independent resources and imperial authority. The smaller states had to be persuaded to relinquish their complete equality of representation with the larger states ; the larger states had to be coaxed into making concessions to the smaller. Can a more difficult problem of practical politics be imagined? It was finally solved, not to the satisfaction of the delegates but in a tolerable way, by practical expedients which were to acquire immense importance, and which were indeed the unconscious development of new faculties in the political organism under the constraint of hard necessity.

At the time of the Revolution, the provincial assemblies seized the powers reft from royal authority and elected executive officials formerly appointed by the crown or the lords proprietary. Just such powers the Parliament of England had exercised in 1689 when William and Mary were elected to fill the vacancy caused by the flight of James II. The first thought, in the reconstruction of a general government for America, was to proceed in the same way. The Virginia plan, prepared in advance of the meeting of the convention, provided that the executive and the judiciary should be chosen by the national legislature. The national legislature should have power to negative all state laws contravening national interests. This would have put the states, in their relations to the general government, in about the same position as the charter colonies had been with respect to the British government, and this was the intention. Writing to Edmund Randolph, while the Virginia plan was preparing, Madison said, " Let it have a negative in all cases whatever, on the legislative acts of the states, as the king of Great Britain heretofore had." Hamilton's proposition, that the national executive should appoint the governors, would have put the states in about the same position as the royal colonies had been. All were agreed that a subordination of the states to the general government was necessary to the extent which its proper functions required ; but what the relative situation of the states would be, under any scheme which might be contrived, was a point of great difficulty. Virginia, on a basis of representation according to population, would elect more members of the national legislature than five of the smaller states. Her vote, combined with that of three other large states, would outweigh the representation of the remaining nine states. The smaller states were determined not to be swallowed up in that way. The hitch at this point balked

E

the business until the idea was hit upon of leaving state autonomy intact by delineating for the general government an orbit which should include the citizenship of the nation upon a plane apart from that in which the state governments revolved.[1] The dual citizenship of Americans, which has had such vast constitutional results, was thus wrought by a casual stroke.

The issue as regards the composition of the national legislature was settled by a compromise giving the states equal representation in the Senate, while in the House representation was according to the population as computed by a special rule which allowed slaves to be counted for only three-fifths of their numbers. The problem as regards the constitution of the executive proved insoluble until the idea was conceived of making the selection of the executive the discretionary act of an élite body appointed by the states expressly for that purpose. "The immediate election should be made by men most capable of analyzing the qualities adapted to the station, and acting under circumstances favorable to deliberation."[2]   In order that the courts should be "the bulwarks of a limited constitution against legislative encroach-

---

[1] John Dickinson, whose championship of state rights led the way in this direction, said, "The proposed system is like the solar system, in which the states are the planets, and they ought to be left to move more freely in their proper orbits."

[2] The Federalist, No. 68.

ments,"[1] it was then settled that the judiciary
should be constituted by executive appointment,
independence of executive control being secured by
establishing a life tenure of office. It is the one
department of the government which has exactly
fulfilled the original conception. It has had an
enormous growth in power and dignity, but strictly
speaking this growth has not been a development,
but rather an increasing exercise of functions
assigned to it from the beginning.

The influence moulding all the conceptions, the
idea regulating all the contrivances of those
ardent politicians and able young lawyers, intent
upon obtaining some practical result to their labors,
was the Whig doctrine of checks and balances of
authority through distribution of the powers of
government.[2] In adapting the English constitution to American use, they endeavored to exclude
influences which seemed to be disturbing the
balance of power in the English constitution, and
they incorporated in the American constitution

---

[1] The Federalist, No. 78.

[2] The work of the convention was done by the young men.
Washington, who was then fifty-five, presided, but took no part in
the debates. Dr. Franklin, who was old and near the close of
his life, exerted himself to promote agreement, but he does not
seem to have concerned himself much about details. He thought
that sooner or later a king would be set up, but desired that republican institutions should have a trial, and he was willing to accede to
almost any arrangement to that end. See Madison's Journal, June
2, 4, and July 24.

restraints suggested by English and colonial experience. The united control of legislation and administration, which was obtained by the practice of selecting the ministers of the crown from among the leaders of Parliament, was an aberration from constitutional theory against which English reformers were in the habit of inveighing. The act of settlement, passed by a reforming House of Commons in 1700, contained an article stipulating that "no person who has an office or place of profit under the king shall be capable of serving as a member of the House of Commons." This article, which was defeated by crown influence, was transferred to the constitution of the United States after suitable revision of its language.[1] An accompanying article of the act of settlement guarded against the irresponsible exercise of power by providing for the transaction of important affairs of state in the privy council, with the requirement that those who should advise and consent to what was done should so record themselves. These ideas are reflected in the provisions of the constitution, adopted after repeated efforts to concert a scheme for a privy council distinct from Congress had failed, by which the Senate is associated with the President as his advisers in the negotiation of treaties and in the appointment of public officers.[2]

[1] Section 6, Article I.

[2] Section 2, Article II. A comparison between the constitution, with the amendments immediately made to it, and the bill of rights

The bestowal of these important functions upon
the Senate made it more powerful than the House
of Lords upon which it was modelled. Great
things were expected of the Senate. Of course it
would represent wealth. The qualifications then
required for membership in the state legislatures
would insure that. John Dickinson, on whose
motion it was decided that the senators should be
elected by the state legislatures, gave as one of
his reasons that "he wished the Senate to consist
of the most distinguished characters, distinguished
for their rank in life and their weight of property,
and bearing as strong a likeness to the British
House of Lords as was possible." James Madison
thought that "the second branch, as a limited number of citizens, respectable for wisdom and virtue,
will be watched by and will keep watch over the
representatives of the people; it will seasonably
interpose between impetuous councils, and will
guard the minority who are placed above indigence
against the agrarian attempts of the ever-increasing
class who labor under the hardships of life, and
secretly strive for a more equal distribution of its
blessings." Gouverneur Morris hoped that the
Senate " will show us the might of aristocracy."

But even the creation of such a body as this was

of 1689, will show other points of resemblance indicating the source
of the political ideas embodied in the constitution. See Stevens'
" Sources of the Constitution of the United States " for a thorough
discussion of this subject.

not a sufficient safeguard against democracy. The great concern of the delegates was to provide effective restraints on the legislative branch. "It is against the enterprising ambition of this department," said Madison, "that the people ought to indulge all their jealousy and exhaust all their precautions."[1] On the other hand, Hamilton remarked that "energy in the executive is a leading character in the definition of a good government."[2] Congress was given no powers except such as were specified. The powers of the President are plenary except as specifically limited. In the one case the language of the constitution is: "All legislative powers herein granted shall be vested in a Congress of the United States, which shall consist of a Senate and a House of Representatives." In the other case the grant is without reserve, "The executive power shall be vested in a President of the United States of America." Language which might imply subordination is avoided. The President's oath of office is: "I will faithfully execute the office of President of the United States, and will, to the best of my ability, preserve, protect, and defend the constitution of the United States." Not Congressional authority alone but executive prerogative also is a fountain of law. Madison declared, "All constitutional acts of power, whether in the executive or in the judicial department, have

[1] The Federalist, No. 48.
[2] *Ibid.*, No. 70.

as much legal validity and obligation as if they proceeded from the legislature."[1] The delegates seem to have looked forward to the possibility that the President might have to act as a saviour of society, on the principle tersely stated by Madison that "the safety and happiness of society are the objects at which all political institutions aim and to which all such institutions must be sacrificed."[2] To obtain their full significance as conceived by the fathers, the provisions of the constitution, requiring that the United States shall guarantee to every state a republican form of government and give protection from domestic violence, should be interpreted in connection with this embodiment of prerogative. The Shays' Rebellion in Massachusetts and the disturbances in New Hampshire and Rhode Island had laid a great fear on the delegates.

At the first session of Congress, the Senate, under the lead of John Adams, endeavored to carry out these ideas of presidential prerogative by attaching titles of royalty to the office; but the House of Representatives defeated all such propositions. Nevertheless the precautions taken by the framers of the constitution, in behalf of the presidency, were so effectual that Congress was made an incurably deficient and inferior organ of government. As the nation develops and the people

[1] The Federalist, No. 64.
[2] *Ibid.*, No. 45.

increase their qualifications for self-government, it will be seen that they will lay hold of the presidency as the only organ sufficient for the exercise of their sovereignty.

In giving shape to the determinations of the convention, the draughting committee seems to have made free use of material afforded by state constitutions.   It is a common legislative practice to consult the statute books for material already shaped for use, and in this respect the behavior of the convention of 1787 was what that of any constitutional convention in our own times might be. In plan and purpose, the constitution is a product of the political ideas of the English race.   It stands in lineal succession to such muniments of public right as Magna Charta, the Bill of Rights of 1689, and the Act of Settlement of 1700.   The embodiment of Whig doctrine in a written constitution was, however, an unperceived revolution in political conditions, since it converted what was simply a working theory, open to modification as times changed, into a rigid frame of government.   The anatomy of the English constitution was completed by the establishment of royalty on a parliamentary title.   Its development since then has been carried on by functional activities.[1]   The constitution of the United States was a sort of Act of Settlement

---

[1] Lecky comments instructively upon this point.   History of England, Vol. III., p. 10.

after the American Whig revolution of 1775–1783 ; but in adapting the traditional structure of government to new uses, the federal composition of the nation compelled changes which, although intended as simple variations, resulted in generic difference. In endeavoring to get back to the old type of government, the fathers originated a new type of more complex organization and larger capacities of development. The old type, from its superior complexity to the simple forms of absolute rule, could not have been developed save in the shelter of England's insular position. The still more elaborate organization of the new type had a remote new world in which to expand. Although its development is still incomplete, its stability is so well established that federal government is now the mould of empire. Guizot says, "Of all the systems of government and political guarantee, it may be asserted without fear of contradiction that the most difficult to establish and render effectual is the federated system : a system which consists in leaving in each place or province, in every separate society, all that portion of government which can abide there, and in taking from it only so much of it as is indispensable to a general society, in order to carry it to the centre of this larger society, and there to embody it under the form of a central government." [1]

[1] Guizot's History of Civilization, Lecture IV.

This distribution of independent powers of government, according to the respective needs of local and general administration, all comprehended in organic union, is the contribution of America to the advance of political science, and it has been evolved from the old Whig doctrine.

CHAPTER V

CLASS RULE

THE constitutional history of the United States begins with the establishment of the government of the masses by the classes. It was expected as a matter of course that the gentry would control every branch of the government. "The administration of government, in its larger sense," remarked Hamilton, "comprehends all the operations of the body politic, whether legislative, executive, or judiciary."[1] This unity was to be maintained by the fact that the conduct of public affairs would be a part of the activity of good society, enmeshed in its usual ambitions, enjoyments, and habits of intercourse. Who, save the gentry, would have the means or ability to attend to such matters? The common people were not regarded as having any direct part in the government at all. It was admitted that "there are strong minds in every walk of life that will rise superior to the disadvantages of their situation, and will command the tribute due to their merit, not only from the classes to which they particularly belong, but from the society in general," but these "are exceptions to the rule."

[1] The Federalist, No. 72.

"The representative body, with too few exceptions to have any influence on the spirit of the government, will be composed of landholders, merchants, and men of the learned professions."[1]

The checks and balances of the constitution were regarded, not as restraints upon the government itself, but as restraints upon the classes who would have possession of the government, to keep them from abusing their trusts for individual advantage. By giving a different constitution to the various branches of government, it was intended to counteract class selfishness by creating antagonistic interests. "Ambition must be made to counteract ambition," said Madison. "The interests of the man must be connected with the constitutional rights of the place."[2] John Adams wrote, "It is the true policy of the common people to place the whole executive power in one man, to make him a distinct order in the state, from whence arises an inevitable jealousy between him and the rest of the gentlemen; this forces him to become the father and protector of the common people, and to endeavor always to humble every proud aspiring senator, or other officer in the state, who is in danger of acquiring an influence too great for the law or the spirit of the constitution."[3] And again, "If the people are sufficiently enlightened to see all the dangers that

---

[1] The Federalist, Nos. 35, 36.   [2] *Ibid.*, No. 51.
[3] Adams' Works, Vol. VI., p. 186.

surround them, they will always be represented by
a distinct personage to manage the whole executive
power ; a distinct Senate, to be guardians of property against levellers for the purposes of plunder,
to be a repository of the national tradition of
public maxims, customs, and manners, and to be
controllers in turn both of kings and ministers on
one side, and the representatives of the people on
the other, when either discover a disposition to do
wrong ; and a distinct House of Representatives,
to be the guardian of the public purse and to protect the people, in their turn, against both kings
and nobles." [1]

A government constituted on these principles
was obviously not a republic, in the sense in which
we use the word, as implying popular rule. A title
fairly descriptive of its nature was that applied to
it by John Adams, in some correspondence with
Roger Sherman, at the time of the adoption of
the constitution. He called it "a monarchical
republic " ; but it must not be supposed that there
is in the term any intimation of a hybrid or unique
species of government. In his writings on government, Adams had classified England under the
same title ; and in now applying it to America he
meant simply that it, too, was a monarchy, iñ that
the custody of the executive power was an individual
trust, and that it was also republican, inasmuch
as the constitution provided for the represen-

[1] Adams' Works, Vol. VI., pp. 117, 118.

tation of the people. It is quite plain that this was the view taken by the authors of the Federalist, though not so bluntly stated. The new government is always referred to as republican; but Madison explained that by republic he means "a government in which the scheme of representation takes place"—a definition which includes England quite as well as America. He argued that the new government should by no means be classed with the democratic republics of antiquity, in which the people ruled. "Democracies have ever been spectacles of turbulence and contention, have ever been found incompatible with personal security or the rights of property, and have in general been as short in their lives as they have been violent in their deaths." Means must be provided "to refine and enlarge the public views, by passing them through the medium of a chosen body of citizens whose wisdom may best discern the true interests of their country."[1] "The true distinction between these (ancient republics) and the American governments lies in the total exclu-

---

[1] The Federalist, No. 10. Adams in one of his letters remarks that in England a republican was regarded as unamiably as a witch or blasphemer. According to Jefferson's Anas something of this prejudice against the word lingered in Washington's mind. Jefferson relates that on May 23, 1793, Washington called his attention to the word "republic" in the draft of a state paper, with the remark that it was a word "which he had never before seen in any of our public communications." On November 28, Jefferson records his satisfaction that the expression "our republic" had

sion of the people in their collective capacity from any share in the latter."[1] There is nothing in the constitution requiring Congress to hold public sittings, although "each House shall keep a journal of its proceedings, and from time to time publish the same, except such parts as may in their judgment require secrecy." Members were not to be simply the delegates of the people; for the purposes of government they were the people themselves. To protect them in the complete exercise of this representative capacity, it was provided that "for any speech or debate in either House they shall not be questioned in any other place."[2] That the people may know

been introduced by Attorney General Randolph in his draught of the President's speech to Congress, and that Washington made no objection to it. Jefferson's Writings (Ford's edition), Vol. I., pp. 231, 271.

[1] The Federalist, No. 63.

[2] Article 1, Section 6, of the constitution. The original source is the Bill of Rights of 1689. This privilege the House of Commons was in the habit of asserting to the extent of forbidding any publication of its debates or comment on its proceedings. Colonial legislatures had as stoutly maintained the same privilege. This is one of the features on which Patrick Henry based his opposition to the adoption of the constitution. In one of his speeches before the Virginia convention he said: "What security have we in money matters? Inquiry is precluded by this constitution. . . . How are you to keep inquiry alive? How discover their conduct? We are told by that paper that a regular statement and account of the receipts and expenditures of public money shall be published from time to time. Here is a beautiful check! Here is the utmost latitude left. If those who are in Congress please to put that construction upon it, the words of the constitution will be satisfied by

what their trustees do with the funds in their keeping, "a regular statement of the receipts and expenditures of public money shall be published from time to time." Thus a certain degree of accountability was established; but the desire was not to enable the people to control the government, but to enable the government to control the people. "In framing a government which is to be administered by men over men," said Madison, "the great difficulty lies in this: you must first enable the government to control the governed, and in the next place, oblige it to control itself." [1]

So, then, the framers of the constitution made no intentional provision for the control of the government by public opinion. The idea could hardly have occurred to them. Public opinion in the modern sense of the word is a very recent thing. As late as 1820, Sir Robert Peel spoke contemptuously of "that great compound of folly, weakness, prejudice, wrong-feeling, right-feeling, obstinacy, and newspaper paragraphs which is called public opinion." If the definition had been attempted in 1787, public opinion would have been described, very likely, as aristocratic greed, knavery, and in-

---

publishing those accounts once in a hundred years. They may publish or not as they please." Wm. Wirt Henry's Patrick Henry, Vol. III., pp. 491, 492. Popular anxiety on the subject was so great that the first amendment to the constitution prohibited the making of any laws "abridging the freedom of speech or of the press."

[1] The Federalist, No. 51.

trigue, compounded with popular stupidity and mob
clamor. Who then could have dreamed of the great
series of inventions which have transformed the
world? These elaborate networks of railroads
and telegraphs, the product of a social activity
which has meanwhile been making corresponding
gains in public education and popular intelligence,
are nerve filaments of the body politic, giving it
an organization and a sensitiveness that constitute
it a new being, unknown before since the beginning of the world. In the eighteenth century, the
possibility of such a phenomenon was unthinkable.
The human animal, alone or in the herd, was about
the same as he always had been, and such as he
was always likely to be. Political characteristics
were much the same as when Aristotle surveyed
party struggles in the Grecian states, or when
Cicero analyzed the faction strifes of Rome. Modern civilization itself seemed to be a barbarian en-
campment in the ruins of the ancient world, the
memorials of whose grandeur were melancholy
portents. Gibbon, whose great history belongs
to this period, concludes his account of the fall
of the Roman Empire with some speculations 'on
the fate of the modern world, whose undertone of
gloomy foreboding is not concealed by their show
of philosophic composure. In the grand French
monarchy, where the stability of government seemed
impregnable, society indulged optimistic dreams of
what might be accomplished by the reign of philos-

ophy. With light hearts and buoyant spirits the ancient régime pushed out into the stream of vanity and glided down towards the Niagara plunge of revolution. English institutions were still too unsettled after the upheavals of the seventeenth century to permit any false sense of security to arise. In England and America, the spirit of the age was pessimistic. There was an away-with-melancholy struggle in the coarse enjoyments of society. Irreligion was as abounding as in France; but it was not mocking in spirit, for the necessity of making use of every element of social order caused statesmen to value even "the authority of superstition."[1] There was a cynic contempt of day dreams and utopist fancies.[2] While doing with Stoic fortitude what it lay in them to do, the men who took the chief part in founding the republic had painful misgivings as to the durability of their work.[3]

[1] The Federalist, No. 38, by Madison.

[2] In the Federalist, No. 30, written by Hamilton, there is a characteristic allusion to the enthusiasts "who expect to see the halcyon scenes of the poetic or fabulous age realized in America."

[3] In a letter written in his old age, John Adams says that Washington was made unhappy in his retirement, after occupying the presidential chair, by fears for his country. Adams' Works, Vol. X., p. 16. Hamilton, towards the close of the great career which was brought to such an untimely end, wrote to a friend, "Perhaps no man in the United States has sacrificed or done more for the present constitution than myself, and, contrary to all my anticipations of its fate, as you know, from the very beginning, I am still laboring to prop up the frail and worthless fabric." Works, Vol. VII., p. 591.

The democratic tendencies which they dreaded seemed uncontrollable. Despite all their pains in fashioning the machine on the old model, it would not work that way. The trouble was, as Fisher Ames acutely remarked, " Constitutions are but paper ; society is the substratum of government." The social conditions were such that the constitution could not escape conversion to democratic uses.

Although the fathers imagined that they were making the government on the old Whig model, they were only copying its external form. In reality, the Whig theory of government was a fiction masking the transfer of administrative authority from the crown to parliament. The attachment of the English people to kingship was such that politicians were bound to defer to it, just as politicians in our day are bound to maintain that their proposals are thoroughly constitutional and realize the true intent of the fathers. The Whigs, in their way, were as sincere in their loyalty to the crown as the Tories, but after the Revolution of 1689 England was really ruled by the landed aristocracy. The personal rule which George III exercised did not proceed so much from the authority of the crown as from its influence. It was the rule, not of a king, but of a political boss, dependent upon corrupt inducements and transient combinations.[1] The crown, lords, and commons were

---

[1] "The power of the crown, almost dead and rotten as prerogative, has grown up anew, with much more strength and far less

not in fact distinct and independent depositaries of authority ; for the landed gentry served as a connective tissue, enfolding the branches of government and establishing a centralized control.   Seats in Parliament were almost personal property, and were frequently sold as such.   Elections, as a rule, were a mere matter of form.   Contests were rare. In the first general election held in George III's reign there were contests only in two counties and sixteen boroughs of England, and none at all in Scotland or in Wales.[1]   At the beginning of the present century, of 658 members of Parliament, 487 were virtually nominated by peers or wealthy squires.

Whatever unity or efficiency of administration existed in the national government when it was first established was due to the fact that the gentry controlled the government in all its branches. Hence the machine did actually go.   The French revolutionary constitution of 1791, which was framed with the same idea of separating the executive and legislative powers, broke down at once for want of such coördinating social influences. Similar failures have attended almost every attempt to imitate the constitution of the United States. The constitutional checks clog the machine. Deadlocks are broken by executive decree, and it

odium, under the name of influence." Burke's Present Discontents, 1770.

[1] Jephson's The Platform, Vol. I., p. 16.

speedily becomes manifest that the true constitution is a military oligarchy. The history of Central and South American republics affords numerous examples of this process.

The class supremacy dexterously reasserted by the gentry was, however, doomed to destruction. The English gentry had to do with a settled population, trained to habits of deference and unable to escape from landlord control. But the American gentry were very differently situated. During the greater portion of the colonial period, the pressure of the French and Indians upon the English settlements confined the field, so that the prestige of the gentry could not be seriously impaired. But with the expulsion of the European powers, and the driving back of the Indians, a profound change in social conditions ensued. The land was practically illimitable in extent, and coercive social arrangements were impracticable, as the fathers soon discovered. " We need as all nations do," wrote Fisher Ames to Rufus King in 1802, "the compression on the outside of our circle of a formidable neighbor, whose presence shall at all times excite stronger fears than demagogues can inspire the people with towards their government."[1] The actual conditions were such as to favor democratic concessions. The desire to obtain settlers caused inducements, which early took the

---

[1] Life and Correspondence of Rufus King, Vol. IV., p. 106.

shape of offers of political franchises.[1]   The restrictions upon the suffrage on which the framers of the Constitution had depended, as guaranteeing the political control of the gentry, soon began to loosen. The breach between society and politics, which was sure to occur when political influence ceased to be a class privilege of the gentry, was not long delayed.[2] Hamilton lamented the growing indifference of the better class of people to the exercise of their suffrage much in the style so common nowadays. That breach was destined to expand until the honorable title of politician should carry with it a social

[1] As early as 1681 William Penn set forth among the attractions which his province of Pennsylvania offered to settlers that "they will have the right of voting, not only for the election of the magistrates of the place in which they live, but also for the members of the provincial council and the general assembly, which two bodies, conjointly with the governor, formed the sovereign power." The desire for settlers in the colonies was so strong that one of the grievances specified in the Declaration of Independence was that the king put obstacles in the way of emigration. The operation of this desire has had marked effects upon American institutions. Fourteen states give foreigners the right to vote on the declaration of an intention to be naturalized.

[2] The danger was foreseen by the framers of the Constitution. Dickinson remarked that the freeholders were "the best guardians of liberty, and the restrictions of the right (of suffrage) to them was a necessary defence against the dangerous influence of those multitudes without property and without principle with which our country, like all others, will in time abound." The qualifications in the different states were so various that it was found impossible to agree on any uniform rule, and the constitution therefore simply adopts in every state the voting qualifications prescribed in elections for representatives in the state legislature.

opprobrium and what is known as good society would hold itself aloof from politics or merely invade it at intervals.

The gentry did not, however, lose their control until they had founded the government and established agencies for operating its machinery in lieu of those which their class interests had provided. Parties were founded whose organization was gradually to develop a strength and an elaboration equal to the intricate tasks imposed by the complex nature of the government. The rigid framework of the Constitution forced political development to find its outlet in extra-constitutional agencies, bringing the executive and legislative branches under a common control, despite the constitutional theory. The new control was to be essentially as aristocratic as the old, for the political class is none the less an aristocracy, although its muniments do not consist of social privilege or territorial endowment, but rest upon proficiency in the management of party organization too complex for any save professional experts to handle. The history of American politics verifies Burke's remark, that "an aristocracy is the most natural thing in the world."

PART II

POLITICAL DEVELOPMENT

—◆—

CHAPTER VI

SETTING UP THE GOVERNMENT

THE new government patterned its behavior as closely as possible after the English style. Hamilton drew up for the President a scheme of etiquette, imitating royal exclusiveness. "In Europe," he said, "ambassadors only have direct access to the chief magistrate. Something very near what prevails there would, in my opinion, be right. . . . I have thought that the members of the Senate should also have a right of individual access on matters relative to the public administration. In England and France peers of the realm have this right." But the Representatives were not entitled to such a privilege.[1]

The address to Congress, with which Washington opened the session, was couched in the style of the speech from the throne. At the first session there was some talk of setting up a sort of throne

[1] Hamilton's Works, Vol. IV., p. 3.

for him in the senate chamber, but the project did
not take well and it was dropped. He used the
Vice-President's chair instead, and the Representatives went to the senate chamber to hear him, as
the Commons proceed to the House of Lords on
similar occasions. He addressed himself to both
bodies, or either, as the nature of his remarks suggested. The tone was personal, such as a king
might use. In his speech opening Congress at its
first session, referring to his constitutional duty
of recommending to their consideration such measures as he should deem necessary and expedient,
he expressed his appreciation of "the talents, the
rectitude, and patriotism which adorn the characters selected to devise and adopt them." In opening the next session, he told the Representatives:
"I saw with peculiar pleasure, at the close of the
last session, the resolution entered into by you,
expressive of your opinion that an adequate provision for the support of the public credit is a
matter of high importance to the national honor
and prosperity. In this sentiment I entirely concur. And, to a perfect confidence in your best
endeavors to devise such a provision as will be
truly consistent with the ends, I add an equal reliance on the cheerful coöperation of the other
branch of the legislature."

Congress, too, conformed to English precedents
in its procedure. The houses would vote a joint
address in reply, containing a due amount of per-

sonal compliment. The members trooped to the President's "audience chamber," and the president of the Senate delivered the address, whereupon the President would renew the assurances of his distinguished consideration.[1]

It is pathetic to read the accounts which have reached us of the embarrassments of General Washington in his conscientious discharge of these irksome duties. The explosion of wrath described by Jefferson in his "Anas," when Washington swore he would rather be living on his farm than be emperor of the universe,[2] was doubtless the expression of the dearest wish of his heart.[3] Maclay tells us that when Washington made his first address to Congress, he was "agitated and embarrassed more than ever he was by the levelled cannon or the pointed musket." A similar spectacle was presented when Congress waited on him to deliver their address in response. Maclay says : —

"The President took his reply out of his coat

---

[1] The joint rules adopted by the First Congress provided "that when the Senate and House of Representatives shall judge it proper to make a joint address to the President it shall be presented to him in his audience chamber, by the President of the Senate, in the presence of the Speaker and both houses."

[2] Jefferson's Writings (Ford's edition), Vol. I., p. 254.

[3] When John Adams was inaugurated he was impressed by Washington's intense gratification on quitting office. Adams wrote to his wife : "Methought I heard him say, 'Ay ! I am fairly out, and you fairly in; see which of us will be the happiest.'"

pocket. He had his spectacles in his jacket pocket, having his hat in his left hand and his paper in his right. He had too many objects for his hands. He shifted his hat between his forearm and the left side of his breast. But taking his spectacles from the case embarrassed him. He got rid of this small distress by laying the spectacle case on the chimney-piece. . . . Having adjusted his spectacles, which was not very easy considering the engagements of his hands, he read the reply with tolerable exactness and without much emotion."

Many a time must this honest, single-minded Virginia gentleman have deplored the fate which made such pretence his duty, when in the ordinary course of affairs he should have had a right to expect that he would be living in comfort on his plantation, engaged in the country employments and recreations of which he was so fond. Mrs. Washington also had to exchange the genial hospitality and easy manners of Virginia for a stiff etiquette and a social parade which made her the target of disparaging gossip.[1] And while Washington, with his best endeavor, thus played his part in this caricature of kingship, it was quite ineffectual. There was no historical prestige attaching to his office; there were no fixed social gradations to buttress his dignity; he had no revenue nor patronage, save what Congress chose to create for him. His brand-new authority was

[1] Maclay records a characteristic sample. Journal, p. 73.

destitute of the sanctions which attach to royal
prerogative and it inspired no awe. Within the
limit of its constitutional powers, Congress might
decide for itself how it would treat the President.
The matter would be determined wholly by its own
disposition. That disposition was not hostile, but
it was very suspicious. In addition to the usual
fear of subjects as to what rulers might do if given
the opportunity, there was a strong apprehension
that the Federal leaders were hankering after something grand and splendid in the way of government,
as close to the monarchical standard as possible.

We have a vivid picture of this attitude of mind
in the diary kept by William Maclay, one of the
senators from Pennsylvania, an honest, well-mean-
ing man, who came to Congress without any
previous share in the councils of the Federal managers. The bent of his mind was critical from the
first. The measures to which the national politicians were forced to resort in managing Congress
offended him and inspired personal dislikes which
he records with amusing simplicity. Jefferson has
" a rambling and vacant look" and "his discourse
partook of his personal demeanor." " He had been
long enough abroad to catch the tone of European folly." Knox has "a bacchanalian figure."
" Hamilton has a very boyish, giddy manner, and
Scotch-Irish people could well call him a 'skite.'"
John Adams, who had been so much abroad that
he felt warranted in giving the Senate occasional

instructions on the way things were done in Europe, the diarist cannot mention without an expression of disgust. He "has a very silly kind of laugh." There "sat Bonny John Adams ever and anon mantling his visage with the most unmeaning simper that ever dimpled the face of folly." Madison is "His Littleness." "There is an obstinacy, a perverse peevishness, a selfishness, which shuts him up from free communication." General Washington himself, as the associate of such men, becomes an object of increasing suspicion. At last the diarist declares : "If there is treason in the wish, I retract it, but would to God this same General Washington were in Heaven! We would not then have him brought forward as the constant cover to every un-constitutional and ir-republican act."

With such a temper in Congress, attempts to establish usages requiring a habit of deference on its part, were doomed to failure. The design of using the Senate as a privy council was baffled as soon as tried. Maclay gives a lively account of the affair. Washington entered the Senate chamber and took the Vice-President's chair. He informed the Senate that he had called for their advice and consent to some propositions respecting the treaty with the southern Indians and had brought the Secretary of War along to explain the business. General Knox produced some papers, which were read. Washington's presence em-

barrassed the Senate. Finally a motion was made
to refer the papers to a committee, and there was
some debate for and against. Maclay spoke in
favor of doing business by committee. The diarist continues : "As I sat down, the President of
the United States started up in a violent fret.
'This defeats every purpose of my coming here,'
were the first words that he said. He then went
on that he had brought his Secretary of War with
him to give every necessary information ; that the
Secretary knew all about the business, and yet he
was delayed and could not go on with the matter."
Finally, the President said that he would have no
objection to postponing further consideration until
the ensuing Monday, but he did not understand
the matter of commitment. There were awkward
pauses. ".We waited for him to withdraw," says
the diarist. " He did so with a discontented air."

It did not take much of such business to deter
Washington from treating the Senate as his privy
council. He finally had to do what every President has done since — make his treaties first, and
submit them to the Senate afterwards, for ratification. The comfortable seclusion of this practice,
once enjoyed, would not willingly be given up.
In 1813 the Senate invited the attendance of the
President to consult on foreign affairs, but Madison
declined the invitation.

The breakdown of the privy council functions
of the Senate had an important result in clearing

the way for the development of the Cabinet. It
was generally supposed at the time of the adoption of the Constitution that the administration
would practically consist of the President and the
Senate acting in conjunction.[1] If the President
had found in the Senate a congenial body of
advisers, so that treaties and appointments to
office would have been made in conference with
it, so much of the policy of the administration
would thus have been brought within the habitual
purview of the Senate that the natural tendency
would have been to draw in the rest likewise. The
language of the Constitution would favor that tendency, while on the other hand the Constitution
is altogether ignorant of the President's Cabinet,
which actually became his privy council. The idea
that the heads of the executive departments are
the personal appointees of each President, the
chiefs of party administration, did not at first
exist.[2] It was assumed that their position was

[1] Mason, of Virginia, refused to sign the report of the constitutional convention because it provided for the rule of an aristocracy.
IIe objected to "the substitution of the Senate in place of an executive council and to the powers vested in that body." Madison's
Works, Congressional edition, Vol. I., p. 355. In the South Carolina convention James Lincoln said: "Pray who are the United
States? A president and four or five senators."

[2] This explains why neither Jefferson nor his opponents thought
there was anything dishonorable in his retention of office while
stirring up opposition to the policy of the administration. Jefferson
continued in office from a sense of public duty for some time after
he wanted to retire. The idea that by so doing he precluded him-

non-partisan and that their tenure of office would
be the same as that of other officials, which was
then regarded as one of permanency during good
behavior.   Hence the Constitution conferred upon
the President as a special privilege, authority to
"require the opinion, in writing, of the principal
officer in each of the executive departments, upon
any subject relating to the duties of their respective offices."   The incongruous superfluity of that
provision, since constitutional usage has made the
selection of Cabinet officers the President's individual prerogative, and has made their tenure of
office subject to his pleasure, shows that the actual
course taken in the development of the government was not altogether anticipated, although the
intentional flexibility of the Constitution, as regards
executive power, gave it an easy permission.

All the members of Washington's Cabinet except
Hamilton were of the opinion that Congress could
not communicate with the heads of departments

self from carrying on an agitation in support of his views of public
policy did not occur to him or his friends, even the most high-
minded of them. . The theory was that the president, like the king,
was above party, so that the idea of treachery towards him or
breach of obligation in party behavior had no place. It was the
same way in England at the same period. Ministers in the same
Cabinet might represent opposing party interests and endeavor to
undermine one another. But conduct like Jefferson's in a statesman of our own times would be thought basely dishonorable. The
same observations apply to Hamilton's conduct in maintaining a
secret control over Adams' administration by his influence with the
Cabinet officials.   .

except through the President. Hamilton, who uniformly acted on his maxim of practical politics that "the public business must in some way or other, go forward,"[1] paid no attention to the scruples of theorists, but entered at once into direct relations with Congress. From the first, he assumed the functions of a crown minister to the fullest extent which circumstances would allow, and his example was soon followed by all the other members of the Cabinet.[2] He organized his department with the view of making it the organ of Congress in the preparation of financial measures.[3] The great series of measures by which he established the finances of the nation were addressed by him directly to the House of Representatives. All his acts consist with the assumption that relations between the heads of the departments and Congress should be practically the

[1] The Federalist, No. 22.

[2] Maclay describes a visit by Jefferson to the Senate chamber to advise the Senate to make a lump appropriation for the diplomatic service to be apportioned according to the discretion of the President. Maclay's Journal, p. 272.

[3] The act establishing the Treasury department became law, September 2, 1789. The nomination of Hamilton as Secretary of the Treasury was not sent to the Senate until September 11. But for months previous he had been active in organizing the government, and the act was drawn in accordance with his ideas. The Federalist, No. 36, written by Hamilton, forecasts the relations of the department to Congress proposed by the act and also indicates that the plan of assuming the debts of the states had already been conceived by him.

same as between the king's ministers and Parliament. He became the premier of the ministry, the channel of communication between the executive and the legislature.[1] This adherence to English precedents appears not only in the manner, but in the character of his work. His scheme for funding the public debt, his plan for a sinking fund, and his proposals for the charter of a national bank, all show recourse to English methods.[2] The powerful influence which the Bank of England had exercised in upholding the Whig government after the English Revolution of 1689, made a suggestion that could not be ignored in devising means to

[1] There was some practical recognition of his position as such. For instance, Jefferson, who was himself Secretary of State, wrote to Hamilton to ask what the Senate would do in regard to certain proposals for a treaty with Algiers. Hamilton's Works, Vol. IV., p. 215. Not the Secretary of War, but Hamilton, wrote to the House "that it is the opinion of the secretary for the department of war, that it is expedient and necessary that the United States should retain and occupy West Point." Works, Vol. II., p. 82. It was Hamilton's practice to revise and alter important state papers prepared by the other Cabinet officers. In a communication to the Attorney General he advised various changes in a paper draughted by him, and even told him that "there appears to me too much tartness in various parts." Works, Vol. IV., p. 544. The extent to which Hamilton's activity pervaded and controlled all the executive departments is extraordinary and it is not to be wondered at that Jefferson should have been chagrined and that Madison should have complained of Hamilton's "mentorship to the commander-in-chief."

[2] For the evidence see Dunbar on "Some Precedents Followed by Alexander Hamilton," *Quarterly Journal of Economics*, October, 1888.

brace and stay the new government. The national bank was founded as much as a political engine as a financial instrumentality. The assumption by the nation of the state debts contracted during the Revolutionary War, had the twofold purpose of diminishing state taxation, so as to clear the field for the operation of the revenue laws of the nation, and of creating a national debt which would be "a cement to the union." With a large body of national creditors in existence, distributed throughout the Union, it was certain that there would be an extensive class of citizens, who would have a direct interest in seeing that a ship of state carrying such valuable freight should be well found and safely handled.

Hamilton's active initiative would not, however, have carried matters far, had it not been supplemented by direct personal management. The public business does not manage itself any more than any other business, and pure reason figures in it as little as in human affairs generally. Politicians have to deal with human nature not as it ought to be, but as it is. The ordinary motives and propensities are more apt to be mean than heroic, so that any man engaged in business must at times admit expedients which have no moral dignity to commend them. In the ordinary affairs of life allowance is made for stress of circumstances, and the fact is recognized that a man of honor may be compelled to make what is called a choice of evils, although it is in truth the selection of a right course in a complicated moral situation. But owing to the curious way in which the public business is idealized by public sentiment, no allowance is made to politicians, and their acts are measured by contemporary opinion according to the abstract ethics which everybody is able to apply to other people. However, in the politics of the English race, ethical theory does not control practice in public affairs any more than in ordinary business. Their institutions have not been made by rule, but have grown, having their roots in race motives and taking their characteristic shape from circumstances of development. In the fulness of time it appears that this growth has had a moral order of its own, but the discovery comes from the appreciation of posterity, and furious censure is apt to be the lot of those whose activities sustained the process of that growth which a later age admires. For all that, there never have been lacking statesmen of the stuff to endure whatever obloquy the discharge of the practical duties of their office may incur. The case of Hamilton is one of the most remarkable examples of this political virtue which history affords. True, such Stoic intrepidity is not rare in politicians of the English breed. Among the statesmen of the Georgian era, there were those who equalled Hamilton in this respect, but they had compensations which he did not have. In England, the government was rich and the management of it lucrative. Men could not only make fortunes for themselves, but could provide well for their relatives and friends. The peculiarity of Hamilton's case is that while he was organizing the government, establishing its finances, and performing prodigies of intellectual effort in the service of the public, to be repaid by calumny and abuse, he was at the same time sacrificing his legal practice and professional advancement for an office paying him $3000 a year, in an age of lavish personal expenditure and social ostentation.

The scale of Hamilton's operations seemed colossal in his day, and to men who did not share his penetration in discerning the extent of national resources, his measures for funding the public debt seemed like fastening a millstone to the neck of the infant nation. The vastness of his plans gave a correspondingly wide scope to the operations of speculators, the advance in the value of public securities opening a rich field of gain. Of course the cry was raised that these speculative opportunities, inevitably incident to any restoration of public credit, were the object of Hamilton's policy. He was accused of setting up an engine of corruption to control the legislature and destroy the purity and simplicity of republican institutions. The political literature of the time is full of references to Hamilton's "corrupt squadron" in Congress, his "gladiators" who by their venal coöperation beat down the opposition of the honest and independent members. Such accusations are the lot of every statesman who has to devise great financial measures. In our own times Secretary Sherman had to move through a storm of abuse in accomplishing the resumption of specie payments, and a like tempest raged around Secretary Carlisle in maintaining the integrity of treasury obligations. But no statesman has ever had to contend against so virulent an opposition with such slender resources as Alexander Hamilton.

Maclay gives an acrid account of Hamilton's negotiation with members of Congress for support to his measures. Various combinations of interest were tried and at last the greedy squabble over the site of the national capital afforded him the necessary leverage. There was really more active concern in Congress about that matter than about the national finances. Even the austere Maclay remarks, that with Dr. Rush he had "puffed John Adams in the papers and brought him forward for Vice-President," because "we knew his vanity and hoped by laying hold of it to render him useful among the New England men in our scheme of bringing Congress to Pennsylvania." Maclay relates that Madison made a motion reducing General St. Clair's salary as governor of the Western territory the very day the general had disparaged the claims of the Potomac site, although previously Madison had favored a larger amount.[1] The bill for assuming state debts was finally carried by means of a bargain arranged between Hamilton and Jefferson, the votes of a sufficient number of Southern members being obtained in return for Northern votes for the Potomac site. The foundations of the national government were laid by "log-rolling."

Although Hamilton's assumption of leadership was made good for a time, from the start it met with an opposition which showed that it could not be permanent. The bill establishing the treasury department made it the duty of the Secretary "to digest and report plans for the improvement and management of the revenue, and for the support of the public credit." Page, of Virginia, immediately moved to strike out that clause on the ground that "a precedent would be established which might be extended until ministers of the government should be admitted on that floor to explain and support the plans they had digested and reported, thereby laying the foundation for an aristocracy or a detestable monarchy." Madison defended the proposed grant of power on the ground that it would promote good administration, which was the chief end of government. Page's motion was defeated, but the word "prepare" was substituted for "report," and it was made evident that the open connection between administration and legislation would continue only so long as the

[1] Maclay's Journal, p. 150.

House should choose to permit it. The temporary splice between the executive and legislative branches was too weak to stand party violence, and at this point the first attack was made when an opposition was organized and the formation of national parties began. Originally the only standing committee of the House had been one on elections. Any matter on which the House desired information, whether a claim, petition, or memorial, was generally referred directly to the head of the proper department. When the House took up an attitude of hostility towards the Secretary of the Treasury, the system of standing committees, which has had such a monstrous development, was begun. In January, 1795, Hamilton quitted an office which had lost the functions that made it useful for his purposes. The effect of the changed relations upon the conduct of the public business was described with prophetic insight by Fisher Ames in a letter to Hamilton, two years after the latter's retirement from office : —

" The heads of departments are chief clerks. Instead of being the ministry, the organs of the executive power, and imparting a kind of momentum to the operation of the laws, they are precluded even from communicating with the House by reports. In other countries they may speak as well as act. We allow them to do neither. We forbid them even the use of a speaking-trumpet ; or more properly, as the Constitution has ordained that they shall be dumb, we forbid them to explain themselves by signs. Two evils, obvious to you, result from all this. The efficiency of government is reduced to a minimum — the proneness of a popular body to usurpation is already advancing to its maximum; committees already are the ministers; and while the House indulges a jealousy of encroachment in its functions, which are properly deliberative, it does not perceive that these are impaired and nullified by the monopoly as well as the perversion of information by these committees. The silly reliance of our haughty House and Congress prattlers on a responsibility of members to the people, &c., is disgraced by every page in the history of popular bodies." [1]

The attempt to maintain the unity of administration by means of ministerial leadership had failed. The political organism was constrained to develop new faculties for that purpose. The necessary control was resumed through the agency of party.

[1] Hamilton's Works, Vol. VI., p. 201.

CHAPTER VII

THE bane of the Whig ideal of government was party spirit. It introduced principles of association inconsistent with the constitutional scheme. Because of party spirit gentlemen betrayed the interests of their order and menaced the peace of society by demagogic appeals to the common people. Instead of the concert of action which should exist between the departments of government as the result of a patriotic purpose common to all, devotion to party was substituted, and the constitutional depositaries of power were converted into the fortifications of party interest.

Throughout the eighteenth century, party was regarded as a gangrene, a cancer, which patriotic statesmen should combine to eradicate. This chord of sentiment was skilfully touched by Bolingbroke in his influential treatise, "The Patriot King," in which he eloquently portrayed the character of the just ruler who should break down party control and command for the state the service of all good men. The policy of George III. was formed upon this ideal, and it influenced the conduct of the greatest statesmen of the age. The elder Pitt prevented the Rockingham Whigs from establishing a stable government by holding aloof on the ground that he thought "any change insufficient which did not comprehend or annihilate every party in the kingdom."[1] He finally upset the Whig government by consenting to take office at the head of a non-partisan administration. This administration — whose power was so compacted by crown influence that when Pitt himself turned against it his tremendous attacks were ineffectual — brought on the American war and lost to the British crown thirteen colonies and eight islands.

Edmund Burke splendidly defended the constitutional function of party organization, but it was the fashion to regard him as a clever Irish adventurer in Lord Rockingham's service, repaying his patron by advocating views which suited the designs of a nobleman who wanted to restore the principles of political monopoly and exclusion on which Walpole had acted. Burke defined party as "a body of men united, for promoting by their joint endeavors the national interest, upon some particular principle on which they are all agreed."[2] This is the modern English doctrine, but in 1770, when Burke propounded it, the attempt to put such a gloss on the machinations of cabal and faction was treated with scorn. The idea of basing government on party seemed like selecting poison as

[1] Lecky's History of England, Vol. IV., pp. 256, 297.
[2] The Present Discontents.

a diet. A section of the Whig party, in whose ranks were conspicuous some statesmen distinguished in a corrupt age for their rigid personal integrity, fought party government to the last. The Whig ministry, which in 1783 succeeded to power after the British defeats in America had temporarily destroyed Tory ascendency, was shattered by a conflict on this point. Shelburne, who stubbornly resisted the efforts of the Rockingham Whigs to organize the Cabinet as a party interest, told the House of Commons that he had imbibed the principles of "his master in politics, the Earl of Chatham, who had always declared that this country ought not to be governed by any party or faction, and that if it were to be so governed the constitution must necessarily expire."[1]

In fact, the principle of party government was never recognized in England until it was firmly established in practice, and it had become manifest that, despite all theory to the contrary, any other mode of government was quite impracticable. The acceptance of the party system involved a profound alteration in the constitutional theory. The old Whig doctrine of checks and balances of power became obsolete. It was found by experience that more efficient checks and balances were inherent in the constitution of party itself, since it is constantly obliged to consider all shades of opinion in order to maintain its strength. The amassing of

[1] Lecky, Vol. IV., p. 256.

the sovereignty of the nation in one organ of government, which according to the old theory was
the very essence of tyranny, became the very
essence of popular rule. The modern theory is
thus stated by Bagehot: "The English constitution is founded on the principle of choosing
a single sovereign authority and making it
good."

The old Whig abhorrence of party spirit raged
in the bosoms of the fathers. It is a topic to
which frequent reference is made in their speeches
and correspondence. The Federalist abounds
with remarks on "the pestilential influence of
party animosities." It forms the chief topic of
Washington's farewell address to his countrymen.
"There is an opinion," he says, "that parties in free
countries are useful checks upon the administration
of the government, and serve to keep alive the spirit
of liberty. This within certain limits is probably
true; and, in governments of a monarchical class,
patriotism may look with indulgence, if not with
favor, on the spirit of party. But in those of a
popular character, in governments purely elective,
it is a spirit not to be encouraged." He re-states
the Whig doctrine of "the necessity of reciprocal
checks in the exercise of political power, by dividing and distributing it into different depositaries,
and constituting each the guardian of the public
weal against the invasions of the others." He
describes in solemn language the "horrid enor-

mities " which party spirit may perpetrate against these constitutional safeguards of government.

Innumerable echoes of that memorable appeal still reach the ears of the public. Non-partisanship is still preached as a civic duty, but it has never been reduced to practice and it never will be. The reason is very simple. No law of human nature is better known than that action is the correlative of desire. The very existence of public opinion implies the seeking of means for giving effect to it in the conduct of public affairs, and in a free country this produces party action. But little reflection is needed to show that what are called non-partisan movements are really new party combinations, and the only distinction marked by the phrase is that the purpose is special and transient.

As with every organism, the natural tendency of party is to obtain sustenance wherever it can. It appeals to the follies and passions, as well as to the virtues, of human nature, so that its activity is as productive of evil manifestations as well as of good as the capacity of human nature allows. Hence it always presents aspects revolting to upright men. In particular, its subordination of all other considerations to the needs of its own organization, is accompanied by a disregard of absolute standards of worth, which is peculiarly offensive to those who do not feel, or sympathize with, its necessities. This defect in accommodation of party functions to ethical ideals is ever a source of complaint, and it has inspired magnificent outbursts of scorn from poets and moralists. Nevertheless, there never has been a time, since the colonies had a life of their own, when party spirit was not active in this country, and never more so than when formal party divisions were temporarily effaced. A party which grows so great as to destroy regular opposition tends to split and fall apart from internal repulsions, no longer counteracted by external pressure. Such times are marked by an abounding partisanship, displaying itself in violent faction strife, eventually producing new party combinations.

A period of this kind was brought on by the success of the Revolution. The Tory party was destroyed, and the Whigs were left undisputed masters of the field, but the triumphant party was rent by faction animosities excited during the course of the struggle. In order to understand the situation it is necessary to consider in some detail the political side of the War of Independence.[1]

Congress was not instituted as a regular government and was altogether unfit to exercise the functions which devolved upon it. It assumed

---

[1] The chief authority for the statements which follow is Wharton's "Revolutionary Diplomatic Correspondence," a government publication. There is a vivid account of the characteristics of the Revolutionary period in W. G. Sumner's "Alexander Hamilton."

the control of the national finances, the regulation
of the army and navy, the appointment of public
officials, and in fine the entire administration of
public affairs. The only practicable way in which
a body of notables, equal in rank and importance,
opinionated and contentious, could handle such a
fund of patronage was by continual bargain and
intrigue. Congress sat in private, and it was
secluded from the control of any public opinion
save that of its own circle. The possession of
such opportunities in a position of irresponsible
control subjected character to a dangerous strain,
and there is evidence that deterioration did take
place. Expressions of the sharpest censure might
be collected from contemporary writings. In
the summer of 1778 a letter written by Henry
Laurens, then president of Congress, in which he
referred to "scenes of venality, peculation and
fraud," was intercepted by the British and published in the London papers. There was always
profusion and waste at the seat of government
however the army might suffer. The festivities
which enclosed the sittings of Congress were
never more extravagant than during the darkest
period of the struggle. Washington wrote that
"party disputes and personal quarrels are the
great business of the day ; whilst the momentous
concerns of an empire, a great and accumulating
debt, ruined finances, depreciated money and
want of credit, which in its consequences is the

want of everything, are but secondary considerations and postponed from day to day and from week to week, as if our affairs wore the most promising aspect. . . . And yet an assembly, a concert, a dinner or a supper, will not only take men off from acting in this business, but even from thinking of it." The low repute of Congress injured the patriot cause in foreign estimation and repelled sympathy. The mainstay of American credit abroad was the great personal reputation of Benjamin Franklin and the marvellous ability with which he managed the interests of the infant republic. But had it not been for the energetic remonstrances of the French court, by representations made through its minister at Philadelphia, Congress might have removed Franklin from his post at a most critical juncture. The generalship of Washington was admired by the ablest European critics, among them Frederick the Great; but Washington, too, had to endure the hostility of a congressional cabal which came near removing him from command.

Still it would be a great mistake to infer that the inefficiency of Congress was due to any lack of honesty or patriotism. Its evil tendencies were the result of a defective organization. It was impossible for a body so constituted to act with the resolution and consistency necessary for successful administration, and in every branch of the public service the results were deplorable. Taxes

H

being unpopular, the members eagerly caught up the idea that they could make money out of paper. Between June 23, 1775, and November 29, 1779, bills to the amount of $200,000,000 were emitted and made a legal tender. Severe laws against the advance of prices, and refusal to accept this paper in lieu of money, were enacted. In effect, such financiering was a vast confiscation of property for public use. Jefferson remarked, "It was a mode of taxation, the most oppressive of all because the most unequal of all."[1] The chief sufferers were, of course, the producers, — the laborers, the mechanics, the farmers. They were constantly being defrauded of their just dues, and the natural consequence was the rapid spread of disaffection. Goods were secreted, provisions hid away, and supplies withheld. In 1777, while General Washington, with wretchedly inferior forces, was striving to keep the field against General Howe in Pennsylvania, he said that he felt as if he were in an enemy's country. The commissary department, which Congress insisted upon keeping under its thumb, seemed unable to do anything. Washington's troops were left to starve, while Howe was able to obtain fresh provisions in abundance. The paper-money plague cheated the troops, as it did all who gave service at a fixed rate of compensation. It became impossible to obtain recruits, and disaffection became prevalent in the

[1] Writings, Vol. IV., p. 165.

army. "No day, nor scarce an hour passes," wrote
Washington, "without the offer of a resigned
commission."[1] There was desertion from the
American camp to the British army.

Meanwhile any reform in administration was
stubbornly resisted. The chief solicitude of Congress was to keep the army under civil control.
Dread of the rise of a Cromwell haunted their
minds. Hence, above all things, they resolved to
control military appointments and prevent the
organization of a regular army. In 1776, John
Adams, referring to the promotion of officers by
Congress, said: "That interest, favor, private
friendship, prejudice, may operate more or less
in the present assembly is true. But where will
you lodge this power? To place it in the general
would be more dangerous to the public liberty
and not less liable to abuse." In 1777, he "hoped
that Congress will elect annually all the general
officers." Wharton remarks that "the leaders of
the opposition, by holding the great military appointments in the hands of Congress, by refusing adequate compensation to the soldiers, had
much to do with protracting the war." The behavior of Congress was such as to invite the very
evil they feared. In letters written by confiden-
tial agents of the British government it was
said that Washington's only course in order to
sustain himself would be to follow the example of

[1] Works, Vol. V., p. 201.

Cromwell. Not until the cause of independence had been brought to the brink of ruin did Congress consent to the creation of independent executive departments for the management of finances, war, the marine, and foreign affairs. The triumph of the Revolution soon followed.[1]

By an ordinary law of political development, the efforts made to strengthen executive authority and the resistance thereto made by interests disturbed by change, tended to produce parties in the government, and doubtless would have done so had the government of the Confederation possessed a stable basis. As it was, there were antagonistic factions — the one administrative, the other parliamentary, which served as centres of party forma-

---

[1] Wharton regards the decisive victory over Cornwallis at Yorktown as the direct consequence of the improved financial administration. A department of finance was established, and on March 13, 1781, Robert Morris was placed at its head. " He started with the position that on taxation, full and equal, must the country depend for its ordinary income; that until it showed its readiness to impose such taxation, it could not either honorably or successfully borrow; that the issue of paper money must be stopped, and that a national bank should be established to equalize exchanges and meet sudden governmental exigencies. To the comparative success of his administration, in the face of an opposition the most bitter, is the final triumph of the Revolution to be largely attributed. Our income from taxation was greatly increased, the bank was prosperous, and France, encouraged by this, continued to make loans and forward supplies, without which the campaign of 1781–1782 could not have been effectively conducted." Vol. I., p. 289.

tion. In the one, the military group was prominent ; the other was wholly civilian. On the one side was the energetic desire to build up executive authority ; on the other, an habitual dread of arbitrary power. The parliamentary faction had it all their own way until their principles were discredited by the wretched results of their meddlesome incapacity, when there was a strong reaction in favor of communicating more executive vigor to the government. A class of national politicians, to which Jefferson and Madison belonged, introduced a more sensible tone of thought. It was the influence of this class which eventually prevailed upon Congress to establish executive departments. It was the alliance of this class with the military group which secured the adoption of the constitution, and its features were chiefly their work. Both groups energetically coöperated in setting up and starting the new government. The successful establishment of constitutional government was a break or starting-point, the natural consequence of which was a new alignment of parties.

The rise of national parties is generally dated from the struggle over the adoption of the constitution ; but the nature of that struggle was such that it could not furnish an enduring basis of party action. When the constitution was adopted and put into operation, Anti-federalism, having been merely a policy of negation, was destitute of any principle of vitality. Party action had to find its place under the constitution, and make its issues on questions of constitutional interpretation and government policy.   At the most, all that can be said is that the struggle over the adoption of the constitution engendered antipathies which supplied material for national party purposes ; but the distribution thereof was determined by the circumstances of the time when national parties were formed.   The natural tendency of the defeated Anti-federal state factions was to recruit the party of national opposition ; but when the Anti-federal leaders happened to be faction adversaries of the leaders of the national opposition, the tendency was just the other way.   Hence the time came when Patrick Henry, who had resisted the constitution with all his might, and who had declared that he would " seize the first moment that offered for shaking off the yoke in a constitutional way," [1] was seen on the stump excusing the alien and sedition laws and condemning the Virginia and Kentucky resolutions.   Other prominent leaders of the opposition to the adoption of the constitution, among them Richard Henry Lee, Luther Martin, and Samuel Chase, also became high Federalists.   On the other hand, Madison, Dickinson, and others, who took an active part in securing the adoption of the constitution, became prominent Republicans.   Jefferson, their party leader, had been in sympathy with the

---

[1] Madison's Works, Vol. I., p. 402.

national movement, although out of the country at the time, and on his return had done service of essential value in getting the new government fairly started.

It is, therefore, impossible to establish any connection between Anti-federalism and the Republican party organized by Jefferson, which implies party continuity. The truth is that the formation of national parties was inevitable from the antagonistic views on national policy held by the political groups which coöperated in the adoption of the constitution. The situation was similar to that in England after the Revolution of 1688. Whigs and Tories coöperated in reconstructing the government; but after the Act of Settlement they soon renewed their party strife as furiously as ever. So it was after the adoption of the constitution of the United States. As soon as the government became sufficiently well established to relax the pressure of their common necessity, the groups began to draw apart. The purpose of the military group, and of those associated with them in interest and sympathy, was to make the national government strong and effective. This consideration presided over their calculations of the effect of measures. Their experience had been such as to concentrate their attention on the apparatus of government. On the contrary, the object of the other group of national politicians had been to set up an orderly government, but not a weighty one, which might rest heavily upon the people.[1] Their ideal was an agricultural community, settled in its habits and steady in its ways, requiring no more apparatus of government than would suffice to subject the common people to the magisterial supervision of their natural protectors — the landed gentry. In his "Notes on Virginia," Jefferson said: "While we have land to labor, let us never wish to see our citizens occupied at a workshop or twirling a distaff. . . . Let our workshops remain in Europe. It is better to carry provisions and materials to workmen there than to bring them to the provisions and materials, and with them their manners and principles. . . . The mobs of great cities add just so much to the support of pure government as sores do to the strength of the human body." He brought up this point again when writing to Madison about the new constitution. He said: "I think our governments will remain virtuous for many centuries, as long as they are chiefly agricultural; and this they will be as long as there shall be vacant lands in any part of America. When they get piled up upon one another in large cities, as in Europe, they will become corrupt as in Europe."[2]

The manifest tendency of Hamilton's measures to develop banking, commercial, and manufacturing

---

[1] This explanation of the origin of parties adopts that given by Chief-Justice Marshall, who spoke from his own knowledge of the men and the times. See his Life of Washington, Vol. V., Chap. V.

[2] Jefferson's Writings, Vol. IV., p. 480.

interests seemed therefore to be a policy whose purpose was to corrupt and alter the character of the government. There was no lack of circumstances to feed suspicion. Obstacles, which ignorance and perversity put in the way of plans for the benefit of the government, were the occasion of expressions of disgust in administration circles. Private talk among party managers is apt to be cynic in tone as regards the public. The courtiers of King Demos, like courtiers in general, revenge themselves for the servility which they have to assume in public, by private sneers at his majesty. It is doubtless quite true, as Jefferson reports in his " Anas," that talk at the executive mansion was disparaging of popular government as compared with the order and decency of royal government ; but it does not follow that there was any idea of establishing royalty. Long after, when Hamilton had been for many years in his untimely grave, and the passions of party controversy had cooled, Jefferson acquitted Hamilton of any idea of subverting republican institutions ; but that was the accusation at the time. By a natural antithesis, Jefferson's party styled itself the Republicans. The supporters of the administration retained as their party name the title of Federalists, originally designating the advocates of the adoption of the constitution, but now used as implying that it was they who were defending and upholding the federal government against its enemies.

CHAPTER VIII

THE RULING CLASS DIVIDED

JEFFERSON and his colleagues believed themselves to be the genuine conservatives. "The Republican party wish to preserve the government in its present form," wrote Jefferson to Washington in justification of their course. What they did do was to give a powerful impetus to democratic tendencies which were destined to transform the government. Men who in the constitutional convention had descanted upon the evils of democracy, and had tried to leave as little room as possible for popular control over the government, cast aside their scruples when the only practicable way of maintaining their influence was to stir up the people against the government. Politicians employ their logic to defend the positions they feel impelled to take; their action is the result of circumstances operating upon their endowment of character and habits of thought. Their personal relation to the events of their times has much more to do with shaping their policy than any abstract theory of government which they may profess. English history notes that some of the greatest changes in government, some of the most radical

principles of reform, have been introduced by conservative parties acting from new considerations
of interest on special occasions. Political structure
grows like coral rock, the product of multitudinous
activities incited by individual needs.

The Republican leaders were very much in the
position of the Rockingham Whigs in 1763, when,
unable to make an effective resistance in Parliament, they subsidized the demagogue John Wilkes
and abetted a pamphlet and newspaper war on the
administration. It was not possible for Jefferson
to emulate the example of the wealthy nobles
who gave Wilkes an annuity of £1000, but he
assisted Callender by presents of money, and he
gave Freneau an office in the state department,
keeping him there despite Washington's complaint
that the publications in Freneau's paper were
"outrages on common decency." When men like
Hamilton or Madison took a hand in the fray,
they addressed themselves to people of their own
class. On setting about a reply to Hamilton's
defence of the foreign policy of the administration,
Madison wrote to Jefferson: "None but intelligent
readers will enter into such a controversy, and to
their minds it ought principally to be accom-
modated." The ephemeral journalism of the day,
however, addressed a different public. Its object
was to excite the passions. Lampoon and invec-
tive were preferred to serious argument. Current
events afforded plenty of material. The whole

world was convulsed by the throes of the French
Revolution, and in America the shocks produced
waves of democratic excitement. The position of
the administration was one of great perplexity,
requiring caution and reserve, so that misrepre-
sentation of its acts and purposes was easy.

The distinct assumption of political functions
by the newspaper press took place during the
eighteenth century. Originally, newspapers were
simply handy mediums of announcement. They
were an improvement on the town crier. For
them to engage in political discussion was out of
harmony with traditional ideas of government.
The criticism of politics, which now addresses
itself to journalism, formerly found its outlet in
pamphleteering. In England, every political tempest brought a shower of ballads, tracts, and pamphlets, falling as thickly as autumn leaves. The
artillery of the law was as ineffectual against such
fugitive writings as it would be against a swarm
of mosquitoes. The ministers of the crown found
that the most practical course was to have their own
corps of pamphleteers to wage war for them. The
great mass of such publications was ephemeral
rubbish, soon swept away; but English literature
reckons among its classics writings which originally had a party purpose. Addison's famous
poem "Blenheim" was written to order for the
Whig ministry of the day, who wanted some verses
on Marlborough's victory for popular circulation.

Most of Swift's writings are Tory pamphlets. His "Gulliver's Travels" continues to be a popular story-book, although the political satire, which originally gave it piquancy, is no longer noticed. Some of the best works of Edmund Burke, which for all time will never cease to be profitable to men who give serious thought to problems of government, we owe to his activity as a Whig pamphleteer.

It was inevitable that this species of writing would seek so convenient a medium of publication as the newspaper press as soon as possible; but the combination of newsgathering and political criticism had to encounter a formidable prejudice. Reports of the debates of Parliament, or comment on its proceedings, assailed a historic guarantee of public liberty. The character of institutions is really an attribute from the service which they render; but the disposition to regard that character as inherent, causes them to be valued for their own sake when they have lost the use which made them valuable. Thoroughly honest and patriotic statesmen insisted upon the secrecy of parliamentary proceedings long after it had ceased to be necessary as a protection of freedom of debate, and had become the shield of corruption. The intrusion of journalism into the field of politics was attended by violent struggles, but the public demand was so imperious that Parliament was literally beaten into submission.

In the American colonies the censorship of the

press had been very strict.   Benjamin Franklin,
in his autobiography, gives some amusing instances
of his collisions with the authorities because of his
audacity in venturing an occasional remark on public affairs.   The Revolutionary movement freed the
press.   The practical convenience of such a medium
for the expression of colonial opinion outweighed
any theoretical objections.   A stream of articles
poured into the columns of the newspapers of the
day.   The celebrated " Farmer's Letters " of John
Dickinson appeared in the *Pennsylvania Chronicle.*
The pens of other leaders of the Revolution were
busily employed in like manner.   The practice continued after the Revolution, and to a series of newspaper articles over the signature " Publius," written
by Hamilton, Madison, and Jay, to influence the
action of the New York convention, we owe that
great commentary on the constitution, commonly
known as " The Federalist."   Communications on
public affairs from Cato, Camillus, Decius, Senex,
Agricola, and such like, frequently appeared in the
newspapers, until gradually political comment was
recognized as an ordinary function of the newspaper
press, and the editorial article became an established institution.   In our own time, the transformation of public sentiment has become so complete
that there is a disposition to regard the press as
being in some way responsible for the conduct of
public affairs, and blame for defects of government
is laid at its door.

Federalism being essentially a movement for the restoration of the old order, the traditional ideas as to the place and duties of the press in a well-regulated government were revived. In one of his essays on government, Fisher Ames said: "The press is a new and certainly a powerful agent in human affairs. It will change societies; but it is difficult to conceive how, by rendering men indocile and presumptuous, it can change them for the better. . . . It has inspired ignorance with presumption, so that those who cannot be governed by reason are no longer awed by authority." These forebodings soon seemed to be in course of rapid fulfilment. The highest privileges of Congress were violated with impunity. The constitutional right of members, that "for any speech or debate in either House they shall not be questioned in any other place," was virtually annulled. The license of speech assumed by the papers was abominable to the supporters of the government. When the Republican journals began to charge that Washington was drawing more from the treasury than the law allowed, and were circulating forged letters to show that during the Revolutionary War he desired to submit to the king, whatever contempt might be felt for such attacks, the effect upon public opinion could not be ignored. The provocation was increased by the fact that the leading Republican journalists were men of alien birth: "a group of foreign liars," John Adams

termed them.   The growth of party spirit, which
was regarded as destructive to constitutional government, seemed to be a direct consequence of the
tolerance shown to a seditious press.   " The very
idea of the power and the right of the people to
establish government," said Washington in his
farewell address, "presupposes the duty of every
individual to obey the established government.   All
obstructions to the execution of the laws, all combinations and associations under whatever plausible
character, with the real design to direct, control,
counteract, or awe the regular deliberations of the
constituted authorities, are destructive of this fundamental principle and of fatal tendency."

It is necessary to understand this attitude of
thought in order to comprehend the remarkable
features which the politics of the times eventually
presented.   The behavior of the Federalist judges
during Adams' administration would seem to be
an amazing exhibition of headlong and reckless
partisanship, if not viewed in the light of their
ideas of constitutional privilege and duty.   They
were trying to uphold the traditional ideal of government.   They let no fair opportunity pass of
instructing the people how monstrous and horrid
a thing it was for them to rebel against magisterial
control and disturb the constitutional balance of
power among the departments of government by
seditious attempts to interfere in the administration of public affairs.   The charge to a grand jury

at times became a political harangue. In western Pennsylvania, Judge Addison, of the state judiciary, delivered a series of charges on Jealousy of the Administration and Government, the Horrors of Revolution, etc., pointing out to the people what terrible things were likely to happen if they were not dutiful in their behavior towards constituted authority. General Washington, then in private life, was so pleased by Judge Addison's performance that he sent a copy of the charge to friends for circulation. Chief Justice Ellsworth, in a charge to a Massachusetts grand jury, denounced "the French system-mongers, from the quintumvirate at Paris to the vice-president (Jefferson) and minority in Congress as apostles of atheism and anarchy, bloodshed and plunder."

The wave of popular indignation which swept the country when Talleyrand's attempt to blackmail the American envoys was made known to the public, temporarily prostrated the Republican party and gave the Federalists control of both Houses of Congress. The Federalist leaders seized the opportunity of suppressing that "fatal tendency" to which Washington had referred, by passing the alien and sedition laws. The President could now send out of the country such aliens as he might deem dangerous to the peace and safety of the United States. It was a crime, punishable by fine and imprisonment, to publish any false, scandalous, or malicious writings against the gov-

I

ernment of the United States, or either House of
Congress, or the President, with the intent to defame
them or bring them into contempt or disrepute.
Such legislation was quite in accord with the traditional theory of government. Washington, in his
correspondence, referred to it approvingly; and
while Hamilton regarded it as impolitic, he did not
question its constitutionality. The laws were vigorously enforced, despite popular clamor. To wag a
loose tongue ran the risk of severe punishment. A
Jerseyman named Baldwin was fined $100 for
expressing a wish that the wad of a cannon discharged as a salute to President Adams had hit
the broadest part of the President's breeches.
Matthew Lyon, of Vermont, while canvassing for
reëlection to Congress, charged the President with
"unbounded thirst for ridiculous pomp, foolish
adulation, and a selfish avarice." That cost him
four months in jail and a fine of $1000. For a
time it seemed as if the conservative reaction had
consummated its purpose, and that the federal
monarchy was perfected, affording an example of
authority which George III himself might have
admired.

The enraged Republicans, unable to make head
in Congress, now developed fresh resources of
opposition by invoking state authority. Then
began the conflict of state and federal powers of
government which constitutes such an important
episode of our constitutional history. It is gener-

ally regarded as peculiar to American politics, so that it has been treated as comprising the substance of American constitutional history, but it is really a very old feature of politics. Wherever independent powers of government have existed side by side, they have served as antagonistic centres of opposition. That was the bane of the feudal system, and led to its overthrow by an exaltation of royal authority sustained by necessities of social order. In England, the consolidation of authority was so complete that when the Rockingham Whigs were helpless in Parliament, during the memorable struggle over the Wilkes' case, the most effective form of opposition they could think of was to get up reproachful petitions to the king from every locality which their influence could sway. From the strength of the passions which were aroused during the struggle, there can be no doubt that, had the territorial strongholds of the Whig aristocracy possessed independent powers of government, those powers would have been brought to bear against the administration. In this respect the Jefferson faction among the American gentry had a peculiar advantage, for the state governments did possess independent political powers which furnished weapons to the opposition for attacks on the government. The famous Virginia and Kentucky resolutions made their appearance. Madison, who had labored hard in the constitutional convention to give the government discretionary authority to veto any state legislation, and who had declared that the people "will never be satisfied till some remedy be applied to the vicissitudes and uncertainties which characterized the state administrations,"[1] draughted the Virginia resolutions. They declare the constitution to be "a compact to which the states are parties," so that they have a right to interpose their authority when the federal government attempts "a deliberate, palpable, and dangerous exercise of other powers not granted in that compact." In 1786, when the states were united only by the loose ties of the Confederation, Jefferson laid down the doctrine that "when any one state in the American union refuses obedience to the Confederation, by which they have bound themselves, the rest have a natural right to compel them to obedience."[2] The time had now arrived when he draughted the Kentucky resolutions, asserting the right of any one state "to nullify of its own authority all assumptions of power by others, within its limits." Thus was developed a resource of opposition which was long in habitual use as a menace to federal policy. During Madison's administration, the New England Federalists carried state opposition almost to the stage of secession. At various times, Pennsylvania, Ohio, New York, North Carolina, South Carolina, Massachusetts,

[1] The Federalist, No. 37.
[2] Jefferson's Writings, Vol. IV., p. 147.

Alabama, Georgia, Mississippi, and Maine have each imitated the example of Virginia and Kentucky and made threats of nullification. All parties in turn have made use of such means of opposition, until it was suppressed forever by the Civil War. The tendency has not ceased altogether, but it is now reduced to such absurd shifts as were displayed during the agitation. over the Force Bill in aid of federal election laws, when the most that state opposition could do was to threaten to withhold appropriations for state representation at the Chicago World's Fair.

The alien and sedition laws doomed the Federalist party. The people rebelled against the yoke, and the Federalists went down in irretrievable ruin. It may seem strange that a party of which Washington had been the head, and which founded the government, was so deficient in vitality that it could never recover from the shock of defeat, but its position was weak and precarious from the first. The combination of interests which produced it never attained true party union. The deep antagonism, originating in the events of the Revolutionary War, divided it in a way that made it incapable of united action after Washington's control and influence had been removed. John Adams had belonged to the old congressional group. Although thrown by circumstances into party antagonism, Jefferson and Adams had a strong personal esteem for each other. When

Adams was elected, Jefferson wrote to Madison, asking if "it would not be worthy of consideration whether it would not be for the public good to come to a good understanding with him." On the other hand, the military group profoundly distrusted Adams. Washington's relations with Adams were marked by formality and reserve, and Adams wrote that he detested "that contracted principle of monopoly and exclusion which had prevailed through Washington's administration." Hamilton, in his famous denunciation of Adams, made it a count of his indictment that Adams, as a member of the Continental Congress, had supported the system of annual enlistments which had been so injurious to the discipline and efficiency of the army. Hamilton would have prevented Adams' election could he have done so, and Adams was so distrusted by his party that his cabinet officials looked to Hamilton for instruction and advice on important points of public policy. For a considerable period Adams' administration was subject to a secret control and was but nominally under his direction. This false situation ended in an open breach between Hamilton and Adams, which shattered the Federal party.

But even had it escaped these intestine disorders, the original Federal party was doomed to extinction. Old-fashioned Federalism was the product of an order of ideas transmitted from the colonial period, and fast becoming obsolete.

Under the new conditions of thought and feeling, created by the progress of the nation, it was inevitable either that it should perish or else be completely transformed. Burr's pistol blew the brains out of the Federal party; for Hamilton's death removed the only leader who might have risen to the occasion and made a new departure. Before it died, Federalism had degenerated into a senile Toryism, as much out of touch with the age, and as incapable of political activity, as Jacobitism in England.

The extraordinary scenes which disgraced the close of Adams' administration were the natural product of Federalist ideas of government. The constitution seemed to have gone to wreck, and the duty of the hour was to make as great a salvage as possible. "In the future administration of our country," wrote Adams to Jay, in offering him the chief justiceship, "the firmest security we can have against the effects of visionary schemes or fluctuating theories will be in a solid judiciary; and nothing will cheer the hopes of the best men so much as your acceptance of this appointment." Jay declined the office. "I left the bench," he said, "perfectly convinced that under a system so defective it would not obtain the energy, weight, and dignity which were essential to its affording due support to the national government, nor acquire the public confidence and respect which, as the last resort of the justice of

the nation, it should possess." Had Jay resolved
to brave the perils he feared, John Marshall might
have passed obscurely into history as a serviceable partisan, instead of as the great chief justice.
Even after his appointment to the bench, Marshall
continued at Adams' urgent request to hold the
office of Secretary of State. He was kept busy
issuing federal commissions, as Federalists were
appointed to every office in the reach of the administration. A bill was hurried through Congress, establishing circuit courts and providing for
thirty-six new judgeships, which were promptly
filled. The work of appointing Federalists to
office went on to the very last hour of Adams'
term of office.

Jefferson's installation in office was an event
that was regarded with gloomy foreboding by the
old school of statesmen. It seemed that the time
had arrived of which Fisher Ames wrote: "The
Democrats really wish to see an impossible experiment fairly tried, and to govern without government. There is universally a presumption in
Democracy that promises everything; and at the
same time an imbecility that can accomplish nothing, nor even preserve itself."

But although it seemed that party spirit had
trampled over constitutional government, there
was at work, quite unsuspected, a principle of
conservatism that seems to be peculiar to party
of the English and American type.

CHAPTER IX

POLITICAL FORCE

THE aptitude of politics to form a party of administration and a party of opposition, which is generally regarded as a normal characteristic, is really a tendency which has to be acquired. The natural tendency is towards a multiplication of parties to correspond with varieties of opinion and groupings of interests, so that instead of opposing parties contending for the management of public affairs, there would be shifting parliamentary groups, such as make French and German politics so perplexing to outsiders. The strong tendency of English politics to party division, rather than faction partition, is evidently not a race characteristic. A sectarian disposition is a conspicuous trait of religious opinion among Englishmen and Americans, and in politics also a sectarian disposition is exhibited by the frequent attempts to organize new parties. In politics, however, such movements are counteracted by other forces which tend to gather all varieties of political sentiment into two opposing party organizations.

The explanation of this curious phenomenon is probably to be found in the circumstances of English political development. Royal authority in England was not built up gradually, as in France and Germany, by centuries of struggle against feudal privilege, but was attained at once by conquest. The prerogative of William the Conqueror, in the eleventh century, was as robust as that of Louis XIV in the seventeenth. The king of England had complete control of the national authority at a time when a French or a German king was merely the primate of a swarm of sovereigns. The royal prerogative was so powerful in England that it did not fear parliamentary institutions as a rival source of power, and instead of aiming to suppress them, as in Continental Europe, the disposition was to preserve them, as an useful means of communication with the people. Milton's reason for desiring to abolish the use of the word "parliament" to denote the English legislature was that it originally signified "the parley of our lords and commons with the Norman kings when he pleased to call them."

The uniformity of jurisprudence, effected by the plenitude of royal authority, was a powerful nationalizing influence, small opportunity being afforded for the growth of the provincial rights and privileges which played such a great part in the politics of Continental Europe. The immense weight of royal prerogative rested upon the nation as a whole, compacting its elements. To make any stand against royal oppression, the nobles had to act together and have the support of the

people. When bounds were set to royal prerogative, they were established, not as a class privilege,
but as a general right, of which Parliament was
the natural guardian. The influences of constitutional progress tended to fuse the various elements
of the population, originally as diverse and antagonistic as anywhere else in Europe, into national
unity. The process consumed centuries, but its
heat and pressure formed English politics into a
substance so homogeneous that, when public opinion
became a factor in administration, the force generated by it exhibited the marked polarity which
has been its characteristic, — a positive phase and
a negative phase, the government and the opposition.

After the overthrow of the Stuarts had practically transferred the executive authority from
the crown to Parliament, the conditions which had
brought about this unique phenomenon were continued by the rule of the nobility. The Whig
oligarchy, which had successfully carried through
the Revolution of 1689, resumed in its class control
the authority of which royalty had been dispossessed. Without such restraints, the establishment of the authority of Parliament would have
allowed such free play to divergent interests that
politics would probably have become a chaos of
turbulent opinion. Such had been the result of
the victory of Parliament over Charles I. Parliamentary government became impossible with

the usual result — the establishment of a military dictatorship. The nation was glad to escape by returning to the ancient constitution. The Revolution of 1689 was aristocratic in its inception and guidance, and did not disturb the forms of the constitution while radically transforming its character. Unity of administration was no longer secured by the king's prerogative, but by aristocratic control. The body of the aristocracy, united by their class interests, were at the same time divided into contending factions by rivalry for the possession of office and power. Their struggles developed party organization and discipline, and set party action in the grooves along which it has since moved. They were like a board of directors, who might quarrel among themselves and split into factions, each aiming to secure control of the affairs of the corporation ; but to whose strife their common interests set bounds which they instinctively respected, so that their disputes were necessarily subject to some regulation, gradually finding expression in rules of procedure. In like manner, parliamentary usages have been established which give to the English government its true character. The cabinet system has no other foundation than a general agreement that the political junto which can secure a majority in the House of Commons is entitled to the administration.[1]

---

[1] Boutmy's English Constitution, Part III., Chap. IV., gives a lucid account of the process of English party development.

Something like the same conditions of control and guidance were established in the United States by the rule of the gentry. This rule was, however, so artificial and factitious that it was always in a condition of extreme delicacy. Had it fulfilled the desire with which it was instituted, of setting a rigid barrier to democratic tendencies, it would have been crushed. The tutelage to which it was intended to subject the nation would not have been endured. Notwithstanding Washington's military renown and the popular veneration for his character, the spirit of insubordination was so strong that the government was a weak, shaky affair. John Adams says that, in the exciting times of 1794, "ten thousand people in the streets of Philadelphia, day after day, threatened to drag Washington out of his house and effect a revolution in the government, or compel it to declare war in favor of the French Revolution and against England."[1] In Adams' opinion, the yellow fever, more than any strength in the government, prevented a revolution. The attempt made during Adams' administration to suppress popular agitation by means of the sedition laws might have caused an explosion of democratic force which would have blown up the government, had it not been for an event which at the time was regarded by the supporters of the government as a dire misfortune — the formation among the gentry them-

[1] Adams' Works, Vol. X., pp. 47, 48.

selves of an opposition party. It was the great unconscious achievement of Thomas Jefferson to open constitutional channels of political agitation, to start the processes by which the development of our constitution is carried on.

It is remarkable how promptly the varied discontents, which might have converted politics into a strife of revolutionary groups, rushed into the outlet provided for them. Everywhere the state factions were gathered into relations with the Federal or Republican parties, and placed themselves under the guidance of their party chiefs. This was the salvation of the government. Change became possible without destruction. Anti-federalism lost its sullen temper, and entertained hopes of the government if only Jefferson and the Republicans should obtain control. The whiskey insurrectionists saw a way open by which they could attack the hated excise without rebellion, and their ablest spokesman, Gallatin, became a Republican party leader. The clubs of social revolutionists which had sprung up in the cities, blazing with incendiary ideas caught from the French Revolution, were converted into party workers, and their behavior was moderated by considerations of party interest. When the more violent factions among the Republicans showed a disposition to follow up their victory in the election of Jefferson by an assault upon the judiciary, their own party leaders held them in check. In

Pennsylvania, Governor McKean, whose election was one of the first triumphs of the Republican party, vetoed a bill reforming the judiciary system. Eminent Republicans, such as Alexander Dallas, Jared Ingersoll, and Hugh H. Brackenridge opposed the impeachment of three judges of the state supreme court, and the state senate gave a majority for acquittal. Even Jefferson's own influence could not procure the united support of his party in the U. S. Senate for the impeachment of Judge Chase. The reform of government which the Republican leaders had really sought was a change in the custody of the powers of government, and they would not support movements aimed directly at the authority of government. As their support was essential to party success, faction animosity had to defer to their ideas.

The distinction between party and faction seems to be this: party aims at administrative control, while faction is the propaganda of a particular interest. Party, therefore, contains a principle of conservatism, inasmuch as it must always seek to keep faction within such bounds as will prevent it from jeoparding party interests. An important consequence of this party instinct of comprehension is the tendency of opposing party organizations to equalize each other in strength. The practical purpose of their formation causes each to compete for popular favor in ways that tend towards an approximately equal division of popular support. Even in the greatest victories at the polls, the preponderance of the triumphant party is but a small percentage of the total vote. If a party becomes so hopelessly discredited that it has no chance of success, it disappears like the Federalists or the old National Republican party, and a new party takes its place based on contemporaneous divisions of public sentiment.

The conservative function of party is not duly appreciated, because its operation is negative. What is done is known, but how far the impulse which produced the act has been moderated cannot be known. It must, however, be apparent on reflection, that even in times of the most contagious excitement there must be some modification of individual opinions to secure an agreement of purpose among large bodies of citizens. It is reasonable to infer that the habitual calculation of consequences, essential to the training of every political leader, must affect his deference to the behests of his supporters. It may be stated as a fact, which acquaintance with the interior workings of politics will verify, that the influence of party leaders is chiefly exerted in soothing the prejudices and moderating the demands of their followers. If party action were an accurate reflection of the passions, animosities, and beliefs of the mass of individuals composing the party membership, politics would be as tremendous in their instability as ocean waves; but party action being a social product is in organic connection with all the processes of thought and feeling which pertain to human nature, and is subject to the play of their influence. A typical result is that curious accumulation of traditions and tenets which give to party communion almost the sanctions of religious faith. On this point, with great sagacity, Macaulay has said : " Every political sect has its esoteric and its exoteric school, its abstract doctrines for the initiated, its visible symbols, its imposing forms, its mythological fables for the vulgar. It assists the devotion of those who are unable to raise themselves to the contemplation of pure truth by all the devices of . . . superstition. It has its altars and its deified heroes, its relics and its pilgrimages, its canonized martyrs and confessors, and its legendary miracles."

American party history conspicuously attests the truth of these observations. The mythic tendency has converted the choleric politicians of the early period of the republic into sages, philosophers, and even saints ! If it were not so difficult to notice that which is familiar, it would be easy to see that this process of canonization is going on in our own time, idealizing and transfiguring men whose real personality is still well within the recollection of the living.

K

CHAPTER X

THE overthrow of the Federalists was marked by an immediate change in the deportment of the administration. Jefferson substituted a written message for the speech to Congress at the opening of the session, giving as his reason that he thus avoided the contention that would have taken place in Congress over the character of the address in reply to the President. He also tried to introduce an easy and informal style of manners at the executive mansion. It is usually the case that those who set themselves against established forms have to give more attention to the subject than those who observe them, and in introducing what he called "the principle of pêle mêle," Jefferson troubled himself a great deal more about questions of etiquette than his predecessors had done.

The agencies of government devised by the Federalists were mostly left intact. The alien and sedition laws were by their terms only temporary measures, and they expired by limitation. The legislation by which the Federalists had packed the bench was rescinded, and thus "the midnight judges" were gotten rid of by extinguishing their office. The internal revenue laws were repealed; but Jefferson became so far reconciled to the United States Bank as to suggest "a judicious distribution of favors" to that and other banks "to engage the individuals who belonged to them in support" of his administration. A bill enabling the United States Bank to establish branches in the territories was approved by him.

In general, it may be said that the Jeffersonian triumph restored the supremacy of the civilian group. They proceeded to put down the army and navy, and rid themselves as rapidly as possible of the burden of national defence; but there was no reluctance about making a large use of the powers of government which had come into their hands. The Louisiana purchase was effected by an assumption of authority quite in Hamilton's style. Jefferson himself salved his wounded sense of consistency by recommending the adoption of a constitutional amendment expressly legalizing his act; but even his own Cabinet would not pay any attention to his scruples. The embargo upon American commerce, which he ingeniously conceived as a dignified retaliation for the insults and injuries which his policy encouraged England and France to inflict, carried national authority to logical extremities to which the Federalists would not have dared to go. The enforcement act passed to sustain the embargo was a greater interference with the ordinary privileges of citizens than would have been necessary in the exercise of war powers. The executive behavior of Jefferson and Madison shows that they were willing to go to any length in the development of authority, so long as it was in its nature such as would remain in civilian hands.[1]

All this was a great stumbling-block to the state sovereignty theorizers, who at a later day declared that they were simply holding out for the ideas of Jefferson. Calhoun, with his habitual intellectual honesty, frankly admitted that Jefferson did not live up to the principles which he had enunciated. Calhoun said: "He did nothing to arrest many great and radical evils; nothing towards elevating the judicial departments of the governments of the several states, from a state of subordination to the judicial department of the United States, to their rightful constitutional position as coördinates; nothing towards maintaining the rights of the states, as parties to the constitutional compact, to judge in the last resort as to the extent of their delegated powers; nothing towards restoring to Congress the exclusive right to adopt measures necessary and proper to carry into operation its own as well as other powers vested in the government, or in any of its departments; nothing towards reversing the order of General Hamilton which united the government

[1] Henry Adams' History of the United States, Vol. IV., pp. 398–400.

with the banks; and nothing effectual towards restricting the money power to objects specifically
enumerated and delegated by the constitution."[1]

In its character the government was as aristocratic as before. Manhood suffrage had been
established in Kentucky and in Vermont, and a
general movement towards the removal of restrictions on the suffrage had begun; but in most of
the states the voters were still a limited class of
the adult male population. In only six of the
sixteen states which voted in 1800 were electors
chosen by popular vote. Political leaders set up
candidates and made nominations in their party
interest in pretty much the same style in which
such matters were done in England. In 1808,
Jefferson wrote to William Wirt: " The object of
this letter is to propose to you to come into Congress. That is the great commanding theatre of
this nation and the threshold to whatever department of office a man is qualified to enter. With
your reputation, talents, and correct views, used
with the necessary prudence, you will at once be
placed at the head of the House of Representatives; and after obtaining the standing which a
little time will assure you, you may look, at your
own will, into the military, the judiciary, diplomatic, or other civil departments, with a certainty
of being in either whatever you please; and in the
present state of what may be called the eminent

[1] Calhoun's Works, Vol. I., p. 360.

talents of our country you may be assured of being engaged through life in the most honorable employments."

No party leader in our time would dare to give so broad a guarantee. Of the early period of our politics, Professor Alexander Johnston remarks : "In both parties the abler leaders assumed the direct initiative in party management to an extent which would be intolerable, if openly asserted at the present time."[1] Nevertheless, the democratic tendencies of the times were very marked, and the circumstances were such that the natural care of the administration for its own interests, in dispensing the patronage of the government, tended to foster those tendencies. It may seem strange that the democratic movement, which eventually overthrew the old régime, should have been promoted by such a close oligarchy as the Virginia dynasty of presidents. But it is a thing of common occurrence in politics to find that special exigencies impel politicians in directions opposed to their traditional tendencies.

In using the patronage for party ends, Jefferson and his successors adopted no new principle of conduct. Such use of the patronage was an inveterate practice of English politics. It dates from the time when the crown, no longer able to overawe Parliament by power, had to resort to influence — that is to say, it dates from the Revolu-

[1] Cyclopædia of Political Science, Vol. I., p. 769.

tion of 1689. The rage for office was quite as great in the colonies as in England. During colonial times, quarrels over questions of patronage were the cause of many conflicts between provincial assemblies and the governors. The state of antagonism, which generally existed between the governor and the assembly, strengthened and perpetuated the original English conception of the speakership as the office of a party leader, a character which has never left it in this country. Most of the time of the Continental Congress seems to have been consumed in disputes about the offices. John Adams says : "Congress was torn to pieces by these disputes, and days and months were wasted in such controversies, to the inexpressible injury of the service."[1] The restoration of the general government made no change of disposition in this respect. So far as the influence of patronage could extend, it was used to secure political support for the administration. Maclay notes in his diary that Washington had begun to consult with representatives as to his appointments, and took this as a sign of "a courtship of and attention to the House of Representatives, that by their weight he may depress the Senate and exalt his prerogative on the ruins."[2] Although the administration was non-partisan in theory, yet it was careful in making appointments to select such as

[1] Adams' Works, Vol. VI., pp. 538, 539.
[2] Maclay's Diary, p. 122.

were zealous in support of the government, and would exert their influence to make it a success. When the break-up of the Cabinet occurred, and an anti-administration party was organized, only staunch Federalists received office. In a letter to Colonel Timothy Pickering, Secretary of War, Washington said: "I shall not, while I have the honor of administering the government, bring a man into any office of consequence knowingly whose political tenets are adverse to the measures the general government are pursuing; for this, in my opinion, would be a sort of political suicide."

During Adams' administration the utterances of Federal leaders in the Senate were very emphatic on this point. Senator Bayard announced "that the politics of the office-seeker would be the great object of the President's attention, and an invincible objection if different from his own."[1] Senator Otis said that "the pecuniary claims of Henry Miller for extra clerk hire," occasioned by his inability to keep up with his office work while electioneering for Adams, was "a paltry consideration infinitely outweighed by the service he was rendering to his country."[2]

The direct influence of patronage was more potent then than it is now; for the conduct of politics was further removed from the people, and was more largely an affair of personal management and

[1] Annals of Congress, 1797–1798, p. 1232.
[2] National Intelligencer, August 14, 1801.

individual negotiation, which could be greatly promoted by executive favors. "This is the great
spring of all in the minds of senators and representatives," wrote John Adams, "to obtain favors
for favorites among their constituents, in order to
attach them by gratitude, and establish their own
influence at home and abroad."[1] Adams attributed his defeat for reëlection to the presidency to
a matter of this sort. Washington, when in command of the little army put on foot during the
French war scare in 1798, refused to give Peter
Muhlenberg an officer's commission. "And what
was the consequence?" said Adams. "These two
Muhlenbergs (Peter and Frederick) addressed the
public with their names both in English and in
German, with invectives against the administration and warm recommendations of Mr. Jefferson.
. . . The Muhlenbergs turned the whole body of
the Germans, great numbers of the Irish, and
many of the English, and in this manner introduced the total change which followed in both
houses of the legislature and in all the executive
departments of the national government."[2]

Removals from office were for a long time hindered by the feeling that they were in the nature
of an attack on property rights. In England, the
disposition to regard public trusts in private hands
as a species of property was so strong that so

---

[1] Adams' Works, Vol. IX., pp. 633, 634.
[2] *Ibid.*, Vol. X., p. 122.

bitter an assailant of political corruption as Junius
conceded that the nomination boroughs were entitled by usage and prescription to rank as property. It is true that removals from office on party
grounds were practised under George III, but the
national instinct of justice was deeply violated. In
1762–1763, Henry Fox broke the power of the elder
Pitt and secured a parliamentary majority for the
Bute ministry by sweeping removals of Pitt's supporters and by the ruthless use of all the patronage
of the government ; but he made himself execrated
by public opinion, and the literature of the day
contains expressions of the deepest abhorrence.
George III personally pursued the same tactics,
with ruinous results, and in the end he had to
abandon the system and rest the administration
of affairs on the talents and popularity of the
younger Pitt. A great purification of politics followed. Having under the cabinet system of government the power of shaping issues by exercising
a direct initiative in legislation, an administration
supported by a popular mandate was to a large
extent relieved of the necessity of using bribery
or trafficking in offices to facilitate the transaction of the public business ; for the administration was in a position to invoke the power
of public opinion to overawe intriguers and
mutineers.

When Jefferson became President he found the
offices in the possession of the Federalists. In

trying to bring in his party friends, he was hampered by this sentiment that a man had a property right to the retention of his office. When he removed Elizur Goodrich from the collectorship of New Haven, he was disturbed by the energy of public remonstrance. Writing in reply, he said: "Declarations by myself, in favor of political tolerance, exhortations to harmony and affection in social intercourse, and respect for the equal rights of the minority, have on certain occasions been quoted and misconstrued into assurances that the tenure of office was not to be disturbed. But could candor apply such a construction? When it is considered that under the late administration those who were not of a particular cast of politics were excluded from all office; when, by a steady pursuit of this measure, nearly the whole offices of the United States were monopolized by that sect; when the public sentiment at length declared itself and burst open the doors of honor and confidence to those whose opinions they approved, was it to be expected that this monopoly of office was to be continued in the hands of the minority? Does it violate their equal rights to assert some rights in the majority also. Is it political intolerance to claim a proportionate share in the direction of public affairs? If a due participation of office is a matter of right, how are vacancies to be obtained? Those by death are few, by resignation none. Can any other mode than that of removal be proposed? This is a painful office; but it is made my duty and I meet it as such."

Nevertheless, the force of hostile sentiment was so strong that he made few removals. So long as the gentry retained their class control of the government, the tenure of office was rarely disturbed on avowed party grounds.

CHAPTER XI

THE forces which broke down the traditional restraint were developed in state politics, where they began to operate with marked effect as. soon as the national government was established. An intermixture of national with state politics was provided by the constitution, for the states were made parties to the administration of the government. The management of state politics was hence an essential part of national politics. As soon as the constitution was framed, the struggle to control state politics on national issues was begun, and it has gone on ever since.

The South preserved longer than any other section the characteristics of colonial politics ; the conditions there were such that the class interests and social connections of the gentry provided an organization that was sufficient for political purposes. Being thus shielded from the necessities which at an early date forced the Northern politicians into a commerce in offices, the original prejudice against assailing a man's property in his office remained acute in the South long after it had been dulled or extinguished in the North.

The political activity of the Southern gentry was a function of their social position. What they chiefly sought from politics was honor and power. Their instinct was to regard office as the due of social eminence or individual ability. The conception of office as payment for partisan servility was revolting to their ideas. The greed and violence of the mob politics of Northern cities filled them with disgust. In Virginia changes of the state administration were not accompanied by changes in the offices until after 1834.[1] Daniel Webster, in a speech at Richmond in 1840, declared that "Virginia more than any other state in the Union had disavowed and condemned the doctrine of removals from office for opinion's sake." As late as 1849 Calhoun boasted of South Carolina: "Party organization, party discipline, party proscription, and their offspring, the spoils system, have been unknown to the state. Nothing of the kind is necessary to produce concentration."[2]

In the North, party divisions in the states, caused by the introduction of national issues, did not simply produce rival factions among the gentry as in the South, but from the first appealed to and drew into the field of political activity an electorate, in whose opinions the offices were good things which ought to go around. The rise of this sentiment was, however, gradual, and even in New York,

[1] Tyler's Letters and Times of the Tylers, Vol. I., p. 524.
[2] Calhoun's Works, Vol. I., p. 405.

where favoring influences were strongest, it made its way with difficulty. When Hamilton began the work of building up the Federal party in New York, state politics had for many years been controlled by family influences, with no more disturbance than was caused by rivalries among the Clintons, Livingstons, and Schuylers. Although party contests were full of personal rancor, yet effective public opinion was still the class opinion of the gentry. The electorate was limited, only freeholders with an estate of £100 above all liens having the franchise. In the state election of 1789, out of a population of 324,270, only 12,300 votes were polled. Hamilton's success was due to the fact that on the issue he presented he was able to combine the Livingstons and the Schuylers against the Clintons. The use the Federalists made of their victory showed the restraining influence of polite opinion. Actual removals from office were few. The Federalists got their party friends into office by seizing vacancies caused by the expiration of terms of office, although reappointment had been the usage. New offices were created by increasing the number of such public officers as judges and justices of the peace. In this way enough Federalists were introduced into the county courts to outvote their opponents. In counties where the numbers of such officers had been about twenty, there were now forty or fifty.

Politics could still be managed by conference and agreement among gentlemen, and the conduct of politics had to defer to their class opinion. But the spread of democratic influence was rapid. The growth of city population developed an electorate, which soon dispossessed itself of habits of deference to social superiors, so that it had to be wrought upon by other influences. There were none so available as those connected with the use of patronage, and this use had to conform to the changing conditions of politics. The change in the political situation was made sharply manifest by Aaron Burr, whose political ambition was so steadily thwarted by Hamilton's ascendency, and who was so jealously excluded from influence, that it was necessary for him to develop a new source of power, or be crushed altogether as a factor in politics. His instrument was the Columbian order, now better known as Tammany Hall. Founded during the second week of Washington's administration, it was originally a social rather than a political organization. It seemed to have become a centre of political activity, largely owing to the fact that it was a place of meeting for the common people, filling the place occupied among the gentry by their clubs and assemblies. By a natural antagonism of classes it gradually became a political power. While the gentry arranged their political deals with their feet under the mahogany and the punch-bowl on the board, there was now in existence a competitive mixture of politics and hospitality to which the common people could resort. A stanza by Fitz-Greene Halleck has embalmed the tradition of those early days : —

" There's a barrel of porter in Tammany Hall,
And the Bucktails are swigging it all the night long.
In the time of my childhood 'twas pleasant to call
For a seat and cigar 'mid the jovial throng."

By the aid of Tammany Hall, in 1800, Aaron Burr wrested from Hamilton the political control of New York City. The election presented the modern features. Voters were sought out and brought to the polls, carriages were sent for the sick, infirm, or lazy, and Tammany Hall kept open house all day. Hamilton, whose power in New York City had rested upon the support of the local moneyed aristocracy, was much impressed by the effectiveness of the new political methods. He came to the conclusion that the Federalists " erred in relying so much on the rectitude and utility of their measures as to have neglected the cultivation of popular favor by fair and justifiable expedients." He drew up a scheme of "the Christian Constitutional Society," whose objects were to be the support of the Christian religion and of the constitution of the United States.[1] Senator Bayard, of Delaware, to whom he submitted the project, did not think favorably of it, and it was dropped.

[1] Hamilton's Works, Vol. VI., pp. 541-543.

L

From such cares as these the Southern leaders were quite free. Politics were so completely under the control of the gentry that scarcely any appeal could be made in any quarter against their class sentiment. The Virginia dynasty was the political expression of the natural hegemony of the great state of Virginia in a compact confederation of social interests which ruled the South, and by means of an united South ruled the Union. The security in which Jefferson and his close successors abided as regards their own section gave them a free hand in the turbulent politics of the North. If a Northern politician became dangerous, the federal patronage could be used against him with effect. Aaron Burr was the first to experience this. Up to the time of the struggle which ensued when the presidential election of 1800 devolved on the House of Representatives, Burr was recognized as the head of the Republican interest in New York. But under Jefferson's administration De Witt Clinton became the party leader in that state. Clinton resigned his seat in the United States Senate to become mayor of New York City, the power and influence of which office gave him the best opportunity of undermining Burr's local interest. Burr, weighed down by the odium of his fatal duel with Hamilton, was unable to maintain himself as a party leader; but before submitting to political extinction he made an instructive test of the fitness of the stage of public affairs for a rôle which at one time or another has been successfully enacted in every other country, and which still affords an opening to political talent in Central and South American states. He turned conspirator. The result showed conclusively that American politics do not afford a field for such adventure. The political habits and instinctive prejudices of the American people are so firmly attached to constitutional government that not in any mood will they hearken to proposals which do not claim its sanction. However fierce an outburst of public sentiment may be, even though it reach to the stage of insurrection or civil war, it must keep under the cover of a constitutional theory.

A Southern politician, who might become recalcitrant, could not be disposed of as easily as was Burr. When John Randolph of Roanoke turned against the administration, Jefferson had to endure his galling attacks, for he could not cut the ground from under Randolph's feet in his own constituency. But when De Witt Clinton, in his turn, assumed an attitude of opposition to the national administration, during Madison's term, he could be dealt with as Burr had been. The federal patronage was turned against him, contributing to the defeat which Clinton then sustained in the struggle for the control of state politics.

Similar interferences of federal influence in the contests of state factions, in furtherance of the party interests of the national administration, were of frequent occurrence, and in this way the federal patronage acted as a stimulus to democratic tendencies. The road to political consideration being thus plainly pointed out, travel naturally turned that way. The organization of political clubs and societies antagonized the family politics of the old state factions and gradually broke down the old methods. Democratic gains increased democratic pressure upon the restraints put against popular activity in politics, and set in motion processes of change which profoundly altered political conditions. A race of politicians grew up who were not the men to entertain scruples about disturbing gentlemen in their snug berths. The longer the office-holders had been in the more reason why they should get out, so as to make room for others and give every one a chance at the public crib. The survival of the old prejudice may, however, be traced in the behavior of Clinton, who, in the violent faction struggles of New York, was several times in power, wielding the state patronage in behalf of his party, and was several times overthrown, to become the victim of a fierce proscription aimed at him and his adherents. At one time he advocated the removal of heads of departments only. Then he took up Jefferson's line of argument and proposed a fair division of minor offices between the two parties. In 1817 he won a great victory by appealing to the rural counties with his scheme for the construction of the Erie canal. Believing himself then independent of New York City politics, he declared his opposition to partisan proscription and, beyond turning out a few Tammany office-holders, made no removals on party grounds. This was the last stand made in New York against the use of the offices for party purposes. Clinton was antagonized by a combination of factions, and during Monroe's administration the federal patronage was so actively employed against him that he made it a subject of formal complaint in a message to the legislature. Clinton was driven back to his former methods, which became the settled practice of all administrations.

Not alone in New York, but in Pennsylvania and in other Northern states, the development of the new method of affecting party concentration for administrative purposes made rapid progress. The transfer of those methods to the sphere of national government was simply a matter of time, but it was not accomplished until the new influences at work in American society swelled in volume until they inundated the whole field of national politics.

CHAPTER XII

THE growth of national parties tended to develop in the people of every state a conception of equitable rights in the political arrangements of all the states. If the party did not receive fair play anywhere, it suffered everywhere. The popular sense of injury in this respect, once excited, was very alert and suspicious, and there was incessant complaint against the unfair discriminations which existed.

The inability of the framers of the constitution to get much beyond general principles in reaching an agreement, had left a latitude to state action in national politics which resulted in gross inequality of political circumstances. The state legislatures elected United States Senators as they pleased, appointed presidential electors as they pleased, and provided for the election of state quotas in the House of Representatives as they pleased. The variety and uncertainty of the conditions to which national party action was subjected were especially exasperating with respect to the presidential election. The system was not made for democratic use, and its unsuitability soon became a sore grievance. When the people sought to say for themselves who should be President, they were outraged by the facility with which the electoral machinery could be used to thwart their desires.

In 1800 the election of Jefferson was put in jeopardy by Federalist manœuvres in Pennsylvania. In that state it had been the practice from the first to choose presidential electors by popular vote. Every four years the legislature would discharge its constitutional duty of providing for the appointment of presidential electors by passing a special act for an election by the people. In 1796 fourteen Jefferson electors had been chosen and only one Adams man. When the election of 1800 came on, the state Senate was Federalist by thirteen to eleven ; the House was strongly Republican. No law was passed for a popular election, and the Senate held out against any action by the legislature until the House agreed that the fifteen electors should be chosen out of a list of sixteen — eight to be nominated by the Senate and as many by the House. In this way seven electoral votes were obtained for Adams, although the sentiment of the people was strongly in favor of Jefferson. In New York, during the same campaign, it became evident that the incoming legislature would appoint Republican electors. Hamilton wrote to Governor Jay, proposing that the expiring legislature should be convoked in special session to pass

a law providing for district elections of presidential electors, so as to enable the Federalists to
secure a number. The letter was endorsed by
Jay, " Proposing a measure for party purposes
which I think it would not become me to adopt."
In Massachusetts, where it had been the practice
for the legislature to appoint the electors, two at
large, on its own motion, and the remainder from
lists of candidates sent up from the congressional
districts, the system was suddenly changed, in 1804,
for fear that some Republicans might slip in, and
a law was passed providing for an election by popular vote on a general state ticket. In New Jersey,
in 1812, calculations of Federalist party advantage
caused just the reverse of the policy of the Massachusetts Federalists to be adopted. The practice had
been to choose the presidential electors by popular
election. The state elections showed a popular
majority for the Republicans, but owing to peculiarities of apportionment the legislature was controlled by the Federalists. Less than a week
before the time when the election by the people
should have taken place, the legislature repealed
the law, and itself appointed the electors, all Federalists.[1]

Fortunately, none of these manœuvres changed
the result of the presidential election, or else a
revolutionary violence might have been engen-

[1] Stanwood's History of Presidential Elections.

dered in politics, fatal to constitutional development. In the Massachusetts case cited, the actual
effect was helpful to the Republican party, for it
carried the state, and hence obtained the solid
electoral vote. The cumbrous machinery of the
electoral college yielded sufficiently to popular control to secure toleration, but its operation revealed
one defect which compelled prompt amendment.
Under the system, as originally established, each
elector voted for two persons, without designating
the office, and the person who received the greatest number of electoral votes became President.
Therefore, as soon as the electors voted as party
agents and cast their votes solidly for both party
candidates, there was a tie vote. Such was the
outcome of the election of 1800, and although it
had been perfectly well understood that Jefferson
was to have been President and Burr Vice-President, yet, when the case went to the House of
Representatives, they stood legally on precisely
the same footing. The ensuing struggle shook
the government so alarmingly that there was a
prompt and irresistible demand that this defect
should be cured. Even at this early date there was
some popular agitation in favor of the establishment of an uniform system of electing the President; but conservative influences were too strong
for it to be effective. The system was amended
so as to provide that electors should designate
their choice for President and for Vice-President;

but the original latitude of action given to the states was not restricted.

There were great diversities of practice in the various states. In some, the electors were appointed by the legislature; in others, they were elected by districts; in others, they were elected on a general ticket. This lack of uniformity was inimical to democratic influence, for it varied the conditions so as to make precarious any concert of action which might be arranged, and placed the people at the mercy of the faction temporarily in control of the electoral machinery. Imagine the resentment of Tammany Hall after achieving a victory for the Republican ticket in New York in 1800, when news came of the Federalist strategy by which the party lost seven electoral votes in Pennsylvania!

In view of the fact that the practical results of the working of the electoral machinery were for a long period after 1800 quite in accord with prevailing popular sentiment, it is a striking proof of the strength of the dissatisfaction with the system that such persistent efforts were made to obtain the passage of a constitutional amendment. During Monroe's administration the agitation of the subject was carried on with great earnestness. Congress was urged to submit to the states a constitutional amendment, providing that all the electors should be chosen by popular vote in districts. This proposition was before Congress from 1813 to 1822. It passed the Senate by the requisite two-thirds majority in 1818, in 1819, and again in 1822, but failed to pass the House. In 1819, it was passed to a third reading in the House by a vote of 103 to 59, but on the question of the passage of the bill, received only 92 votes in favor to 54 against — less than the necessary two-thirds.

The truth was that political control had been gotten into a shape that was satisfactory to the dominant group of Southern politicians. Chief-Justice Marshall noticed early in Jefferson's administration that it was his policy to "embody himself with the House." This policy was so successful that it was the usage to make up the committees with regard to the President's wishes, and to reserve important chairmanships for members who enjoyed his confidence. The original functions of the electoral college were quietly taken over by the administration, and the presidential succession was arranged through the agency of the Congressional Caucus.

The American people are a singularly accommodating democracy, but only on condition that they are humored. There was no objection whatever when the Republican members of Congress met in 1804, and cut out the work of the electoral college by nominating Jefferson and Clinton. But in 1808, when the Caucus chairman, Senator Bradley of Vermont, convoked it "in pursuance of the powers vested in me as president of the late convention of the Republican members of both Houses of Congress," the newspapers at once began to harp upon his authoritative language, and to ask upon what meat this Cæsar fed. This system of nomination aggravated the inequality of the electoral system by complicating with it the inequality that existed in the system of congressional elections. While in some states the district system prevailed, in others the representatives were elected on a general ticket, constituting a solid party phalanx. The violation of democratic instincts, perpetrated by this diversity of political circumstances, caused a simultaneous demand for reform here, as well as in the electoral system, and the two propositions were generally coupled. In 1818, Senator Sanford of New York, by instruction of his state legislature, introduced an amendment providing for an uniform district system in the election both of members of the House and of presidential electors, the appointment of the two electors, allotted to each state in addition to those corresponding to the number of its representatives, to be made by the legislature. This was the one of the various propositions submitted from time to time which came the nearest to passing Congress.

The combination of interests which established the Virginia dynasty was too strong to be seriously disturbed. The presidency was handed along from Jefferson to Madison, and from Madison to Monroe with some perturbation, but with no great difficulty. Pennsylvania, the heterogeneous character of whose population prevented the establishment of a family political control, like that of the Clintons in New York, was always attentively cared for by the Virginia dynasty, and her adhesion made it impossible to form a sectional combination against Southern ascendency. New York went into revolt against the Congressional caucus, and set up De Witt Clinton against Madison when he was a candidate for the second time; but, although the remains of the Federalist party rallied to Clinton, he was crushingly defeated, and then the federal patronage was used to overthrow his control of New York politics. The state was brought back to its former subordinate relation, and again received the vice-presidency as its reward.

The time was not ripe for a successful revolt against the rule of the Congressional Caucus until the older generation of statesmen should cease to furnish a presidential candidate upheld by their collective prestige. That period arrived when Monroe had received the usual renomination. Every one of the four candidates for the presidential succession were men of the post-revolutionary age, and among them was a typical representative of democratic aspirations. General Jackson's career had marked him as the natural leader of the democratic movement. His success as a military man had been in brilliant contrast with the pompous impotence of generals set up by the Washington gentry. His victory at New Orleans over the flower of the British army uplifted the national pride which had been humiliated by the incapacity of the government. As a politician he represented the new states, the chief source of the democratic leaven which was stirring the whole mass of American society. In the splendid force of his indomitable manhood, he realized a popular ideal which his frontier training and his educational deficiencies made only the more genial and inspiring.

Having found such a leader, the triumph of democracy was inevitable. Although in six states, among them the great state of New York, there was no election by the people, yet such was the strength of the Jackson movement that he received the greatest number of electoral votes. Crawford, the nominee of the rump, which in 1824 was all that was left of the Congressional Caucus, stood third in the poll. John Quincy Adams, who stood second, was elected to the presidency by the House of Representatives, but he was the last President of the old order. The Jackson movement went on without intermission. Before Adams had sent his first message to Congress, the Tennessee legislature had nominated Jackson to the succession and he had formally accepted the nomination. The force of public sentiment compelled Vermont, New York, Georgia, and Louisiana to accept the popular system of choosing electors, leaving only Delaware and South Carolina to continue the system of appointment by the legislature. Jackson was triumphantly elected, and the subserviency of the electoral machinery to popular control was forever established. Before the next presidential election, South Carolina, which had taken up an independent rôle and was outside of the communion of national party organization, was the only state which retained the old system of appointment by the legislature.

During Jackson's administration, efforts were made to obtain the passage of a constitutional amendment providing for a direct election by the people, but they were unavailing. The President repeatedly urged it on the attention of Congress, and the agitation of the subject continued for a number of years; but the conditions required for the amendment of the constitution are so many and so rigorous that in the ordinary course of politics it is impossible to satisfy them. The end sought was, however, step by step attained through party activity. With the establishment of the system of nominating conventions, which took place at this period, the superior weight in party councils of a state which cast a solid electoral vote, over a state whose vote was apt to be divided by the district system, caused a general abandonment of the latter method. In 1832, the method of choosing electors was uniform throughout the country, with the exception of Maryland and South

Carolina. Before the next presidential election, Maryland abandoned the district system for the general ticket ; but South Carolina clung to the system of appointment by the legislature until after 1860. Since the Civil War the general ticket has been everywhere used, except in Michigan in 1892. The Democrats, having secured the legislature at the election of 1890, revived the party trickery of the Federalist period, and passed a law establishing the district system ; but the next legislature repealed it.

Lack of uniformity as regards the method of congressional elections ceased to disturb the Democratic party after its triumph, as it speedily found a party advantage in the complete suppression of minorities in some of the states. The correction of this injustice was a fruit of the Whig victory of 1840. In May, 1842, an act was passed requiring the election of members of the House by districts. At that time the members from New Jersey, Georgia, Mississippi, Missouri, and Louisiana were elected on a general ticket. The national regulation of senatorial elections did not take place until the present Republican party[1] rose to national dominion. The law for this purpose was enacted

---

[1] There have been three Republican parties in United States history, viz.: The Republican party of Jefferson, of which the Democratic party claims to be the lineal successor; the National Republican party established by the Adams and Clay men, which was soon merged into the Whig party; and the Republican party still existing, organized in 1856.

July 25, 1866. Thus step by step the states have been brought into a uniformity of system in national politics, and this again has reacted in various ways upon state politics, so as to produce a general conformity in political methods.

A fact of the highest importance, which has been made manifest by this process, is the plastic nature of constitutional arrangements, however rigid their formal character. The electoral college has been entirely divested of its original functions, without a change of a letter of the law. Instead of possessing discretionary powers, it has become as mechanical in its operation as a typewriter. The case is conclusive evidence of the ability of public opinion to modify the actual constitution to any extent required. It has also revealed wherein the true strength of a constitution resides. There is not a syllable in the organic or in the statute law to safeguard the present constitutional function of the electors, and yet such is the force of public sentiment that there is practically no danger that any elector will ever violate his party obligations, although it cannot be doubted that those obligations have been established in opposition to the expectation of the constitution.

M

CHAPTER XIII

DEMOCRATIC REFORM

AT the time Jackson was elected to the presidential office, Congress had acquired great weight in the government, and had practically become the seat of administrative control. The idyllic conceptions of government proclaimed by Jefferson had not fared well in this rough and bustling world. A strong reaction in favor of more vigorous and efficient government set in and made itself felt in Congress. In a speech delivered in the House, January 31, 1816, Calhoun remarked : " In the policy of nations there are two extremes : one extreme, in which justice and moderation may sink in feebleness ; another, in which the lofty spirit which ought to animate all nations, particularly free ones, may mount up to military violence. These extremes ought to be equally avoided ; but of the two, I consider the first far the most dangerous." Such language indicated a change of heart in the Republican party. It began to lean to a policy which could be distinguished from the old Federalist policy only by nice discrimination. Internal improvements were begun under Jefferson's administration, and before

Madison left office another national bank had been chartered with the same general powers as the one of Hamilton's creation against which Jefferson had fulminated. Such changes provoked the taunt that the Republicans were turning Federalists, but in reply it was argued that with Republicans at the head of affairs things could be allowed that might justly have been regarded as dangerous while Federalists were in control. This ingenious view of the case was Madison's own, produced during his philosophic retirement at Montpellier after the close of his public career. Writing under date of May 22, 1823, he said, "It is true that, under a great change of foreign circumstances, and with a doubled population and more than doubled resources, the Republican party has been reconciled to certain measures and arrangements, which may be as proper now as they were premature and suspicious when urged by the champions of Federalism."

Notwithstanding such soothing lotions, the sense of consistency in the old Republican leaders smarted under the necessity of having to reconcile themselves to theories and measures which they had formerly denounced, and an easy way of avoiding it was to throw the responsibility on Congress. As for themselves, they admitted the desirability of enlarged powers of government, if only the constitutional authority could be found. So Jefferson, Madison, and Monroe each recommended that the constitution should be amended for this purpose. Congress hearkened respectfully, and then assumed the necessary authority. In 1806 the government began the construction of the Cumberland road. In 1808 Secretary Gallatin submitted an elaborate plan of internal improvements, including the construction of both roads and canals, which was received with enthusiasm. The financial embarrassments caused by the embargo put an end to that scheme, but in 1816 a scheme of the same nature was brought forward in the House by Calhoun. The bill passed Congress, but was vetoed by Madison in the last hours of his administration. His message was in effect a plea to Congress to amend the constitution so as to obtain the undoubted right to enact such very desirable legislation. Nevertheless, the policy of internal improvement continued to take shape in Congress. Monroe was so hard pressed that, in his turn, he was compelled to vindicate the consistency of his principles by sending in an elaborate veto message, which in a stately and dignified way performed the dialectic feat vulgarly known as beating the devil around the stump. After arguing at great length that he could not really be expected to sanction internal improvements unless authorized by an amendment to the constitution, he contrived this loophole for Congress: "My idea is that Congress have an unlimited power to raise money, and that in its appropriation they have a discretionary power, restricted only by the duty to appropriate it to purposes of common defence and of general, not local, national, and state benefit." Congress promptly acted upon this hint and exercised its discretionary power. Items on account of internal improvements became a regular feature of the ordinary appropriation bills.

Such an attitude of the executive department connived at the concentration of power and responsibility in Congress, and promoted the establishment of a parliamentary régime. The party arrangement by which the Congressional Caucus named the President, gave a parliamentary origin to the administration, and the government began to take its tone and character from Congress. The presidency seemed on the way to becoming the headship of a permanent bureaucracy, at the top of which stood the Cabinet. After the traditional two terms had expired, the incumbent retired to private life, to be revered as a sage, and the Secretary of State was promoted to fill the vacancy. For more than a quarter of a century after the accession of Jefferson, the Cabinet resembled the Senate in being a continuous body, each president as he stepped into the office from the Cabinet retaining his old associates. Such was the permanency of tenure that a sense of individual right in the retention of Cabinet office grew up. The force of this sentiment is displayed in some correspondence which took place between William Wirt and ex-President Monroe after the election of Jackson. Wirt had been attorney-general during the administration of Monroe and John Quincy Adams. He consulted Monroe whether he should be expected to offer his resignation to Jackson. Monroe expressed the opinion that from some points of view Cabinet officers "may be considered as holding an independent ground — that is, depending on their good conduct in office and not on the change of the incumbent." If the Cabinet were subject to change, "the danger is, by connecting the members with the fortune of the incumbent, of making them the mere appendages and creatures of the individual." He concluded, however, that "as the heads of departments are counsellors and wield important branches of the government, I do not see how they can remain in office without the President's sanction." [1]

The people naturally got into the habit of looking altogether to Congress for decisions on questions of national policy. Furious contests took place in Congress in regard to the tariff, internal improvements, and slavery, without entering into the presidential election. All such issues were confined to the parliamentary arena. The struggle over the admission of Missouri, which from 1818 to 1820 kept the country in boiling excitement, and caused the Representatives from the free states

[1] Kennedy's Memoirs of William Wirt, Vol. II., pp. 221, 222.

to present a more solid front against slavery than at any time previous to the election of Lincoln, did not have any effect upon the presidential election. Monroe was reëlected almost unanimously.

Congress was strong, not only in the ascendency it had acquired in the management of public affairs, but also in the dignity and influence of its membership. Lustre was given to its proceedings by the presence of a singularly able group of statesmen, strong in personal force and parliamentary experience. It was the age of Clay, Webster, and Calhoun.

The democratic upheaval which lifted Jackson to the presidency was a consequence of the great extension of the suffrage which had been going on since the beginning of the century. Ohio, Indiana, Illinois, Mississippi, Alabama, Maine, and Missouri had entered the Union with manhood suffrage either specifically provided by law, or virtually established in practice. Their example had reacted on the older states, so that a demand for like privileges to their citizens could not be denied by the politicians. Maryland in 1810, Connecticut in 1818, New York in 1821, and Massachusetts in 1822 abolished their property qualifications.[1] The last stand of the statesmen of the old school was made against the spread of this movement, the survivors among the original leaders of the Federalists and the Republicans joining hands in

[1] Cyclopædia of Political Science, Vol. I., p. 774.

defence of their order. John Adams, in Massachusetts, stood on common ground with Madison, Monroe, and Marshall in Virginia in resisting the breaking-down of property qualifications to the franchise. In 1830 there were 80,000 white male inhabitants of Virginia who were disfranchised. They were the mechanics and artisans of the commonwealth, and their exclusion from the franchise was a perpetual inducement to this valuable class of citizens to emigrate to the West. But Madison made his last fight in opposition to their demand for the franchise, and, aided by the vigorous support of Monroe and Marshall, carried the constitutional convention of his state in favor of his views, so that the freehold qualification was continued in Virginia for twenty years more.[1]

In most of the states, however, property qualifications had become either nominal in amount or in enforcement. At the same time population had increased with amazing rapidity. The census of 1830 showed that the 4,000,000 of 1790 had grown into 13,000,000. Jackson's triumph was the result of political forces generated by this great increase of the electorate. It was an earthquake extending over the entire area of politics. The old Republican party was shattered to fragments. The old relations between Congress and the presidency were destroyed. The whole struct-

[1] Thorpe's " A Century's Struggle for the Franchise," *Harper's Magazine*, January, 1897.

ure of administration was shaken and displaced. A period of reconstruction necessarily followed. The force which regulated the process was supplied by the establishment in national politics of the principle of rotation in office, already reduced to practice in the politics of New York, and to a large extent adopted in all the states outside the area of Southern plantation politics.

Although its definite assertion in national politics was somewhat of an innovation, the doctrine was not a new one. It had been advocated for centuries as a sovereign remedy for political corruption. A great deal was made of it in the political writings of the Commonwealth period in England. Harrington in his "Oceana," proposed that every officer, magistrate, or representative should be excluded from his place of power and trust for a term equal to that of his employment. Burgh, whose "Political Disquisitions" was the text-book of reform in the last quarter of the eighteenth century, elaborately set forth the benefits to be derived from the application of this principle. John Adams, in some thoughts on government published in 1776, favored the principle "if the society has a sufficient number of suitable characters to supply the great number of vacancies." Jefferson favored rotation in office, to prevent the creation of a bureaucracy. Some enunciation of the principle was a staple article of the bill of rights which it was the fashion to affix to the state constitutions adopted by the colonies after the Declaration of Independence. During Monroe's administration, this principle obtained practical recognition in the federal service by the passage of the act of 1820, limiting the commissions of district attorneys, collectors, naval officers, navy agents, surveyors of customs, paymasters, and some other classes of officers, to a term of four years. The ground on which this law had been enacted was the protection it would afford to the public revenues by compelling the settlement of accounts at regular intervals ; but what was that, it was now asked, but an admission of the efficacy of the principle of rotation in office ?

What with Jefferson had been abstract philosophy, Jackson was willing and able to put into practice. The circumstances of administration in Jefferson's time had restrained such tendencies, but now the circumstances were such as to make them peculiarly energetic. Reform was the watchword of the new administration, and heedless of the shrieks of remonstrance, the reform of the civil service was carried on unflinchingly. The number of removals during the first year of Jackson's administration is variously computed at from 690 to 734 — less than the number of changes which now soon follow the installation of a reform administration ; but the contrast with the behavior of previous administrations in this respect was so startling that the event has become the mark of a new era in politics. The changes that took place were far from being a clean sweep. Benton avers that, with all his removals, Jackson still left a majority in office against him, even in the executive departments at Washington. Nevertheless, the practice of making changes in office on party grounds had been established as a national system.

The effect of the distinct conversion of the government patronage into a party fund was obviously pernicious in its adulteration of the standard of official worth. Scandalous exhibitions of the consequences in this respect were not long delayed. At the same time it is incontestable that in this way the means were obtained of readjusting the political system in conformity with the changed conditions. The energy of the force is exhibited by the results of its operation. The wrangling factions were rapidly aligned in party ranks. There was no opening for an independent rôle. Factions had to choose one side or the other, or be cut off from present enjoyment or future possibility of office. Appropriate party issues were shaped by executive policy. The administration of the patronage on party grounds carries with it the power of defining party issues, for it implies on the part of the appointing power a conception of what constitutes party membership. Whatever else may be said of it, the test has the advantage of being practical and efficient. · Dissenters may contend that they represent the true party tradition, but that does not help their case any. They must submit or go into opposition; and unless they are able to wrest control of the party organization from the President, they must organize a party organization of their own.

Some appearance of continuity with the party of Jefferson had been preserved by the very magnitude of Jackson's triumph. Such was the strength of the movement that it had, in the modern phrase, "captured the organization," taking over its name so as to enable the new party to set up the claim of being the direct lineal successor of the Republican party of Jefferson. For a time the title of Republican was retained in use as part, at least, of the party name, and is still so retained officially, but the organization soon became known simply as the Democratic party. The opposition to Jackson claimed to be the true Jeffersonian Republican party, and it was at first known as the National Republican party; but in broadening out so as to include all the elements of opposition, it finally abandoned that title for the good old revolutionary party name of Whig. The Whig party was a coalition of the National Republicans, or Adams and Clay men, with the Anti-Masons, Conservatives, and Nullifiers. The Whigs, however, always contended that they represented the true Jeffersonian principle — the maintenance of the constitutional checks and balances of power. Both Whigs and Democrats were really new parties, but the Democrats obtained possession of the Jeffersonian tradition.

It was soon made evident that the basis of administrative control had been shifted from Congress to the presidency. The reluctance of Congress to make a party issue of the rechartering of the Bank of the United States was strongly exhibited. The President forced that issue upon it. To the will of Congress, the President opposed his will, and his will prevailed. When Congress refused to authorize the removal of the government deposits, the President himself assumed that authority. The Senate placed upon its records a censure of his acts. Inside of three years it had to reverse its judgment and expunge the censure from its records. Thus at a time when its prestige was at the highest, and it had been accustomed to exercising a controlling influence in the government, Congress was overborne by the weight of presidential authority. There was no uncertainty as to the nature of the instrument by which the power of the presidential office was made effectual. During the debate of January, 1837, on the final passage of the expunging resolution, Henry Clay said : —

"The Senate has no army, no navy, no patronage, no lucrative offices, nor glittering honors to bestow. Around us there is no swarm of greedy expectants rendering us homage, anticipating our wishes, and ready to execute our commands. How is it with the President? Is he powerless? He is felt from one extremity to the other of this republic. By means of principles which he has introduced, and innovations which he has made in our institutions, alas! but too much countenanced by Congress and a confiding people, he exercises uncontrolled the power of the state. In one hand he holds the purse and in the other brandishes the sword of the country! Myriads of dependents and partisans scattered over the land are ever ready to sing hosannahs to him and to laud to the skies whatever he does. He has swept over the government like a tropical tornado."

CHAPTER XIV

THE VETO POWER

THE state of mind in which the framers of the constitution addressed themselves to the task of forming a national government was such as to cause them to attach great importance to the veto power, to make it strong, searching, and effective. They had been familiar with its exercise in colonial relations with the British government, and the character of legislation since such control had been removed was regarded as demonstrating the necessity of reëstablishing it. The original proposition of the Virginia plan was that the national legislature should have a right to negative all state laws contravening national functions ; then in their turn the acts of the national legislature, including such as negatived state laws, should be subject to the approval of a Council of Revision, to be composed of "the Executive and a convenient number of the national judiciary." The opposition of the delegates from the smaller states was so stubborn that the scheme of direct national control over state legislation was gradually reduced until only two marks of it were left in the constitution as it was finally adopted. One of these is the clause

175

giving Congress power to make or alter regulations prescribed by state authority for elections of Senators and Representatives ; the other is a clause relative to state imposts on imports or exports, providing that "all such laws shall be subject to the revision and control of Congress."

The veto power, as attached to the presidential office, had a different experience in passing through the constitutional convention. Although the debates were carried on by taking up in their order the propositions of the Virginia plan, the committee of detail seems to have used the draught of a constitution submitted by Charles Pinckney of South Carolina as a skeleton which was gradually filled out according to the resolves of the convention. Pinckney's original draught gave the President power to veto bills substantially as was eventually provided in Article I, Section 7, of the constitution, the only new matter added by the convention being the clauses requiring the vote to be taken by ayes and nays, and entered upon the journals of the two Houses. The veto power, in the shape it finally assumed as regards bills, closely resembles the corresponding section in the constitution of Massachusetts, adopted in 1780. In "The Federalist," Hamilton remarks that this power is "precisely the same with that of the governor of Massachusetts whose constitution, as to this article, seems to have been the original from which the convention has copied." The clause of the constitution of the United States, conferring also a veto power over "every order, resolution, or vote to which the concurrence of the Senate and House of Representatives may be necessary," however, stands alone. In the Massachusetts constitution, "bills" and "resolves" are coupled as subjects of the veto power. The added provision in the constitution of the United States has peculiar force. It was put in towards the latter part of the proceedings, when the convention was reviewing its work to see where any weak points were to be found. Among a number of resolutions adopted for the guidance of the committee of detail was the following: "Resolved, that the national executive shall have a right to negative any legislative act; which shall not be afterwards passed, unless by two-third parts of each branch of the national legislature." In satisfaction of this resolution, the committee draughted the constitutional provisions as they now stand, making the President a party to every legislative proceeding requiring the concurrence of the two Houses. This was perfectly well understood at the time. When the phraseology of the enacting clause of the laws was under consideration, at the first session of the Senate, Ellsworth of Connecticut, who had been a member of the convention, argued that the President should be named as a party to the enactment, because of "the conspicuous part he would act in the field of legislation,

N

as all laws must pass in review before him, and were subject to his revision and correction." [1]

In thus reviving royal prerogative as an attribute of the presidential office, there was considerable uneasiness among the founders of the national government as to the success of the attempt. In "The Federalist," great pains were taken to reconcile public sentiment to so autocratic an authority. Hamilton explained that such a power is necessary to protect the executive from encroachments by the other departments of government. The fear that it might enable the executive to encroach upon congressional authority was treated as chimerical. He said : —

"The superior weight and influence of the legislative body in a free government, and the hazard to the executive in a trial of strength with that body, afford a satisfactory security that the negative would generally be employed with great caution ; and that, in its exercise, there would oftener be room for a charge of timidity than of rashness. A king of Great Britain, with all his train of sovereign attributes, and with all the influence he draws from a thousand sources, would at this day hesitate to put a negative upon the joint resolutions of the two houses of Parliament. . . . If a magistrate, so powerful and well fortified as a British monarch, would have scrupled about the exercise of the power under consideration, how

[1] Maclay's Diary, p. 19.

much greater caution may be reasonably expected in a President of the United States, clothed for a short period of four years with the executive authority of a government wholly and purely republican."[1]

It was a fortunate circumstance that the first veto, which was exercised upon an apportionment bill, fell in with the interests of the South and received the support of Mr. Jefferson and his political connection, so that in this case there was an overpowering concentration of political influence in support of the President. Jefferson remarks in his "Anas" that "a few of the hottest friends of the bill expressed passion, but the majority were satisfied, and both in and out of doors it gave pleasure to have at length an instance of the negative being exercised." Up to Jackson's time it was exercised sparingly and cautiously, rather in the way of counsel than of opposition. Neither Jefferson nor the Adamses used the veto power at all. Madison and Monroe used it to express their dissent from the broad doctrines which, under the lead of Clay and Calhoun in his liberal early period, Congress was adopting in regard to internal improvements ; but there was no settled resistance to the deliberate purposes of Congress. There were in all nine instances only of the exercise of the veto power up to the time Jackson became President. In his hands it ceased to be a mere advisory function, as with Madison and Monroe.

[1] The Federalist, No. 73.

It developed a terrible power. His twelve vetoes
descended upon Congress like the blows of an iron
flail.

The parliamentary leaders raged against a power
which could be put to such use.   Henry Clay
pointed out that "it is a feature of our government
borrowed from a prerogative of the British king."
He declared : " The veto is hardly reconcilable
with the genius of representative government.   It
is totally irreconcilable with it if it is to be employed in respect to the expediency of measures,
as well as their constitutionality."   If such behavior should be tolerated, "the government will
have been transformed into an elective monarchy."
Webster devoted some of his strongest speeches
to an exhibition of the dangers to the constitution
from executive encroachments.   " The President
carries on the government ; all the rest are sub-
contractors. . . .   A Briareus sits in the centre of
our system, and with his hundred hands touches
everything, moves everything, controls everything."
Calhoun denounced the arrogance of the President's
attitude.   "He claims to be not only the representative, but the immediate representative, of the
American people ! What effrontery ! What bold-
ness of assertion ! The immediate representative ?
Why, he never received a vote from the American
people. He was elected by electors — the colleges."

Outside of Congress, the agitation against the
President's vetoes was carried on with vehemence.

The newspapers teemed with denunciations of the bank vetoes. "No king of England," said an editorial article in *Nile's Register*, "has dared a practical use of the veto for about two hundred years, or more, and Louis Philippe would hardly retain his throne three days, were he to veto a deliberate act of the two French chambers, though supported by an army of one hundred thousand men." Under the head of "Effects of the Veto," many newspapers established a regular department of reports of business depression and industrial distress. The veto message and the speeches of Webster, Clay, Clayton, and Ewing upon it were used as campaign documents. The supporters of Jackson did not evade the issue. They also used the veto message as a campaign document, and as a result of this combination of effort no public document ever had a more thorough distribution. The people sustained their President. Jackson's triumph was even more decisive than before. He received 219 electoral votes out of 286. Of the states which had been opposed to him before, he carried Maine and New Hampshire. Of the states which he carried before, he lost South Carolina, where there was no election by the people, and Kentucky, which in the new division of parties stood by her great leader, Henry Clay.

Support of the veto power became a Democratic principle. The Whig party was timid of confronting that issue ; the Democratic party was always ready to present it. After their great victory in 1840, the plans of the Whig leaders were paralyzed by the veto power in Tyler's hands. In January, 1842, Clay proposed constitutional amendments, empowering Congress to pass a bill over the presidential veto by a majority vote. He supported his proposals in a carefully prepared speech. His argument, setting forth the colossal proportions which the presidential authority had obtained by virtue of the veto power, was a strong one. In legislative strength it made the President the equal of anything short of a two-thirds majority of both Houses. He contended with great force that "really and in practice this veto power drew after it the power of initiating laws, and in its effects must ultimately amount to conferring on the executive the entire legislative power of the government. With the power to initiate and the power to consummate legislation, to give vitality and vigor to every law, or to strike it dead at his pleasure, the President must ultimately become the ruler of the nation."

Notwithstanding this weighty exposition of the importance of the issue, the sole reference to it, ventured in the Whig platform of 1844, was the mention of "a reform of executive usurpations" as one of the principles of the party. The Democratic convention, which met soon after, was bluntly outspoken. One of the resolutions adopted declared that " we are decidedly opposed to taking

from the President the qualified veto power, by
which he is enabled, under restrictions and responsibilities amply sufficient to guard the public interest, to suspend the passage of a bill, whose merits
cannot secure the approval of two-thirds of the
Senate and House of Representatives, until the
judgment of the people can be obtained thereon."
This resolution was specifically reaffirmed in 1848,
1852, and 1856. The Whig deliverance of 1844
was, however, the last intimation of an appeal to
the people in opposition to the veto power.

The use of the veto power has increased until
its exercise has become an ordinary executive
function. In our own time there is no power of
government which displays more vigor. At the
time the constitution was adopted, only two states
conferred the veto power upon executive authority,
— New York and Massachusetts. At the time
Clay proposed his constitutional amendment, only
nine of the twenty-six states then in the Union
gave to the governor such a veto power over bills
as the President possessed. At present the governor still has no veto power in Rhode Island,
North Carolina, and Ohio. The veto is annulled
by a majority vote of the legislature in nine states,
— Alabama, Arkansas, Connecticut, Indiana, Kentucky, New Jersey, Tennessee, West Virginia, and
Vermont. In Delaware, Maryland, and Nebraska
it takes three-fifths of the members of both Houses
to pass a bill over the veto, and in the remaining

thirty states it requires two-thirds of the votes of
each House to overrule the veto. Not only is it
the tendency of American constitutional law to
favor the deposit of such an authority in the executive department, but there is a growing disposition to stimulate its exercise. In thirteen states
the governor is specifically authorized to veto
items of appropriation bills. In some states, nota-
bly New York and Pennsylvania, it may be exercised upon bills after the legislature has adjourned,
thus leaving it quite uncontrolled and absolute in
its operation as regards the legislature, and in the
states named the veto power is now chiefly exercised in this field. Of the acts passed during one
session of the New York assembly, 335 were vetoed
by Governor Hill after its adjournment. In the
official publication of the vetoes by Governor
Hastings of Pennsylvania in 1897, fifty-four pages
are occupied by veto messages sent to the legislature, while the curt vetoes filed after adjournment
occupy 238 pages. The revisionary nature of the
veto power is strikingly displayed in this field of
its exercise, by the fact that it is at times used
to reduce particular items of appropriation bills.
Thus in a number of cases, Governor Hastings
refused to pass certain items until the beneficiaries
agreed to execute and file their acquiescence in an
abatement of the appropriation.

The veto power vested in the President of the
United States has not as yet been exercised ex-

cept as regards bills and joint resolutions; but
every vote of the two Houses is subject to it, and
unless it can be successfully contended that the
items of appropriation bills obtain place and enactment without the vote of the two Houses, they
are fit subjects for the exercise of the veto power.
Action, which in effect occupies this position, was
taken by President Grant. On August 14, 1876,
he sent a message to the House, relative to the
River and Harbor bill, in which he expressly stated
that if he regarded it as obligatory upon the executive to expend all the money therein appropriated, he should have returned the bill without his
approval. Referring to the fact that " many appropriations are made for works of purely private or
local interests, in no sense national," he remarked;
" I cannot give my sanction to these, and will take
care that during my term of office no public money
shall be expended upon them."

This doctrine, that appropriations are discretionary and not mandatory, has found expression in
Congress, as it is a convenient apology for extravagance, and passes the responsibility on from Congress to the executive. In the course of a debate
on the River and Harbor bill, June 3, 1896, Senator
Sherman remarked : —

" I cannot conceive a case where one of the ordinary regular appropriation bills should be vetoed
by the President; for, after all, it is a mere permission granted by Congress to the executive officers

to do certain things. It does not require them to do it, but only permits them to do it, and authorizes the money to be paid out of the common treasury of the United States for that purpose. But if the officers who are allowed discretion in the matter say, 'There is no money in the treasury for that purpose; it is otherwise appropriated,' or if the President of the United States should see proper to say, 'That object of appropriation is not a wise one ; I do not concur that the money ought to be expended,' that is the end of it."

While the veto power has had an astonishing development in this country, the kingly prerogative upon which it was modelled has disappeared. Neither George III nor any of his successors ever used it. There is no instance of a veto from the crown upon a law of Parliament since Queen Anne's reign. In the hands of the President, who, in the estimate of "The Federalist," would have to be even more cautious in exercising this power than the British king, it is in robust operation. Either monarchical prerogative has found a more congenial soil in the republic than in the kingdom whose sovereignty was thrown off, or else a remarkable transformation has taken place in the constitution of the presidency, and instead of an embodiment of prerogative, it has become a representative institution. The history of the phases of the development of the veto power shows that the latter view of the case is certainly the true one. Jackson's democratic instinct correctly informed him of the source of his power when he told the Senate that it was "a body not directly amenable to the people," while the President "is the direct representative of the people, elected by the people, and responsible to them."

All the circumstances go to show that the veto power is sustained, not by strength of prerogative, but by the representative character of the presidential office. The development of executive authority has been sustained by public sentiment because it has forged an instrument of popular control. Congress represents locality ; the President represents the nation. Congressional authority is founded on a combination of interests which the people instinctively feel to be beyond their control. The people, parcelled into districts, elect their delegates, but they have nothing to do with the places those delegates may obtain in the shuffle. When the units are supplied, the politicians work out the sum to suit themselves. Presidential authority is founded on the direct mandate of the people. This is the secret of the strength of the veto power. Levi Woodbury, who was a cabinet officer under Jackson and Van Buren, and became a justice of the supreme court, in a speech at Faneuil Hall October 19, 1841, described the constitutional function exactly when he said, " The veto power is the people's tribunative prerogative speaking again through their executive."

CHAPTER XV

THE new character impressed upon the presidential office by the democratic movement at once
made it the basis of political control. Every
national party which has come into existence since
Jackson's time, no matter how purely legislative
its programme, has felt impelled to nominate a
presidential ticket. Unless it is able to control
the presidential office, no party can accomplish its
purposes. The Whig party, which was animated
by the old spirit of parliamentary control, was the
first party to find this out by experience. In electing Harrison in 1840, it secured a President who
fully assented to the parliamentary principle of
government. In his inaugural address he contended that by no fair construction could anything
" be found to constitute the President a part of the
legislative power." His duty to recommend legislation was simply " a privilege which he holds in
common with every other citizen." He regarded
it as "preposterous to suppose that a thought
could for a moment have been entertained that
the President, placed at the capital, in the centre

of the country, could better understand the wants
and wishes of the people than their own immediate
representatives " ; so, therefore, "to assist or control Congress in its ordinary legislation could not
have been the motive for conferring the veto
power on the President." In particular he held
that the President "should never be looked to for
schemes of finance."

This was very satisfactory doctrine to the Whig
party leaders in Congress, but there was no way by
which it could be made obligatory. When Harrison died, his doctrine died with him. Tyler,
although elected on the same ticket with Harrison,
did not scruple to use the veto power to defeat the
Whig schemes of finance adopted by Congress.
Polk, the next President, had occasion to review the
whole subject of the relations between the President and the Congress, and in his message of
December 5, 1848, he laid down the constitutional
principles governing the case as follows : —

"The people, by the constitution, have commanded the President, as much as they have commanded the legislative branch of the government, to
execute their will. They have said to him in the
constitution, which they require he shall·take a
solemn oath to support, that if Congress pass any bill
which he cannot approve, ' he shall return it to the
House in which it originated, with his objections.'
If it be said that the representatives in the popular branch of Congress are chosen directly by the

people, it is answered, the people elect the President. If both Houses represent the states and the people, so does the President. The President represents in the executive department the whole people of the United States, as each member of the legislative department represents portions of them."

The course of our political history since Jackson's time has conformed to the constitutional principle that the President is the direct representative of the people as a whole. The establishment of this principle was accompanied by a marked change of popular habit in the exercise of the suffrage. Originally, the House of Representatives was not only the designated medium for the expression of public sentiment, but in most of the states there was no means of popular participation in the government of the United States, save in the election of members of the House. And even in states where presidential electors were chosen by the vote of the people, the interest in such elections was small as compared with that taken in congressional elections. *Nile's Register* of November 18, 1820, reports that very few votes had been polled for presidential electors in Maryland and Virginia. In the whole city of Richmond only seventeen votes were cast. Yet this was the period when the country was convulsed over the admission of Missouri with a slavery constitution, and congressional elections were attended by great excitement. Even during the presidential election of 1824, with four candidates in the field, each with enthusiastic partisans, the total vote cast in Virginia was less than 15,000; and Massachusetts, which had cast more than 66,000 votes for governor in 1823, cast only 37,000 votes at the presidential election. Ohio polled 50,024 votes; but the election for governor two years before had drawn out 10,000 more votes, and in the same year as the presidential election the vote for governor aggregated 76,634. The Jacksonian era marks the beginning of a concentration of popular interest on the presidential election. After 1824, the popular vote shows a rapid increase. The aggregate in 1824 was 356,038. The aggregate vote cast by the same states in 1828 was 817,409. The increase in some of the states was amazing. In New Hampshire, the vote rose from 4750 to 45,056; in Connecticut, from 9565 to 18,286; in Pennsylvania, from 47,255 to 152,500; in Ohio, from 50,024 to 130,993. The popular tendency thus suddenly developed has been constant. It is now a commonplace of politics that the presidential vote is the largest cast at any election. In the presidential election of 1896 there were cast for President 218,658 votes more than were cast for Congressmen. When it is considered that the practice of putting presidential and congressional candidates on the same ballot is almost general, this popular disposition is certainly very remarkable.

This change in the attitude of the people towards
the President took away much of the importance
of Congress, and had effects upon its character
which soon became very manifest. The framers of
the constitution anticipated for the House of Representatives a brilliant career, something like that of
the House of Commons. The natural ascendency
which the House would possess as the immediate
representative of the people, is the stock argument of "The Federalist" in justification of the
exclusive privileges conferred upon the President
and the Senate. It was held that no danger to
the constitution could result from an excess of
power in them, since "the House of Representatives with the people on their side will at all times
be able to bring back the constitution to its primitive form and principles"; while, on the other hand,
the coördinate branches of the government could
not withstand the encroachments of the House
without special safeguards.[1] The result, on the
whole, during the early period of the republic,
verified this calculation. Although never developing such an authority as that of the House of
Commons, the House of Representatives was the
most important branch of the government. The
Senate was composed of provincial notables who
sat as a privy council, transacting business behind
closed doors. The floor of the House was the

---

[1] The Federalist, No. 63.

field where political talent might obtain distinction. The Senate became tired of its dull seclusion from popular interest, and in 1799 admitted the public to its debates; but the superior prestige of the House was maintained until the Jacksonian era. Calhoun remarks that the House was originally "a much more influential body than the Senate."[1] Benton says, "For the first thirty years it was the controlling branch of the government, and the one on whose action the public eye was fixed."[2] The democratic revolution overthrew the pillars of its greatness. It ceased to make presidents; it ceased to control them. Instead of being the seat of party authority, — the motive force of the administration, — it became in this respect merely a party agency. National party purposes, having to seek their fulfilment through the presidential office, had nothing to ask of the House but obedience to party demands, and at once began the task of devising machinery to enforce submission.

Burke long ago had foretold, "If we do not permit our members to act upon a very enlarged view of things, we shall at length infallibly degrade our national representation into a confused and scuffling bustle of local agency." Precisely such a change rapidly took place in the House of Representatives.

---

[1] Calhoun's Works, Vol. I., p. 341.
[2] Thirty Years' View, Vol. I., p. 208.

Its decadence was rapid and soon became notorious.[1]

From this period dates the disposition of the people to make use of the House to reflect their passing moods rather than their settled habits of thinking. The early contests between the Federalists and the Republicans were faction struggles that did not establish strict party lines in the House. Although in the Fourth Congress the opponents of the administration were strong enough to vote down a resolution of confidence in the President, a Federalist was chosen speaker. Under the Virginia dynasty the political complexion of the House was constant, and its membership exhibited a stability of composition approximating that of the House of Commons at the same period. Henry Clay was elected speaker five times in succession, and might have continued to hold the position had he so desired. But after the Jackson upheaval the House became the shuttlecock of politics. A graphic delineation of changes of party strength appears like storm waves in ascent and reflux. In the Twenty-first Congress the party division in the House was 152 to 39; in the Twenty-second Congress, 98 to 97. In the Twenty-fifth Congress the majority in the House was Democratic; in the Twenty-sixth, it was Whig. In the Twenty-seventh

---

[1] Benton makes some doleful comments on this fact, which he greatly deplores and tries to extenuate. Thirty Years' View, Vol. I., Chap. LVII.

Congress, it was Whig; in the Twenty-eighth, it was Democratic. In the Twenty-ninth Congress, it was Democratic; in the Thirtieth, it was Whig. During the Civil War the waves were flattened down, so to speak; but the fluctuation was still remarkable.[1] Since the reconstruction period the vicissitudes of party strength in Congress are so enormous that they simply daze and confound the politicians. They come in exultingly at one election, on a wave of victory that seems to have swept away the opposition, and a few years later they find themselves swept from power in a condition of utter rout and demoralization, wondering what on earth has befallen them.

So periodic is the fluctuation of public sentiment that it is expected as a matter of course that " the off-year "— the congressional election intervening between presidential elections — will show a gain in the strength of the opposition. Nothing being at stake but the composition of the House, the particular interests of localities are not so heavily weighed upon by the necessities of national party interest, so that faction aims and individual pre-dilections have more to do with shaping results. The popular vote is smaller, opposition is active and ardent, while support is languid, so that it is a common thing to hear of candidates defeated by "the stay-at-home vote." The popular mandate is

[1] Johnston's American Politics gives the congressional strength of parties down to 1889.

delivered at the presidential election. Many people do not vote at any other time. Other elections, so far as they bear upon national affairs, are used for correction, warning, or reproof.

Alexander Hamilton once remarked to a friend that the time will "assuredly come when every vital question of the state will be merged in the question, 'Who shall be the next President?'"[1] That time arrived when the President became the elect of the people, and the presidential office became the organ of the will of the nation.

[1] History, by John C. Hamilton, Vol. III., pp. 335, 346.

CHAPTER XVI

THE CONVENTION SYSTEM

An immediate effect of the conversion of the presidency into a representative institution was the establishment of the convention system. It is a typical development of American politics, and its origin and growth as the result of the operation of democratic forces may be distinctly traced.

The idea was an old one, but was long ineffectual, owing to popular jealousy of any mediation in the election of public officials. In Pennsylvania in 1792, as the time for the election of representatives and of presidential electors approached, it was proposed that a convention should be held "of conferees from all parts of the state to meet at Lancaster and fix on suitable candidates to be recommended to the choice of the citizens." The object was to secure "such an unanimity of suffrage among the electors as would return to the House of Representatives of the United States — men whose attachment to the federal constitution, whose concern in the national prosperity, and whose knowledge of its best interests, should qualify them to administer that government."[1]   The Republican papers at once opened fire on this proposition.   "A Mechanic" sarcastically commends the plan because it relieves the common people of any concern in politics, by providing them with a ticket ready made to their hands.   "Sidney" tells the people: "A congregation of men to frame a ticket, sanctioned by you, is in fact a body of electors, clothed with your authority.   Are you incapable of judging for yourselves, that you must hazard a transfer of your most important rights?"   Hugh H. Brackenridge, the distinguished Republican leader of western Pennsylvania, dissected the proposal with arguments that are as keen to-day as when first penned.   After presenting considerations, showing the improbability that the conferees would be so chosen as fairly to represent the people of their districts, he adds that even if they were, the system would not work fairly, "because the persons that go forward will have attachments and resentments, interests and partialities, hopes and fears, which those at home know nothing of, but which will be fully exercised when they come to form a ticket."   "Leave it," he concluded, "to every man to frame his ticket, or be immediately instructed by others how to do it; but let it be his own act, and there is no deception or injustice."

These comments fairly set forth popular sentiment, but practical experience was constantly

[1] The American Museum, Philadelphia, for August, 1792.

showing that to compass party ends means were necessary for the concentration of votes in the party interest, or else people of like minds on political issues might defeat their desire by disagreement in the selection of representatives. Hence caucuses and mass-meetings were held, and committees of correspondence became busy whenever an election was on hand, in order to set forth the claims of candidates and afford guidance to voters. In matters requiring a concert of action, extending over a state, it became the practice for the members of the legislature to caucus for the purpose of recommending candidates. Travel was slow and costly, the members were from all parts of the state and were already convened, so that the ease and convenience of the arrangement commended it. Men of political prominence, who were not members, could attend and participate in the proceedings if they cared to take the trouble to do so. A practical defect of the system, revealed at an early date, was that in a party caucus of members of the legislature, districts from which members of another party had been elected would not be represented. This could be remedied by the election from those districts of delegates to represent them in the caucus, thus giving it the character of a party convention. The New York legislative caucus, which nominated De Witt Clinton for governor in 1817, was completed in this way.

These methods came into existence, not by theoretic design, but as practical expedients. In just the same way, the nomination of candidates for President devolved upon the Congressional Caucus. Anything like express authority for such action was disavowed. In 1808 the Republican Congressional Caucus, in announcing its candidates, declared "that in making the foregoing recommendation the members of this meeting have acted only in their individual characters as citizens; they have been induced to adopt this measure from the necessity of the case; from a deep conviction of the importance of union to the Republicans throughout all parts of the United States in the present crisis of both our external and internal affairs; and as being the most practicable mode of consulting and respecting the interests and wishes of all upon a subject so truly interesting to the whole people of the United States." Some such explanation was regularly appended to the announcements of the action of the Caucus so long as it undertook to make presidential nominations.

While this method might serve an established party already in possession of legislative control, it would not do for a party whose legislative representation was too weak for it to presume to speak for the whole. Consequently, the Federalists had to make use of other means of pooling their votes. Generally, the old-fashioned method of correspondence between party leaders, in the states where they still had some strength, was sufficient for their needs. In 1812, when the Clinton revolt in New York against the Virginia dynasty inspired the Federalists with some hope, they held a convention in New York, at which eleven states were represented, and endorsed the Clinton presidential ticket, already nominated by the legislative caucus at Albany. This convention, although more like a ratification mass-meeting than a nominating convention in the modern sense, led to an attempt to establish a regular convention system in New York. The Clinton bolt, although it controlled the Republican Caucus at Albany, did not carry with it the entire party organization in New York. Tammany Hall, with the support of Madison's administration, began a vigorous war on De Witt Clinton, and in 1813 formally proposed that a state convention should be called for the purpose of nominating the governor. The movement failed, but the tendency of political opposition to resort to the convention system became strongly marked. This was particularly the case with new political movements, whose power had yet to be developed in the composition of the legislature. Their interests naturally antagonized the legislative caucus, in which established political interests were intrenched. Hence the Anti-Masonic party, which sprang up in 1826, was driven to the expedient of holding conventions of its own. Its propaganda was actively carried on during the period in which the new conception of the presidential office was formed, and obedient to that impulse a national convention of the party was held in Philadelphia in 1831. This may be regarded as the first regularly constituted national party convention, congressional representation being taken as the rule of party representation.

The popular dislike of party machinery was, however, deeply rooted. The Jackson movement had derived a great deal of strength from this sentiment, and in overthrowing the Congressional Caucus there was no intention to substitute for it the still more elaborate and cumbrous convention system. The desire was to procure a constitutional amendment, enabling the people to vote directly for President. In the ordinary course of politics, however, the constitution is unamendable. A two-thirds majority of both Houses of Congress, and the sanction of three-fourths of the states, can be commanded only at rare and tremendous junctures. As the close of Jackson's first term approached, the newly formed Democratic party found itself exposed to dangerous hazards of dissension from the lack of any method of securing party agreement as to the ticket to be supported by the presidential electors who might be chosen in the party interest. While it was settled that Jackson should be renominated, the vice-presidency was an open question, to decide which some mode of party action was necessary. There was some inclination to restore the Congressional Caucus. This was the preference of Van Buren and the Albany agency. Of course candidates apprehensive of the influences controlling Congress were opposed to this, and moreover public sentiment had been too deeply incensed against the Caucus to be won over. Meanwhile, the convention system had been adopted by the opposition. After the Anti-Masonic party had held its national convention, the National Republicans held theirs. William Wirt was the presidential candidate of the Anti-Masons. Henry Clay was the candidate of the National Republicans. The hope of the opposition to Jackson was that the electoral vote would be split up so as to throw the election into the House of Representatives, where the states would vote as equals. The necessity of concentrating the Democratic vote became manifest, and the convention system appeared to be the only practicable method. The New Hampshire legislature led the way by issuing a call for a national convention, and Jackson gave his approval to the movement. Every state responded except Missouri. The system of national conventions was thus adopted by all parties.

The position of the national convention, as the supreme authority in party organization, was not established without opposition. The Pennsylvania Democracy bolted the nomination of Van Buren for Vice-President in 1832, and the electoral votes of the state were cast for William Wilkins for that office.   In 1832 and 1836 South Carolina cast her electoral vote for candidates of her own, who received no votes from any other state.   In 1836 the Democratic party was the only party which held a national convention.   The plan of the opposition was to take the greatest possible advantage of local elements of hostility to the national administration by running a number of tickets, and thus endeavor to throw the election into the House of Representatives.   The Democratic party organization in Virginia bolted the national convention nomination for Vice-President, and the electoral votes of the state were cast for an independent candidate.   Van Buren, the convention candidate for President, was elected, but no one had a majority of votes for Vice-President. The election devolved on the Senate, which chose the convention nominee — Richard M. Johnson of Kentucky.   In 1840 the Democratic-Republican national convention did not venture to nominate a candidate for Vice-President, but adopted a resolution, leaving "the decision to their Republican fellow-citizens in the several states, trusting that before the election shall take place their opinions shall become so concentrated as to secure the choice of a Vice-President by the electoral colleges."   The Democratic party did not obtain many electoral votes in that election.   While all were given to Van Buren for President, they were divided among three candidates for Vice-President.

Declarations of party principles naturally accompanied the nomination of party candidates, and so the party platform had its origin. As in the case of the convention system the germ of the platform may be traced a long way back. In 1800 the Congressional Caucus of the Republican party adopted resolutions, setting forth the principles represented by Jefferson's candidacy. In 1812 the New York legislative caucus, which nominated Clinton to the presidency, set forth the grounds of opposition to Madison in a series of resolutions. During the Jackson movement the adoption of resolutions at meetings and conventions became a regular practice. When national party conventions regularly assumed the function of selecting candidates, they could not well avoid making statements of party principles. Public opinion demanded such explanations, and the politicians had to comply. In 1840, the first formal national platform of the Democratic party was adopted. The Whigs, a party of political odds and ends, did not formally present a platform either in 1840 or in 1848. The prepossessions in favor of parliamentary control which clung to the Whig party made the laying down of platforms in connection with presidential nominations a disagreeable duty. Its real feeling on the subject was probably that which it declared when, reduced to a mere rump under the name of the Constitutional Union Party, it met at Baltimore in 1860 and nominated Bell and Everett. It then adopted resolutions setting forth that "experience has demonstrated that platforms adopted by the partisan conventions of the country have had the effect to mislead and deceive the people, and at the same time widen the political divisions of the country by the creation and encouragement of geographical and sectional partisan parties."

That party never held another convention, and never since then has any party failed to submit to the people some statement of its purpose.

But while the adoption of a platform is now an accepted party obligation, the duty is not discharged with complete sincerity. Platform utterances have become so vague and ambiguous that the tendency of public sentiment is to attach much less importance to them than to the declarations of the presidential candidates. Mr. Blaine, in a review article, thus described the change which has taken place : —

" The resolutions of a convention have come to signify little in determining the position of President or party. Formerly the platform was of first importance. Diligent attention was given, not only to every position advanced, but to the phrase in which it was expressed. The presidential candidate was held closely to the text, and he made no excursions beyond it. Now, the position of the candidate, as defined by himself, is of far more weight with the voters, and the letter of acceptance has come to be the legitimate creed of the party."

The establishment of national control over party organization, against the obstructions raised by popular prejudice and state pride, could not have been effected without the influence of the federal patronage. The resistance to the system in the Democratic party was strong and stubborn, and some marks of it still appear in convention procedure. The rule requiring a two-thirds majority to nominate, which is peculiar to the Democratic party, was a precaution taken by state party organizations against submergence of their interests. The subsequent adoption of the unit rule, by which a majority of each delegation was allowed to cast its full vote, recognized a practice begun in the Van Buren interest, the inequitable character of which was mitigated by making it uniform.[1] It required the full pressure of Jackson's authority to make the party organizations in a number of states submit to the convention system at all. The great edifice of national party organization has the presidential patronage for its corner-stone.

[1] These famous rules are usually ascribed to the influence of state sovereignty ideas, but the facts of the case do not sustain this theory. Calhoun, who was the great champion of state sovereignty, always contended that the people should elect convention delegates by districts. He also contended that if delegations voted as states, they should have an equal vote, as in an election of the President by the House of Representatives.

CHAPTER XVII

THE TRANSFORMATION OF THE CONSTITUTION

An effect of the convention system, which was at once noted, was the complete effacement of the constitutional design for the election of President. Senator Benton, a leader of the Jackson movement which was the great agent of change, was startled by the consequences of the new system. He said, "The election of the President and the Vice-President of the United States has passed, — not only from the college of electors to which the constitution confided it, and from the people to which the practice under the constitution gave it, and from the House of Representatives which the constitution provided as ultimate arbiter, — but has gone to an anomalous, irresponsible body, unknown to law or constitution, unknown to the early ages of our government. . . ."[1] Benton's remedy was "the application of the democratic principle — the people to vote direct for President and Vice-President." This was the original demand of the Jackson party. Benton drew a fancy picture of American citizens going to the polls, each declaring who, in his individual opinion, was the fittest man for President.

[1] Thirty Years' View, Vol. I., p. 49.

He likened it to "the sublime spectacle" that was seen in the city states of antiquity, "when the Roman citizen advanced to the polls and proclaimed: 'I vote for Cato to be Consul'; the Athenian, 'I vote for Aristides to be Archon'; the Theban, 'I vote for Pelopidas to be Bœotrach'; the Lacedæmonian, 'I vote for Leonidas to be first of the Ephori.'" That there would be any difficulty in exercising a real choice does not seem to have occurred to Benton, but the point was clearly discerned by Calhoun's penetrating intellect. He argued that the natural incompetency of the people to judge in such a case would inevitably transfer the real selection to a few managers. Like Benton, he held that "the complex and refined machinery provided by the constitution for the election of the President and Vice-President is virtually superseded"; and that "the nomination of the successful party, by irresponsible individuals, makes, in reality, the choice."[1] But so far from holding popular election to be the cure, he found it to be the cause of the evil, so that the extension of the principle would only aggravate the malady. In his own state of South Carolina he successfully opposed the choice of presidential electors by popular election, on the ground that "so far from giving power to the people it would be the most effectual way that could be devised of divesting them of it and transferring it to party managers

[1] Calhoun's Works, Vol. I., p. 224.

P

and cliques." In his "Disquisition of Government"
he sets forth with impregnable logic the sequence
of cause and effect. He points out that parties
will rule because associated effort is more powerful than individual action.

"The conflict between the two parties in the
government of the numerical majority, tends necessarily to settle down into a struggle for the honors
and emoluments of the government ; and each, in
order to obtain an object so ardently desired, will,
in the process of the struggle, resort to whatever
measure may seem best calculated to effect this
purpose. The adoption by the one, of any measure, however objectionable, which might give it an
advantage, would compel the other to follow its
example. In such a case, it would be indispensable to success, to avoid division and keep united;
— and hence, from a necessity inherent in the
nature of such governments, each party must be
alternately forced, in order to insure victory, to
resort to measures to concentrate the control over
its movements in fewer and fewer hands, as the
struggle became more and more violent. This in
process of time must lead to party organization
and party caucuses and discipline ; and these to
the conversion of the honors and emoluments of
the government into means of rewarding partisan
services, in order to secure the fidelity and increase
the zeal of the members of the party." [1]

[1] Calhoun's Works, Vol. I., pp. 40, 41

Calhoun's writings exhibit a mental attitude in which the nullification doctrine and attachment to the Union meet in harmony. Taking for his starting-point the fact that the intention of the constitution was to establish, not a government by popular majority, but one of checks and balances, he showed how the constitutional checks and balances had been destroyed by party spirit. While the form of the constitution had remained, its restraint had been avoided by transferring the selection of Presidents and the initiative of administration to an extra-constitutional body, free from all restriction, save such as public opinion might impose. Members of Congress and office-holders are constitutionally disqualified from serving as electors, but nevertheless they swarm in national conventions and in practice act as electors. Calhoun's point was that, since the original checks had been overthrown, new ones were necessary if the constitution was to be preserved. The fittest check was one which he held to be inherent in the nature of the union — the exercise of state sovereignty.

"The practical effect is to give to each interest or portion of the community a negative on the others. It is this mutual negative among its various conflicting interests, which invests each with the power of protecting itself; and places the rights and safety of each, where only they can be securely placed, under its own guardianship.

Without this there can be no systematic, peaceful, or effective resistance to the natural tendency of each to come into conflict with the others ; and without this there can be no constitution. It is this negative power — the power of preventing or arresting the action of the government — be it called by what term it may — veto, interposition, nullification, check, or balance of power — which in fact forms the constitution." [1]

It is easy to see how this line of reasoning eventually led to Calhoun's proposal of a dual executive, the final expedient suggested by his patriotism as a means of reconciling to his ideas of constitutional liberty the Union which he loved. The secession movement naturally emerged from this state of thought. It was as constitutional in its temper as the Revolution of 1776. There is no more pathetic reading in all political literature than Calhoun's writings on government. They are a noble monument over the grave of the Whig theory of government, slain in its constitutional intrenchments by victorious Democracy.

The profound change which Jackson's administration effected in the character of the government, makes it a landmark of the divergence between the English and American constitutional systems. To subject the administration of public affairs to the superintendence of public opinion, has been the tendency of constitutional develop-

[1] Calhoun's Works, Vol. I., p. 35.

ment in both countries. In England, the democratic movement made executive prerogative subservient to the national will, through the agency of Parliament; in America, it seized prerogative by the immediate act of the people. There was no conscious selection of means. The choice was determined by necessity. There are instances of popular appeals to George III to exercise the royal veto upon acts of Parliament. The nature of the tenure of royal authority, however, puts it out of the reach of direct popular control. The people have no choice who shall be king. In England, the only organ of government on which democratic forces could act directly was Parliament. When George III was compelled by circumstances to rest his administration upon the popularity of the younger Pitt, the form which democratic development would take was settled. Thenceforth the basis of governmental authority was not the king's will, but public opinion, as reflected in the composition of Parliament and embodied in its leadership. To make the composition of Parliament a fair expression of public opinion was the object sought by the English reform movement which was contemporaneous with the democratic uprising in America. The parliamentary reform bill, which marks the establishment of popular control in England, was passed in 1832, during Jackson's first administration.

In this country democratic progress found in

the President its most convenient instrument. Public opinion suppressed the constitutional discretion of the electoral college, and made it a register of the result of the popular vote as taken by states. The President became the elect of the people, the organ of the will of the nation. Hence the power of the presidential office exhibits an enormous growth, while royal prerogative has withered. The right to choose the ministers of the crown has long since been resigned by English royalty. The President selects the members of his cabinet to suit himself. The constitutional participation of the Senate has become a mere matter of form. The veto power of the crown is extinct. Writing in 1828, Macaulay described it as "a prerogative which has not been exercised for a hundred and thirty years, which probably will never be exercised again, and which can scarcely in any conceivable case be exercised for a salutary purpose." That is just the time when the veto power of the President began to display an exuberant vitality. English royalty has dwindled away into a ceremonial function. The power of the presidential office has increased and is increasing.

In England the formation of the parliamentary type of government was completed when it became a settled principle that party control of the House of Commons carried with it the custody of crown authority. The presidential type of government which democratic progress is shaping in America is still imperfect. While the presidential office has been transformed into a representative institution, it lacks proper organs for the exercise of that function. The nomination of a presidential candidate is accompanied by a declaration of party principles which he is pledged to enforce in the conduct of the administration ; but no constitutional means are provided whereby he may carry out his pledges, and it is due solely to the extra-constitutional means supplied by party organization that the presidential office is able to perform the function imposed upon it of executing the will of the nation. Party organization acts as a connective tissue, enfolding the separate organs of government, and tending to establish a unity of control which shall adapt the government to the uses of popular sovereignty. The adaptation is still so incomplete that the administrative function is imperfectly carried on and the body-politic suffers acutely from its irregularity.

American politics are in a transition state. Throes of change rack the state with pain in every limb and evoke continual groans. A cry for relief is the burden of public utterance. A ready ear is given to quackery, and many political nostrums are recommended with pathetic credulity by large bodies of respectable people. Fortunately for the safety of the state and the development of the constitution, the character and circumstances of the mass of the people are such that efforts to physic American politics are futile.   The agencies which have carried on the process of change will continue to do so, in spite of all outcry and remonstrance, until the democratic type of government is perfected.

PART III

THE ORGANS OF GOVERNMENT

—◆—

CHAPTER XVIII

INSTRUMENTS OF RULE

THE preceding chapters sketch the development of American politics down to our own times. The stage of growth, whose beginning is marked by the Jacksonian era, still continues, and the actual constitution of the government, in its typical characteristics, still remains as it was then moulded. The conclusions which have been reached may be summarized as follows : —

The government began as a magisterial control, the product of a conservative reaction against impending anarchy. This control was founded according to the principles of the English constitution, as then understood, by distributing the authority and balancing the powers of government so as to give representation to different social orders and interests, and enable each to protect itself. The organs of government were constituted upon the English pattern, monarchical prerogative being represented by the presidential office, the House of Lords by the Senate, and the House of Commons by the House of Representatives. In framing the government care was taken to exclude what were regarded as corruptions impairing the constitutional model, — in particular, the formation of a cabinet of ministers from among the members of the legislature, — and extra precautions were taken to confine the democratical element in the constitution by restricting the powers of the House of Representatives to limits narrower than those of the House of Commons.

The government was put up and set going by a concert of action among leading men in the various states, who possessed an aristocratic ascendency strong enough, when dexterously and energetically exercised, to impose their determinations upon the mass of the people. These national politicians comprised two groups formed during the Revolutionary struggle : the one, from the associations of the Continental Congress; the other, from experience of administrative necessities ; the one, wholly civilian ; the other, largely military ; the one, intent upon parliamentary checks upon authority ; the other, intent upon executive efficiency. As soon as the government was fairly established, and the stress of circumstances which brought them together was relaxed, these groups with their adherents drew apart and formed rival parties, each seeking to control the administration.

Party competition for popular favor and support stimulated democratic tendencies, at the same time supplying a leadership which moderated their force and confined them to constitutional methods. As the suffrage was extended and political power was diffused among the masses, the supremacy of the classes which had possession of the government was undermined. Their control of the electoral college — which, although constituted as a deliberative body, had always acted in a ministerial capacity — became precarious, and in the election of Jackson was overthrown. The electoral college was finally divested of any semblance of its original constitutional discretion and became distinctly a party agency. The presidential office was thus placed within reach for use as an instrument of popular control over the administration of public affairs. The office experienced a democratic transformation, making it a representative institution — the organ of the will of the nation. All its powers were invigorated.

This profound change in the nature of the constitution was accomplished without any change in its formal provisions, and the separation of the legislative and executive branches of administration, so carefully ordained by the framers of the constitution, remained intact ; while the coördinating influences upon which they had relied were extinguished. The establishment of a new joint control became the instinctive object of party effort.   To supply the place of the class interests and social connections which originally provided the necessary unity of control, the convention system was developed, and gradually its jurisdiction was confirmed until local, state, and national politics were bound together in national party organization and all their activities were subordinated to national interests.   The magnitude and extent of the functions assumed have been sustained by an appropriate elaboration of structure, giving to party organization in America a massiveness and a complexity unknown in governments whose constitution leaves to party only its ordinary office of propagating opinion and inciting the political activity of citizenship.   In England party elicits the expression of the will of the nation ; in this country it must also provide for its execution, so that it is virtually a part of the apparatus of government itself, connecting the executive and legislative departments, and occupying the place which in the parliamentary type of government is filled by the ministry.   An account of the organs of government would therefore be incomplete unless, to the House of Representatives, the Senate, and the Presidency, there is added Party Organization.

CHAPTER XIX

LIKE the Continental Congress which preceded it, the Congress of the United States is essentially a diplomatic body — a convention of the envoys of locality. This fact determines its essential character, and refers one to the ordinary methods of a diplomatic congress rather than to those of a parliament for an explanation of its usages. The essential characteristic of a genuine parliament is that it embodies national control. The government appears before it, like the general manager of a company meeting the board of directors. The measures he submits for their consideration have been prepared in advance. He explains them, replies to criticism, and when sufficient opportunity has been allowed for discussion, he demands the decision of the board. It is part of his ordinary duties to be prepared to give information as to the condition of the company's affairs, and at all times he must be able to sustain the responsibilities of his trusteeship. Under such circumstances discussion cannot but be direct and practical. When people are talking business, they are intolerant of futile palaver. Hence parliamentary bodies are notoriously rude to bores. Among the traditions of the House of Commons is the story of a member, caught pulling out a written speech in the course of an exciting debate, who was handled in a manner that drove him out of the House and extinguished his parliamentary ambition.[1] It is a well-known incident of Disraeli's career that the first time he attempted to make a speech, his affected manner provoked such a tumult of derision that he could not make himself heard, and he sat down in disgust.

Nothing of this kind could happen in Congress, for the underlying principle of its procedure is that its members, like the delegates to a diplomatic congress, meet as peers, each one having in theory all the rights and privileges that any one has.[2] In the Senate this principle is in no way circumscribed. Nothing can be done so long as any one desires to talk and is able to do so. Even in the House, where under compulsion of necessity limitations have been put upon debate, a member cannot be so dull and incapable but what he may not at least have his opportunity at an evening set

[1] Trevelyan's Early Years of Fox, p. 169.

[2] January 18, 1814, Representative King of Massachusetts contended that the rules should be amended so as to prohibit the House from refusing to consider any resolutions offered by a representative. In his speech he said, "I never can for a moment concede that it depends upon the will and pleasure of this or any other majority of this House, whether the people of the United States, by their representatives, shall, or shall not, be heard upon this floor."

apart for speechmaking only; or, if he like it better, be permitted to print a speech in the Record as having been delivered, with the privilege of free use of the mails to send it to his constituents.

The truth is that in Congress the rôle of orators is the subordinate one of advocating and supporting policies imposed by party, and they may figure brilliantly in this capacity without thereby obtaining much authority. A man may have genuine, forensic ability, which attracts the attention of the House and of the country, and yet his political career may be suddenly ended by the displeasure of party managers whom he has somehow offended or whose plans it suits to bring some one else forward. On the other hand, men who would be utterly lost in a parliamentary debate, and would simply make a show of themselves if they should make an attempt at oratory, may exercise great influence in Congress by their prominence in party councils.[1] The ablest orators cannot compare with them in real power, for they represent an authority superior to Congress — the authority of party organization.[2]

[1] The career of Senator J. Donald Cameron is a case in point. He was indisputably an influential member of Congress, although his incapacity as an orator was a perpetual subject of newspaper ridicule.

[2] In the Republican caucus at Harrisburg, which nominated Mr. Cameron for reëlection to the Senate, Mr. Toweler of Forest County said: "Ingalls and Evarts are orators, and I would like to know

Business is shaped and arranged for consideration, as in a diplomatic gathering, by the action of the Congress itself. It supplies itself with the necessary organs by subdivision into as many committees as it sees fit. The Pan-American Conference which met at Washington 1890–1891 exhibited in its proceedings the ground plan of the methods by which Congress does its work. That conference had so many subjects to consider that it appointed sixteen standing committees. Their reports to the conference presented those subjects in shape for action. Congress works in precisely the same way. It breaks itself up into numerous segments, each a little congress in its way, with both the dominant party and the opposition represented in its membership. The formative stage of legislation is carried on in diplomatic privacy, while the public feeds on gossip about what is going on behind the closed doors. Hidden influences are at work determining results. The conduct of business is a negotiation between diverse interests, and it is only after the conclusions reached are reported that Congress gets a chance to act. And yet the committees assume no responsibility, for the theory is that they are simply agents of Congress, appointed for its convenience. Jefferson's "Manual of Parliamentary Practice," which forms a part of

what they ever got or ever did, except blow off their mouths. Pennsylvania gets everything she wants through her senators." Philadelphia Inquirer, January 8, 1891.

the rules of the House, holds that the proceedings of a committee are not to be published, as they are of no force until confirmed by the House.

Congress originally pursued parliamentary methods, and did not begin to develop its peculiar characteristics until it had rejected the offices of the chiefs of administration on which it had originally depended, and threw itself upon its own resources. The rules of order adopted by the House when it first organized did not provide for the appointment of any standing committees, although before the first session was over the rules were amended so as to provide for a standing Committee on Elections. The recommendations of the President and reports of heads of departments supplied the subjects of legislation, which were considered in Committee of the Whole. The sense of the House being thus ascertained, a select committee would be appointed to prepare the bill.[1] There was close contact between Congress and the heads of administration. Until the government was settled in Washington, all its branches were so bunched together in their quarters that communication was easy, and so long as Congress

---

[1] An entry of January 10, 1794, says: "The House went into Committee of the Whole on the statements and estimates of appropriations for the current year. Resolved, on certain appropriations, and moved that a committee should be appointed to prepare and bring in a bill for that purpose." Annals of Congress, 1793–1795, p. 169.

Q

was willing, the executive departments were almost
as closely in touch with legislation as they would
have been if the Cabinet officers had been actually
present on the floor of the House.   Indeed, it was
not unusual for them to come personally into
Congress with the business they had to propose.[1]

The Third Congress, which adopted the plan of
internal taxation, the preparation of which was
Hamilton's last important official act before leaving the Cabinet, had only two standing committees,
— Elections and Claims.   The Fourth Congress,
which met December, 1795, added two more, —
Commerce and Manufactures, and Revisal and
Unfinished Business.   On December 16, 1796, the
party breach between the House and the administration being then complete, it was resolved on
motion of Mr. Gallatin that a standing Committee
of Ways and Means should be appointed to watch
over the national finances.   Thereafter, motions to
increase the number of standing committees were
made at every session.   Under the Virginia
dynasty, when the House was the seat of administration, the list of standing committees was
extended so as to cover by name every executive
department and all the business of the administration — such as Indian Affairs, Foreign Affairs,

[1] Senate Document, 837 ;   Forty-sixth Congress, third session,
gives a number of instances.   See Appendix.

Military Affairs, Naval Affairs, etc. This completed the committee system, but it still continued
to expand, and from time to time the list of committees has been extended.

The Senate was slow to follow the example of
the House. In its executive functions it acted as
a council of state considering business submitted
by the President. Its legislative functions were
exercised upon business already put in shape for
action by the House. The Senate, being a small,
permanent body, always able to consult its own
wishes, could get along conveniently by the
appointment of select committees as occasion
arose. For the same reason, it did not experience the embarrassment, in choosing its own
committees, which at an early date caused the
House to turn that business over to the Speaker.[1]
The Senate has always adhered to the practice of
choosing its own committees. It was not until
the second session of the Fourteenth Congress, in
1816, that it established standing committees, but
the process once started moved on rapidly. In
the Fifty-fifth Congress the House had fifty-four

---

[1] The rules of the House at first provided that the Speaker
should appoint all committees unless over three in number of members, when they should be balloted for by the House. The rules
adopted at the first session of the Third Congress, November, 1794,
provided that the Speaker should appoint all committees unless
otherwise specially directed by the House. The House found it so
troublesome to undertake this duty that appointment by the Speaker
became the settled practice.

standing committees; the Senate had forty-nine standing committees and ten select; and there were three joint committees.

All this vast development of organization is due to the separation which took place between executive management and legislative control. The English Parliament, with much more authority to exercise, continues to do its work with an organization as simple as sufficed Congress a hundred years ago. The House of Commons has only four standing committees, and but two of these consider bills.[1] The House of Commons still resolves itself into Committee on Supply to consider appropriations, or into Committee on Ways and Means to consider revenue measures, just as the House of Representatives did at first. In other words, the directors, having the management of the concern before them all the time, subject to their supervision and control, do not need to keep up a staff of standing committees to gather information and prepare business for their consideration. Neither do they have to bother about getting their resolves into legal shape, and so moil over questions of phraseology, as Congress is continually doing. A salaried staff of legal experts are there to serve them in this

[1] For the consideration of private bills there is a system of committees, but these are really courts at whose bar eminent counsel practice. For an interesting account of how Parliament does its work see the chapter under that title in Porritt's The Englishman at Home.

respect, giving exact and uniform expression to the legislative intent.

On the contrary, it is in just such work as this that Congress consumes its powers, so that its proper functions of deliberation and criticism are impoverished just as Fisher Ames said they would be.[1] The committees are very industrious, and at every session they turn out an enormous amount of business. That is the main occupation of Congress. The popular characterization of it as "the legislative mill" hits it off exactly. Congress does the best it can do in the circumstances, for it is really the most diligent legislative body in the world, but the harder it works the more it flounders in the mass of legislation thrust upon it. Only a small proportion of the bills on the calendar can ever be reached. Contending interests struggle for attention and pull this way and that. An interest that gets on top in the scramble plunges violently towards its goal, anxious above all things to attain its object while the opportunity serves. Of course there is a great deal of haphazard work. Imagine the plight of a large board of directors, who, instead of dealing directly with the general officers of the company, have to deal with numerous busy committees of their own, possessed by all sorts of ideas, and abounding with schemes conceived in behalf of all sorts of interests ! What opportunity would there be for the establishment

[1] See Chap. VI., p. 88.

of a steady and consistent policy and for the exercise of judgment and deliberation in the dispatch of business?

The Senate is less the victim of circumstances in this respect than the House, for it is so small a body and has such settled habits that it is easy for it to understand itself and know what it wants, so that it can act promptly and easily whenever it so desires.[1] Much of its business is matured before reaching it. The revenue and appropriation bills, which take up the greater part of the time of every Congress, are put in shape by the House, and the Senate is familiar with their provisions before it has to pass upon them.

In the House, however, where all have so much to do and are so eager to do it, the push of legislation is so violent that special precautions have to be taken for the orderly guidance of business. A complicated system of rules has grown up, a curious feature of which is the manœuvring by which business of special importance may be carried around the blockade of measures on the regular calendar. Certain committees have leave to report at any time. Bills for raising revenue, general appropriations, and bills for the improvement of rivers and harbors always have precedence over other bills on the calendar. There are times when the rules may be suspended altogether, to permit

[1] On January 23, 1897, the Senate passed 104 bills in ninety-five minutes. They were bills granting pensions.

any desired measure to be taken up and put upon its passage, but it takes a two-thirds vote to do this, and in such a case debate is limited to forty minutes. The regular channels of legislation are always so hopelessly clogged that the last six days of the session are devoted to legislation under suspension of the rules, and then a legislative crevasse takes place.[1]

Instead of securing deliberation, the practical effect of the committee system, with its numerous entanglements, is to incline Congress towards hasty and violent methods of despatching business. It is difficult to know what is being done in the hurly-burly. The mass of members record their votes for measures about which they know little or nothing, counting in return on a similar indulgence towards the measures in which they are interested.[2] The inevitable consequence is that legislation is frequently crude, obscure, and uncertain. The courts are kept busy construing and

[1] Of the 433 pages of general legislation enacted at the last session of the Fifty-first Congress, 284 pages are covered by the enactments of the last day.

[2] Here is a typical instance culled from the Congressional Record : —

Mr. Broderick. — Do you see any objection to the bill with that feature in it ?

Mr. Brosius. — I do not care anything about the bill. I think I will support the bill because you say it is all right ; but I have given it no attention at all. I only rose to reply to some statements of my friend from Ohio. . . . Congressional Record, February 23, 1897, p. 2254.

interpreting the laws. The litigation that ensues after every tariff act, before its exact meaning is settled, involves millions of dollars, and affects business interests to an incalculable extent.

Where, in this struggle of interests, this jostle of legislation, does the government come in? Writing home about the manner in which he negotiated the reciprocity treaty of 1854, Lord Elgin said: "There was no government to deal with. . . . It was all a matter of canvassing this member of Congress or the other."[1] By "government" Lord Elgin meant a responsible management, defining national policy and shaping legislative proposals. For such a government, our present constitutional system makes no provision. Government is supposed to be a by-product of the normal activities of Congress. The theory is that Congress reflects with tolerable fairness, subject to correction when it fails to do so, the interests, opinions, and desires of the people. This theory blinks such an awkward circumstance as the oligarchic constitution of the Senate, and it quite ignores the fact that public opinion is for the most part a static force, while force in action is the only kind which Congress notices. It may seem like a sarcasm to say that Congress represents every

[1] Letters and Journals of Lord Elgin, p. 121. Laurence Oliphant, who was Lord Elgin's secretary on this diplomatic mission, gives a very racy account of this transaction in his Episodes of a Life of Adventure, pp. 43, 44.

interest except the public interest,[1] but just that is implied by the attitude which Congress takes with regard to public demands. It disclaims the position of a trustee, and seeks to confine its responsibility to the faithful discharge of ministerial functions. It insists that, before anything can be done, the public shall reach definite conclusions and create specific political interests such as Congress is able to take cognizance of. That is what Speaker Reed told the delegation which waited on him, March 26, 1897, to urge financial legislation. The Associated Press despatches report him as saying: "Congress rarely moves faster than the people in matters of legislation, and when public sentiment became crystallized in favor of any particular form of financial legislation, Congress would be apt to respond with little delay. If the people demanded changes in the banking system, and brought pressure to bear upon Congress, they would secure the changes."

In thus avoiding the responsibility of determining legislative policy, Congress really abandons itself to the control of special interests but re-

[1] In the course of a debate in the Senate, Mr. Allen remarked: "In the imposition of tariff taxes the interests of all persons concerned must be considered. The senator from Kentucky (Mr. Lindsay) says to me, 'except the consumers.' The consumers seem largely to get the worst of it in the framing of a tariff bill. That is true largely, possibly, because they have nobody here looking after their interests particularly. They are not organized." Congressional Record, June 29, 1897.

motely concerned about the general welfare. The mass of the people simply desire good government, and leave questions of ways and means to the administration.   The particular interests which bombard Congress may misrepresent the real state of public opinion altogether. In a general way the politicians are aware of this, and endeavor to take the fact into account, but sometimes they make woful miscalculations, and the result is a great revulsion of popular sentiment, producing what is called "a tidal wave" or a "landslide."

Whatever may be the theory, however, a practical consideration which is quite well understood is that the make-up of the committees moulds the character of legislation. In the House of Commons the Speaker is simply a moderator. His party connection is a matter of no importance. But in the House of Representatives everything turns upon the election of the Speaker, for his action in constituting the committees determines the character of legislation.[1] Thus the effect of

[1] A striking illustration of this is furnished by the tariff policy of the Democratic party. When Mr. Randall, the head of the protectionist wing of the Democratic party, was elected Speaker, he thwarted the plans of the tariff reformers by refusing to reappoint Mr. Morrison to the chairmanship of the Ways and Means Committee. The make-up of this committee was the issue in the election of the Speaker at the opening of the Forty-eighth Congress, when Randall was defeated by Carlisle. Mr. Randall was then appointed chairman of the Committee on Appropriations. His influence was still so great that at the first session of the Forty-ninth Congress he

the rules is really to narrow the control of business to a group of party leaders, to whose exercise of authority no direct and open responsibility is attached.

The final stage of legislation exhibits a still more remarkable development of irresponsible control. The rules of the House provide that "all motions or propositions involving a tax or charge upon the people; all proceedings touching appropriations of money, . . . shall be first considered in a Committee of the Whole." But reports from conference committees are excepted from the operation of this rule. A committee of conference may introduce matter into a bill which has not been considered in either House, or it may change items concerning which there has been no disagreement between the two Houses. This is not merely theoretically possible, but has often been done.[1] The report of a conference committee

was able, with Republican assistance, to defeat the tariff bill reported from the Ways and Means Committee. The rules of the House were changed at the next Congress, so that much of the work of the Appropriations Committee was distributed among other committees. Having thus broken Mr. Randall's influence, the Democratic party leaders were at last able to get their tariff bill through the House.

[1] In one case, when the House had fixed a duty of $20 on bar iron, and the Senate had made the rate $20.16, the conference committee fixed the rate at $22.40. Once, when both Senate and House had fixed the duty on iron ore at 50 cents a ton, the conference committee made the rate 75 cents. Taussig's Tariff History, p. 233. New items, which have not been discussed in either

may not be amended or divided or laid on the table, as other reports, but must be adopted or rejected in its entirety. Under such duress, in order to secure the passage of important bills, Congress has time and again passed measures which but few wanted and to which the great majority were opposed.

Thus the system of committee supervision over details of legislation accomplishes its own suicide. In its practical operation it delivers the House, bound and helpless, into the hands of the Senate. Senators take care to load bills with matter for use in making mock concessions, while they extort from the House everything they really want. This arbitrary control of senators over legislation was the issue really involved in the conflict between the two Houses over the tariff bill of 1894. Fear, lest the bill might be defeated altogether, caused the House suddenly to pass the bill just as it came back from the Senate. This unprecedented action made a chance exposure of the way in which legislation is really shaped. Some senators found themselves badly caught at their own tricks, provisions which they had introduced with a jockey-

House, are sometimes introduced. A notorious case was the clause in the tariff bill of 1897, imposing an additional duty of 10 per cent on all goods brought into this country from Canada, which was inserted in the bill by the Senate conferees for a purpose which was not disclosed until after the passage of the bill, and of which a number of the conferees themselves, according to their statements, were quite ignorant.

ing purpose being converted into law. Senator Sherman complained that "there are many cases in the bill where the enactment was not intended by the Senate. For instance, innumerable amendments were put on by senators on both sides of the chamber . . . to give the Committee of Conference a chance to think of the matter, and they are all adopted, whatever may be their language or the incongruity with other parts of the bill." [1]

Altogether, the legislative methods of Congress afford a striking verification of Madison's observation that "in all legislative assemblies the greater the number composing them, the fewer will be the men who in fact direct the proceedings." [2] This holds true alike of a parliament or of a congress, the difference being that in a parliament the men who direct the proceedings assume a definite responsibility under public scrutiny, whereas in Congress they are behind the scenes, and it is only a matter of conjecture who really produce the results which the public experience.

The abandoned character of Congress is exemplified by the Congressional Record. The Record is not a report of actual proceedings, but is a repository of all such matter as members of Congress desire to put in print. Speeches are published that were never delivered, and speeches that were delivered are changed at pleasure. The law

[1] Congressional Record, August 19, 1894, p. 10,109.
[2] The Federalist, No. 58.

allows members of Congress to send the Record free through the mails, so that it is extensively used for the purpose of circulating campaign literature. Compilations of statistics, pamphlets, songs, and even entire books are introduced as part of the record of congressional proceedings. This abuse has increased enormously of late years, swelling the Record to absurdly vast dimensions. The proceedings of Congress during the entire period of the Civil War occupy less space by thousands of pages than the proceedings of any one Congress in the past decade.

CHAPTER XX

THE House of Representatives takes its character from the fact that it represents, not the nation, but the districts into which the nation is divided. It is powerfully acted upon by external agencies of party rule, but there is in its constitution no embodiment of national control to which particular demands and impulses must be subordinated. Hence it lacks the faculty of self-government which, whether in the state or in the individual, implies the supremacy of reason over desire. The consequence is that, when the House is not acting under a party mandate, it is a scuffle of local interests in which every member must take his part under penalty of losing his seat. "What has he done for his district?" is a question which applies the test by which ordinarily the value of a representative is gauged. While eminent party service will add to his reputation, it does not lessen his dependence upon his local constituency. The dominant idea is that it is the proper business of a member to represent his district, and most

239

people would be surprised to hear that any other idea could be entertained.[1]

This idea of particular representation works in the district itself. The county in which the representative may happen to reside "has had the nomination," and that is a reason why another county or part of the district should have the nomination next time. Men of distinguished ability or powerful influence may override such considerations, but the tendency towards change is apt to prevail in the end. Joshua Giddings represented his district for over twenty years, but lost the nomination when he was at the height of his national renown, and when the party in whose cause he had fought so long and valiantly was on the verge of success. National leaders such as Seward and Sumner deplored the loss to the party, and this feeling was generally expressed by the party press, but as the *New York Evening Post* at the time remarked, "The people of a congressional district

---

[1] No other idea than that of local representation penetrates congressional thoughts. For instance, Senator Hawley said: "I remember that when John Morrissey, the pugilist, was elected to the House of Representatives from a district of New York City, it was freely said by some that he was the best man in the district, the fairest representative that could be selected. He would not lie and he was not afraid, and those are two great virtues. In addition to that, he stood by his friends, and he knew what his district wanted. He was their champion in Congress as well as in the fistic arena." Congressional Record, Fifty-fourth Congress, second session, page 2957.

of course have the right to manage their own affairs in their own way."

The gerrymandering schemes by which the state legislatures keep reconstructing congressional districts also contribute to the process of change. In any parliamentary system the absence of Mr. McKinley from the national legislature at the time when the measure which bore his name was a party issue, would be regarded as a grave aberration from the regular working of party government, and his party would see to it that he should be provided with a seat. No such idea is extant in this country. His party denounced the action of the Ohio legislature in putting the bulk of his constituency into another district ; but to ask that other district to give him a seat would have been regarded as equivalent to asking it to forego its right to direct representation. The farthest that party esteem of his services could go was to advance the suggestion that he should move into the other district.

As a result of these various influences, a continual change goes on in the composition of the House irrespective of vicissitudes of party strength. At every Congress there are a large number of new members, and by the time they have gained useful experience they give place to other new members.[1] Men strong enough to keep their foot-

---

[1] Each succeeding House in the ten Congresses (1861–1881), with a single exception, contained a majority of new members. Blaine's Twenty Years in Congress, Vol. II., p. 675.

R

ing feel the strain of the continual watchfulness and effort that are required, and would greatly prefer a seat in the Senate, where the term of office is longer.

Service to local interests being the test of capacity, members must admit any method of rendering such service, or else relinquish their seats to others not so scrupulous. Hence the long-established practice of "log-rolling," by which many minority interests are united to form an overwhelming majority. This is the way in which extravagant River and Harbor and Public Buildings appropriation bills are passed. The many absurdities of the River and Harbor bills are often pointed out in debate,[1] but they are passed just the same, and against such raids the presidential veto is not an effective barrier, as members will unite regardless of party lines to pass the bill over the veto.

Another manifestation which excites the surprise of those who do not understand the devotion of the House to particular interests, is the flood

---

[1] In the course of debate, March 13, 1897, Mr. Hepburn, of Iowa, called attention to the fact that there were appropriations for the improvement of the Chickasay River, the commerce of which in 1895 consisted of 30 tons of cotton, 100 tons of rosin and turpentine, and 3 tons of miscellaneous produce; also of the Leef River, on which one small stern-wheel steamboat makes occasional trips, the total commerce borne by this stream in 1895 being 50 tons. The speaker justly remarked that the government might as well spend money on county roads as on such streams. Congressional Record, Fifty-fourth Congress, second session, p. 2970.

of bills of a freakish character which pour into it at every session. A part of the service required of a member is that he shall introduce bills of any nature desired by local interests, and his industry in this respect is one of the ways in which he may show his ability as a representative of his district. All that is really desired in most cases is that the bills shall be printed at the expense of the government, and copies furnished for distribution.

A body of such character could hardly be expected to form or maintain traditions of conduct which imply an active sense of corporate honor and responsibility. The House is neither proud nor sensitive in regard to its prerogatives. At the time the constitution was formed, the House of Commons had established the right of originating all money bills. Even if an amendment proposed by the Lords should be acceptable, the House would maintain its dignity by throwing out the bill and then passing another bill embodying the amendment. In pursuance of the design of limiting as much as possible the powers of the House of Representatives, the framers of the constitution provided that "all bills for raising revenue shall originate in the House of Representatives, but the Senate may propose or concur with amendments as on other bills."[1] With the exception of the

[1] The rules of the House originally provided that "no bill amended by the Senate shall be committed," but this rule was stricken out, January 12, 1791.

right of impeachment and the power to elect a President in default of a choice by the electors, the clause quoted sets forth the only exclusive privilege allowed the House by the constitution; but the House has been so careless about it that the Senate may, if it pleases, extend its right of amendment to the origination of an entirely new measure. The tariff act of 1883 really originated in the Senate, where it was added to a small internal revenue reduction bill which came over from the House, and the new bill with some changes was accepted by the House. When the Mills bill passed the House in 1888, the Senate under the form of an amendment proposed a substitute measure. In the discussion which followed on the comparative merits of the two bills, the point of constitutional authority made no figure at all. The House bill was the Democratic party measure, and the Senate bill was the Republican party measure, and so the matter rested. The manner in which the enactment of the tariff bill of 1894 was taken from the House by the Senate is still fresh in the public mind. The House then did make some show of standing up for its privileges, but soon made a hasty retreat, passing the bill just as it came from the Senate. As regards special appropriation bills the Senate may, without question, originate and pass all it pleases. Its right to do so has been admitted by the House.[1]

[1] House Reports, No. 147, Forty-sixth Congress, third session.

In order to reach the susceptibilities of the House it is necessary to touch it upon points relating to its service to local and personal interests. The greater ability of the Senate in providing for itself in the way of patronage and perquisites, and the address with which it carries its point in the frequent squabbles over such matters, causes much sore feeling in the House ; but it is moved rather by envy than indignation. The House is also irritable in regard to the treaty-making power when it is applied to commercial subjects, which may affect district interests. The constitution confides this power to the President and the Senate. In Washington's time the House attempted to take jurisdiction of treaties, and made a formal demand for all the documents relating to the Jay treaty of 1794 with Great Britain. This demand was firmly resisted by the President, and the House has never been able to extend its power in that direction. The ratification of a treaty by the Senate makes it the law of the land ; on the other hand, the regulation of commerce is vested in Congress, so that, as regards commercial treaties, there is ground on which the House might intervene. The matter has been the occasion of angry contention between the two Houses, but the House of Representatives has never failed to enact legislation required to carry out the provisions of a treaty.[1] The truth of the matter is — and this is

---

[1] The action of the House on the Mexican reciprocity treaty of 1883 is really no exception to this rule. Out of consideration for

the secret of its behavior — that the time of members is so taken up with the affairs of their districts [1] that the natural disposition of the House is to pay no attention to other matters, save as party obligation requires, and party has no regard for anything save its own convenience, using indifferently either the House, the Senate, or the executive branch, to the extent of its power, just as may suit its ends for the time being.

For these reasons, the abiding fear of the framers of the constitution, lest, notwithstanding all their checks and limitations, the House would engross power at the expense of the other branches of government, has not been justified by events. The House is not so strong and influential now as when Congress first met. Its highest prerogative, which

ex-President Grant, who had taken a personal interest in the negotiation, the Senate did not reject the treaty, but a stipulation was inserted that it should not take effect until Congress should pass laws to put it into operation. This was an indirect mode of defeating it. In 1886 Mr. Hewitt introduced in the House a bill to give effect to the treaty, but it was adversely reported on by the Ways and Means Committee, and the House refused to consider the bill by a vote of 162 to 51. This ended the matter.

[1] The *Washington Star*, which has Congress within its local field, says: " In actual experience the new Congressman learns this, after he has been in Washington for a while: that he is an attorney, a claim agent, an office broker, a bureau of general information, and an errand boy, with occasionally the addition of public entertainer and Capitol guide. Even the Speaker of the House, Mr. Reed, ' the Czar,' may be seen at times pointing out things of interest to visitors, or calling up the echoes in statuary hall for their entertainment."

the framers of the constitution regarded as the foundation of its authority, — control of supplies, — has been relinquished. Madison remarked : " The House of Representatives cannot only refuse, but they alone can propose the supplies requisite for the support of the government. They, in a word, hold the purse : that powerful instrument by which we behold in the history of the British constitution an infant and humble representation of the people, gradually enlarging the sphere of its .activity and importance, and finally reducing, as far as it seems to have wished, all the overgrown prerogatives of the other branches of the government." [1] In our times the spokesmen of the House plead its impotence as its excuse. At the close of the second session of the Fifty-fourth Congress, the chairman of the Appropriations Committee, reviewing the work of the session, declared that "the General Deficiency bill, in recent sessions, as it leaves the House, providing for legitimate deficiencies in current appropriations for the support of the government, is transformed into a mere vehicle wherein the Senate loads up and carries through every sort of claims that should have no consideration by either branch of Congress except as independent bills reported from competent committees." He confessed that "the appropriations are, in my judgment, in excess of the legitimate demands of the public service." But he contended

[1] The Federalist, No. 58.

that this condition of affairs was not the fault of the party in power. " It is the result of conditions accruing out of the rules of the House and out of the rules, practices, and so-called courtesies of the Senate, together with the irresponsible manner in which the executive submits to Congress estimates to meet expenditures for the conduct of the government."[1]   Admissions almost as abject as these are frequently made in the House.

In its final development the committee system has completely destroyed the control of the House over the national finances. Down to the year 1865 something of the nature of a budget existed from the fact that all revenue and appropriation bills were referred to the Ways and Means Committee. All the great revenue measures and all the vast appropriations required by the Civil War were reported by that committee. But, in 1865, the Committee on Appropriations was created, and that branch of legislative business was transferred to it from the Ways and Means Committee. In 1880 the Agricultural appropriation bill was taken over by a committee of that name, and in 1883 the practice of having the River and Harbor bill reported by a distinct committee was begun. In 1885 a wholesale distribution of the powers of the Committee on Appropriations among other committees took place. But six of the great annual

[1] Speech of Mr. Cannon, March 9, 1897. Congressional Record, pp. 2943-2944.

appropriation bills remained in charge of the Committee on Appropriations, the remaining appropriation bills, eight in number, being turned over to seven other committees. Mr. Randall, who was chairman of the Appropriations Committee, when its powers were thus mutilated, told the House at the time, "You will enter upon a path of extravagance you cannot foresee the length of or the depth of, until we find the Treasury of the country bankrupt." In ten years his prediction was fulfilled. The distribution of the appropriations made just so many additional points upon which local interests could mass their demands. The total appropriations (exclusive of pensions) for the decade 1887–1896, as compared with the decade 1877–1886, show an increase of $688,487,376. The appropriations increased 46.43 per cent, while the population increased 24.85 per cent. All sense of proportion between income and expenditure has been lost.[1] The Fifty-third Congress voted appropriations greatly in excess of the revenues of the government, and at the same time it refused to enable the government to borrow money to meet the obligations so profusely created. The government had to use authority conferred upon

[1] The effect of the distribution of the appropriation bills in promoting extravagance has been commented upon in Congress. For a detailed statement, see speech of Mr. Pitney of New Jersey, Congressional Record, February 17, 1897, Fifty-fourth Congress, second session, p. 2009, *et seq.*

it by an old statute, not made for such an emergency, and not suited to the occasion. Bonds of
longer term and higher interest rate than were
at all necessary had to be sold to enable the
Treasury to meet its engagements. The Fifty-
fourth Congress, without having done anything
to increase the revenues, increased the appropriations. Never were the exactions of local interests
so monstrous as during this period. The largest
River and Harbor appropriation bill ever reported
in the history of the country was passed by the
House without debate, and it was eventually passed
by Congress over the veto of the President by a
confederation of interests embracing members of
all parties. To preserve the Treasury from the
bankruptcy prepared by Congress, government
bonds to the amount of $262,000,000 were sold.
The blame of this shameful situation was bandied
from one party to another, but there was a common agreement that it was a matter beyond the
power of Congress to control.

The House is not oblivious to the shame of its
situation, but such is its subserviency to local interests that it is unable to practise any self-control. The best it can do is to put it out of its
power to act at all by surrendering its liberty of
action, in cases when party interests make it necessary to impose restraint. From this condition of
affairs has emerged the strangest system of control ever generated in political procedure — an ab-

solute, discretionary negative upon action, vested in the Speaker. This authority has grown up from force of party necessity, and is extremely simple and arbitrary in mode of exercise. The Speaker refuses to recognize a member who has a proposition to make that is not acceptable to the chair.[1] This authority, which was to a large extent exercised by many preceding Speakers, reached its full development under Speaker Carlisle, and he made it an effectual interdict upon legislation calculated to obtain the support of local interests in a way antagonistic to his party policy. Hence the Blair Educational bill, although it passed the Senate three times, was never voted on by the House because Mr. Carlisle would never recognize a member to make a motion to take it up for consideration. He refused to allow the House to consider a bill for the repeal of the internal taxes upon tobacco, and in a written communication to the advocates of the measure declared his unwillingness to recognize any member of the House for the purpose of moving the consideration of that bill. Subsequent Speakers have exercised the same power quite as absolutely. It has become the practice for members to petition a Speaker to permit the House to consider its own business, and the Speaker does not hesitate to disregard such petitions, even when signed by enough mem-

[1] See Chap. IX. of Follett's The Speaker of the House for a discussion of this curious subject.

bers to remove him from the chair and elect another in his place.   Such an anomaly can be explained only by the fact that members value the protection thus afforded against a pressure of local interests injurious to the general welfare of national party organization.[1]

The characteristics which have been described are reflected in the behavior of the House.   A visitor sees a noisy body, whose least concern seems to be that of deliberation.   Members are sitting at desks writing, or are lounging on sofas, or are talking together in little groups.   There is a constant movement in and out of the smoking rooms under the galleries.   Hands are clapping to summon pages, who are constantly going up and down the aisles on errands for members. There is a ·continual noise and bustle, whose aggressive volume frequently provokes the pounding of the Speaker's gavel.   A member may be addressing the chair, but few members seem to be paying any attention to him.   The manual of parliamentary law, prepared by Jefferson from

[1] "Congressman Ernest F. Acheson was in Pittsburg yesterday. He said he had been forced to agree with Speaker Reed in refusing to give a place to the Omnibus bill, providing appropriations for seventy public buildings, three of which were to be located in Wilkesbarre, Altoona, and his own town of Washington.   Speaker Reed showed that the deficit for the month current was already $8,107,118, and for the fiscal year $46,009,514.   And thus it was he refused to grant a petition signed by 308 members of the House." The Pittsburg Dispatch, January 24, 1897.

the rules of Parliament when it was supposed that the House would be likewise a deliberative body, remarks that "if a member finds that it is not the inclination of the House to hear him, and that by conversation or any other noise they endeavor to drown his voice, it is his most prudent way to submit to the pleasure of the House and sit down." If this advice were followed, there would be few speeches in Congress. But members are not concerning themselves about the pleasure of the House; they are speaking for their districts — "for Buncombe County," as one of them once explained, thus furnishing a generic phrase to describe congressional oratory. It is difficult to hear any speaker all over the big hall, and when a really interesting speaker is on the floor, members leave their seats and crowd around him. Outside of the impromptu mass-meeting which he is addressing, members continue at their writing or other occupations. There is very little real debate. When a measure before the House is a party issue, an equitable division of time is made, and speechmakers follow one another according to a set programme. The speeches are party pleas made, not to the House, but to the districts. It is a regular practice to write out speeches in advance and furnish copies to the press agencies. Before a party spokesman takes the floor, his speech will have been put in type in the newspaper offices.

As soon as he begins, the press agencies send a bulletin to their clients, announcing that the speech is "released"—that is to say, that it may be published. Afternoon papers will come out with as much as they choose to give of the speech, most of which may have been unspoken at the time they went to press. Now and then wrangles take place and spiteful remarks pass between members, communicating to the proceedings something of the interest which attaches to the cockpit or the prize-ring; but the rule is to prearrange everything said and done. The proceedings are quite formal, the object being not debate, but to accomplish what is called "making up the record."

In recent times the powerful influence of party has been prominently displayed by the way it keeps shaping the rules of the House of Representatives so as to compel obedience to its behests. In proportion as rules designed to secure consideration of legislation are used by minorities to obstruct the passage of party measures, partisan ingenuity has been stimulated to find a remedy, until finally expedients have been devised by means of which the avenues of legislation, crowded as they always are, may be temporarily cleared so as to give an open way to the passage of measures to which party urgency is conceded. A measure, which in the regular course of procedure it might take weeks or months to reach, if it could be reached at all, can be called up and put to vote at any time, if the Speaker of the House and his two party colleagues, constituting the majority of the Committee on Rules, decide to have it so. Thus the bill which the Senate substituted for the Wilson Tariff bill was taken up in the House and passed, and then four supplemental tariff bills were reported and passed, all in one day. The various devices of filibustering have been met by modifications of the rules, until it is impossible to prevent a majority in the House from proceeding with any business it is determined to transact. The Senate has not been subjected to the same control, for the reason that it is a body which until recent times possessed more self-control than the House, and was less impeded by its rules in the despatch of business. But since experience has shown that it is no longer to be trusted to act with party honesty, the same pressure of party organization for control of proceedings to which the House. has been subjected is rising against the Senate.

CHAPTER XXI

THE SENATE

THE Senate has had a singular career, and its character was slow in taking definite form. Originally intended to combine the functions of a privy council and a House of Lords, the first part of the scheme was soon found to be impracticable. The only instance of any exercise of such a function since Washington's unsatisfactory experience was during Polk's administration, and his action was a political manœuvre rather than a sincere consultation. There had been a good deal of party jockeying over the Oregon boundary question, but the President pulled the Senate up sharp by inviting its advice whether he should accept or decline Great Britain's proposition to settle upon the forty-ninth parallel from the Rocky Mountains to the Pacific. The Senate shrank from advising rejection, and thus it precluded itself from blaming the administration for the surrender of the extreme claims which demagogues in Congress had been making. In the ordinary procedure of the Senate, all that remains of its privy council function is the fossil imprint preserved in the phrase "the Senate advises and consents" used in ratifying treaties or confirming appointments.

As an adaptation of the House of Lords, the Senate soon bettered the model in grasp of authority. It had not been expected that it would equal the House in political weight. "Against the force of the immediate representatives of the people," wrote Madison, "nothing will be able to maintain even the constitutional authority of the Senate, but such display of enlightened policy and attachment to the public good as will divide with that branch of the legislature the affections and support of the entire body of the people themselves."[1] This expectation had much to do with reconciling the larger states to the admission of the smaller on an equal footing with them in the Senate. At the outset the course of legislation seemed to verify the forecast. The Senate was quite unable to control the situation. Its schemes for surrounding the presidency with monarchical ceremonial were brushed aside by the House in a way that made it appear ridiculous. But it soon regained its poise, and before the first session was over it had manifested in its relations with the House those superiorities of address and management which have since become its recognized characteristics, and to which the House of Lords can offer no parallel. In this respect the framers of the constitution were entirely out in their calculations. They had as-

[1] The Federalist, No. 63.

S

sumed that the Senate, as the institution corresponding with the House of Lords, would encounter
the same resistance from the popular branch of
the government.   But the case was quite different.
The House of Lords represented a distinct order
in the state.   Its natural disposition was to use
its influence and opportunities in behalf of its own
class, and this fact insured the jealous antagonism
of the body representing the mass of the people.
The political position of the Lords was unassail-
able, so that their political privileges could be
confined only by the collective weight and dignity
of the House of Commons.   On the other hand,
aristocratic influence was so strong in the House
of Commons that it could pursue its interests
there with the advantage of avoiding jealousies
and resentments that would be excited by the
same measures if proposed by the House of Lords.
But the Senate and the House of Representatives
did not represent different orders.   At the most
they represented only gradations in the general
class of politicians.   The official tenure of senators
was different from that of members of the House,
but it was likewise based upon party interest.
State attachments established groups of senators
and representatives united by bonds too powerful
to be seriously disturbed by jealousies and antag-
onisms arising out of the parliamentary relations
of the two Houses.   It was an early practice for
the members of state delegations to meet together

and act in concert, so that a disposition was soon created to regard any special facilities which either Senate or House possessed as belonging to the same general fund of political opportunity. What members of the House could not accomplish in their branch, they sought to obtain through their allies in the Senate. The first Congress had been in session just one month when Maclay noted in his diary, "The moment a party finds a measure lost or likely to be lost, all engines are set to work in the upper House." This tendency gave the Senate a free hand in legislation, and it was soon altering and amending bills at its pleasure without exciting any serious contention as to the extent of its powers. Its privileges in this respect being put on an equality with those of the House, its advantages of position soon made themselves felt. Having a small membership, it could act quickly, and, since its organization was perpetual, it had time to wait in order to carry a point, so that it was apt to get the best of the House when disputes occurred. This superiority, which it has always since manifested, was fully developed during the first session.

While the Senate thus successfully stretched its legislative authority to lengths beyond the reckoning of the framers of the constitution, it was equally as prompt in seeking to extend the powers which it derived from its partial association with the President in executive functions. An abuse of the power of confirmation in order to coerce the President's exercise of his right of making appointments to office was perpetrated by the Senate during Washington's administration. Speaking of the agency of the Senate in regard to appointments, Hamilton had remarked that "there will be no exertion of choice on the part of senators."[1] But while the Senate was still fresh from the hands of its creators, Washington's nomination of a naval officer for the port of Savannah was rejected because he was unacceptable to the senators from Georgia. This action elicited a special message from Washington, defending the fitness of his first nomination; but he avoided further contention by making a new nomination. The distrust with which the Federalist party leaders regarded Adams caused an extraordinary degree of interference with his freedom of choice, and Madison also had to endure much dictation from the Senate.[2]

Nevertheless, in political prestige, the Senate long remained inferior to the House. The House

---

[1] The Federalist, No. 66.

[2] These instances do not seem to have attracted the attention of the early commentators on the constitution. Kent, in 1826, said of the Senate : "Having no agency in the nominations, nothing but simply consent or refusal, the spirit of personal intrigue and personal attachment must be pretty much extinguished for a want of means to gratify it. Commentaries, Vol. I., p. 288. Story, writing in 1833, spoke of the Senate as having "but a slight participation in the appointments to office." Commentaries, section 752.

took the lead in legislation of all kinds, the Senate devoting more time to the revision of House bills than to originating bills of its own. The Senate originally sat with closed doors. It was a private conference of provincial notables, affording no opportunities to talent ambitious of political renown. Its members might be really influential in dispensing patronage or directing legislation, but they did not appear upon the stage of affairs. In this respect the situation was somewhat like what it was in England, when the famous statesmen were those who, like Pitt or Fox or Burke, had the ear of the people ; while lords and privy councillors were determining the personnel of ministries and really controlling the management of public affairs. This distinction was, however, more important in the United States, for it meant for the Senate the exclusion of its members from the highest office in the state — the great goal of political ambition. Presidential timber was not grown in the Senate.

The parliamentary régime which grew up under the Virginian dynasty depreciated the Senate in a peculiar manner. The Congressional Caucus determined the presidential succession, and senators as Caucus members were in about the same position as the delegates-at-large to a modern national convention — few in number as compared with the district delegates, and undistinguishable from them in privilege and opportunity. In this field the

united influence of the Senate could not rival
that of a popular Speaker like Henry Clay.   The
House made Presidents and exercised a controlling influence upon public policy.   Madison could
not be reëlected President until he had accepted
the policy of the leaders of the House, which
brought on the War of 1812.

The Jacksonian revolution had a remarkable
effect upon the Senate.   It seemed actually to be
exalted by the general overthrow of parliamentary
rule, even as a tower shows its height more im-
pressively when the edifice which it had buttressed
lies in ruins.   The permanency of its organization,
and the independent foundation of authority which
it derived from the principle of state authority on
which it was constituted, protected it from the
sharp vicissitudes to which the House was exposed,
so that its chamber became the refuge of the great
parliamentary leaders, — Webster, Clay, and Calhoun,—and public attention was concentrated upon
its proceedings.   The prestige of the Senate both
at home and abroad was the creation of this period.
The superior dignity and intellectuality of the
Senate made a deep impression upon foreign observers.   De Tocqueville contrasted the two Houses
with expressions of wonder that one body should
be "remarkable for its vulgarity and its poverty of
talent, while the other seems to enjoy a monopoly
of intelligence and sound judgment."   The only
reason by which he could account for this was that

"the House of Representatives is elected by the populace directly, while the Senate is elected by an indirect application of universal suffrage." The Senate still retains a higher reputation abroad than it has ever had in this country. So late as the year 1896, Mr. Lecky referred to it as "this illustrious body, which plays so important a part in American history, and has excited the envy and admiration of many European statesmen and writers on politics." [1]

It was very natural to conclude that the conservatism and dignity of the Senate were the normal characteristics of a body so constituted, for the course of events long tended to impress such qualities of behavior upon the Senate. The War of 1812 caused a strong reaction against the strict and narrow views of national authority to which Jefferson and Madison had resorted in combating the Federalist administrations; and a movement towards a broad and liberal interpretation of constitutional powers was started under Southern leadership. This movement was checked by the struggle over the admission of Missouri and the passage of the Missouri compromise, which excluded slavery from so large a section of the country as to make it certain that the preponderance of congressional influence would pass to the free states. It therefore became the policy of the Southern leaders to limit as strictly as possible the field of

---

[1] *Democracy and Liberty*, Vol. I., p. 445.

federal authority and to exalt state rights. Their
control, being proportionately much stronger in
the Senate than in the House, had the practical
effect of causing the Senate to exert a restraining and moderating influence upon congressional
action, thus exhibiting it as the more conservative
body.

Influences which tended to make the Senate
illustrious were also developed by the new turn
given to political activities. Throughout what
may be called the middle period of our politics,
extending from the Jacksonian era down to the
Civil War, the dominant issues turned upon questions of principle that made the most thrilling appeals to the moral sentiments of the people, while
their scope comprehended the very nature of the
constitution and the respective rights of the general government and of the states. Political
necessity, as well as the demands of public sentiment, tended to procure the selection of men
strong enough to maintain themselves with credit
in such a forum as the Senate had become, and
so the line of statesmen came into being, whose
powers were evoked by the slavery contest, making the debates of the Senate a school of political
education for the nation.

During its first period the Senate does not
appear to have been a very dignified body. The
ceremonious politeness of the times was a crust of
formality that sometimes gave way explosively

when passions boiled up, and such records of the debates as have come down to us indicate that controversy was apt to degenerate into peevish contention.[1] The reputation of the Senate for gravity and decorum was the creation of its second period, when it had become a parliamentary forum. Those traits were the result of a reciprocity of consideration between men who sat as state ambassadors and whose character was strongly braced by state pride, and they were also upheld by the respect felt by statesmen for the means by which they obtained parliamentary distinction. By exalting the dignity of the Senate, they elevated the stage upon which they stood to address the nation. Privileges of unrestricted debate were not originally possessed by the Senate. The rules adopted at the first session provided that "in case of a debate becoming tedious, four senators may call for the question," and this expedient for shutting off debate was freely used. Writing under date of March 2, 1791, Maclay says, "Every one that attempts to speak is silenced with the cry of 'question.'" But such restraints came to be regarded as incompatible with the dignity of a body

[1] Maclay relates that, on his making a motion which injured the pride of the Senate, by putting them on an equality with the House in the matter of compensation, "such a storm of abuse never, perhaps, fell upon any member. 'It was nonsense,' 'stupidity,' 'it was a misfortune to have men void of understanding in the House.' Izard, King, and Mr. Morris said every rude thing they could." Journal, p. 141.

whose self-respect would keep it from abusing
its privileges.   Still cases may be found when
debate was protracted to a tedious extent.   After
the Whig victory of 1840, Henry Clay complained
that the minority was abusing the privilege of unrestricted debate, and he proposed the reintroduc-
tion of the previous question; but the proposition
met with so much opposition that it was abandoned.
It was felt, and not unjustly, that the privilege was
safely confined by the dignity of the Senate.   Debate, as a filibustering practice, carried on for the
purpose of legislative extortion, was a moral impossibility.

This reputation of the Senate for dignity and
conservatism not only helped to sustain the authority it had seized, but at one important juncture
facilitated such an augmentation of it as to raise
the Senate to an extraordinary pitch of power.
During the Johnson administration, when by a
combination of circumstances unlikely to recur, a
parliamentary opposition to the executive was
developed of such strength as to overbalance the
weight of the presidential office, the victory of
Congress was in effect the triumph of the Senate.
Its advisory executive function was conveniently
at hand for asserting congressional mastery of the
situation.   The Tenure of Office act was passed,
virtually substituting the discretion of the Senate
for that of the President in making removals from
office.   What was taken away from the President's

authority by the united force of Congress was thus given to the Senate, while the House as a body gained nothing. In this way there came about a development of oligarchical power under a republican form of government that was the wonder of the age. It seemed that while everywhere else upper Houses were decaying and their authority was becoming effete, the principle of aristocratic control was renewing its vigor in the constitution of the American Senate, making that body the envy and admiration of Tory statesmen the world over.

This was the culmination of the overt authority of the Senate. As soon as the temporary exigency, which produced the Tenure of Office act, had passed by, the House sought to repeal it. In deference to the appeal of President Grant in his inaugural address, the Senate modified the requirements of the law, but insisted on the point that its consent should be essential to removals from offices. In his message of December, 1869, President Grant declared the law "inconsistent with a faithful and efficient administration of the government," and the House soon after voted for its repeal by a majority of more than six to one. The Senate, however, adhered to its oligarchical power, and under it perfected the practice known as "the courtesy of the Senate," by which the power to make appointments to office in a particular state was in practice vested in the senators from that state.[1]   The attempt of President Garfield to break down the senatorial usurpation caused a faction war which incited an assassin to take his life.   The Senate, however, still clung to its powers and used them to harass President Cleveland's administration, evoking his memorable message of March 1, 1886.   The issue had now become so menacing that considerations of party expediency compelled the Senate to surrender. The Tenure of Office law was repealed by the act of March 3, 1887.

The force of public opinion has not only repelled the extension of the powers of the Senate, but it has to some extent curtailed them.   The Senate would not now as a body dare to interfere with the President's selection of the members of his Cabinet, although originally the appointment of Cabinet officers was just as contingent upon its consent as the appointments of any other class of public officers.   Neither would it dare openly to dispute the right of the President to select members of his own party to fill the public offices under his administration, although quick to find pretexts for embarrassing him in the exercise of that right.   With

[1] In a speech April 6, 1893, Senator Hoar said: " When I came into public life in 1869, the Senate claimed almost the entire control of the executive function of appointment to office. . . . What was called 'the courtesy of the Senate' was depended upon to enable a senator to dictate to the executive all appointments and removals in his territory." Congressional Record, Fifty-third Congress, p. 137.

these exceptions, however, the Senate does not seem to have been sensibly abridged in its powers, and in all functions which it possesses in common with the House it still enjoys better opportunity with superior ability for accomplishing its purposes. Comparing its present with its original state, the authority of the Senate has on the whole greatly increased, while that of the House has diminished.

The peculiar influences which created and sustained the prestige of the Senate have, however, passed away. The principle of state sovereignty is extinct, as a political force, and no longer interposes any check upon congressional action. Ability in the public championship of party principles has declined in importance, as compared with assiduity in service to party organization.[1] Claims of distinction resting upon capacity in party service, either by craft of management or by ability to finance party organization, receive increasing recognition.[2] Senators quite different from the provincial notables of the first period, and still more different from the parliamentary leaders and

---

[1] In an article in the Forum for August, 1897, Senator Hoar remarked, as denoting changed conditions and without intention of disparaging the Senate as now constituted: " Were Webster, or Clay, or Calhoun, alive to-day, his career as a senator must be, from necessity, of a different character from what it was. His leadership and guidance of the public thought would be exercised by writing or speech elsewhere than in the Senate chamber."

[2] These two types are distinguished in popular parlance as " the boss " and " the man with the barrel."

constitutional statesmen of the second period, have made their way into the Senate in such number as to determine its character as a body.

The Senate, by its constitution, is protected against sudden change. Renewal of its membership is a slow and gradual process, so that the Senate at all times contains representatives of different periods of our politics. Then again, the variety of political conditions and party circumstances in the various states is always reflected in the Senate by marked diversities of temperament and mental capacity among its members. A general tendency towards a deep change in the character of the Senate is, however, quite discernible. This tendency has been towards the conversion of the Senate into a Diet of party lords, wielding their powers without scruple or restraint in behalf of the particular interests which they represent. The privileges of unrestricted debate, which were once regarded as opportunities of distinction, have become the intrenchments of particular interests, the shelter of party treachery, and the ready instrument of extortion.[1] The debate

---

[1] In a speech, August 16, 1894, Senator Vest of Missouri remarked : "Sir, after my experience in the last five months, I have not an enemy in the world whom I would place in the position that I have occupied as a member of the Finance Committee under the rules of the Senate. I would put no man where I have been, to be blackmailed and driven in order to pass a bill that I believe is necessary to the welfare of the country, by senators who desired to force amendments upon me against my better judgment, and

on the Silver Repeal bill of 1893, during which a minority endeavored to extort a compromise by refusing to allow a vote to be taken, was an exhibition of the degradation of the Senate, which made a profound impression upon public opinion.

Notwithstanding the great change that has taken place in the character of the Senate, the general tone of its proceedings is superior to that of the House in decorum. It is composed of older, graver, more experienced men, but there have been occasions when it has been shown that all these moderating qualities are unable to stand the strain. It is a small body, so that excitement finds less fuel than in the House, and the dignified traditions of the Senate have not quite lost their hold. The fundamental distinction, however, lies in the circumstances which set senators apart as a distinct class. The greater permanency of their tenure causes them to become residents of the national capital, while members of the House are, as a rule, transient sojourners. Connections of social interest have time to form, and these establish a community of feeling and a reciprocity of consideration which affect the tone of debate and modify party spirit. One of the difficulties which every administration has to encounter is the disposition of senators to stand together on issues affecting senatorial con-

compel me to decide the question whether I will take any bill at all or a bill which has been distorted by their views and objects." Congressional Record, p. 1015.

trol over patronage.   A senatorial faction in revolt against the administration is certain to receive as much comfort and assistance from their fellows, irrespective of party attachment, as can be extended without endangering party position.

While the manner differs, the method of legislative procedure is essentially the same as in the House ; but senators, being individually more powerful to obstruct, exhibit greater hardihood in making demands for concessions in return for their support to measures.   Instead of having to resort to "log-rolling," as in the House, they practise what is known as "the legislative hold-up."[1]   Legislation is managed on the principle of give and take, each interest exacting conditions as the price of its support, and blocking action until satisfied.

[1] Senator Plumb of Kansas, in a speech March 3, 1891, said: "The Senate last year passed an amendment giving a bounty of two cents a pound on maple sugar, which is not only not a national industry, but is the production of an article of luxury.   After it was passed as a matter personal to himself (Mr. Morrill), on statements made by members of the Finance Committee, that it would help to reëlect him to the Senate from Vermont, it was kept on because his colleague (Mr. Edmunds) threatened in writing that if it was not kept on he would vote against the tariff bill."   Congressional Record, p. 3953.

Senator MacPherson of New Jersey, in a speech March 8, 1894, said: "I find a very severe criticism is being made upon the Finance Committee for not reporting the tariff bill back to the Senate.   As to delaying its report, I wish to state that the delay is mine and mine only. . . .   Whatever delay has happened has been owing to the fact that I have been struggling for a little higher rates of duty."   Congressional Record, p. 3281.

This has been defended as being the only way of obtaining fair-play for all interests. In a speech June 8, 1897, Senator Stewart of Nevada said: "What do we have representatives of different sections here for except to represent the interests of our constituents? A senator near me suggests that we are here to get offices for our friends. That is not true, because only a part of us ever have a chance to do that. The offices are always monopolized by one side or the other. We are all here to see to the various interests in our parts of the country, to enact laws to protect them equally, and to live under equal laws. . . . If the tariff laws are unfair, it is because senators in different sections have not looked after the interests of their constituents."

With the deterioration of its character that has taken place, the composition of the Senate makes it inferior to the House in balance and moderation. In the House the weight of particular interests is proportioned to their popular strength, but in the Senate there may be a very great disproportion. Nevada, with a population of 45,761, has the same representation in the Senate as New York with 5,997,853. Thirty-two million people in ten states are represented by twenty senators, while 29,-000,000 people in other states have a senatorial representation of sixty-eight. On February 1, 1896, the Senate substituted a free silver bill for the Treasury Relief bond bill passed by the House,

T

by a vote of forty-two to thirty-five, but the minority represented nearly 8,000,000 more people than the majority. Vagaries of popular sentiment and transient delusions of opinion may be magnified in the Senate far beyond their real strength. Already the consequences are such that the reputation of the Senate for conservatism has become a faded tradition, and instead of regarding the Senate as a check upon the House, the people have gotten into the habit of looking to the House for restraint upon the extravagance and impetuosity of the Senate. The change of public sentiment in this respect has been so great as to force itself upon the recognition of the Senate itself. A Senate committee in a formal report has regretfully admitted that "the tendency of public opinion is to disparage the Senate and depreciate its usefulness, its integrity, its power."[1]

[1] Senate Reports, No. 530, Fifty-fourth Congress, first session.

CHAPTER XXII

ACCORDING to the intention of the constitution it is the business of the President to run the government. It is the business of other branches of the government to condition the operation of the executive department in accordance with the constitutional principles on which the government is founded; but to take care of the government, to attend to its needs, to shape its policy, and to provide for its responsibilities is the special business of the President.

This might seem to be a better statement of the duties of the British ministry than of the President of the United States; but the constitutional provision requiring the President to "recommend" to the consideration of Congress "such measures as he shall judge necessary and expedient" contemplated the discharge of just such duties of foresight and provision as are performed by the British ministry. Gouverneur Morris, who did the actual work of draughting the constitution, gave precisely this illustration of the functions of the presidency when the office was under discussion. "Our President," he said, "will be the British minister." [1]   There was no dissent as to that; the controversies of the convention turned upon the mode of constituting the office, and the means by which it should be confined to its appointed sphere and at the same time be protected in it.   The fathers knew very well that the king himself had been superseded by the ministry as the actual agency of government.   In the same debate Morris referred to the fact that "the real king" was "the minister."   At that period the interception of royal duty by ministerial combinations, based upon parliamentary interest, was regarded as an aberration from the principles of the English constitution and as the chief source of political corruption.   The framers of the constitution took special pains to guard against a parliamentary control.   The President himself was to carry on the administration.   In order that he might be able to impress his policy upon Congress with vigor and effect, the patronage of the government was placed in his hands.   Appointments to office were referred to as "the principal source of influence."   The fathers did not mince words in speaking of such matters; Morris bluntly declared that "the loaves and fishes must bribe the demagogues." [2]   It should be borne in mind that the very object in view in framing the constitution was to enlist the passions and selfish interests of men on the side of social stability and public order.

[1] Madison's Journal, July 24.   [2] *Ibid.*, July 2.

This duty of management was fully conceived by Washington and was habitually acted upon by him in his relations with Congress and in his use of the patronage ·of his office. The President's responsibility for national policy was the ground on which Hamilton appealed to Jefferson to exert his personal influence to secure votes to carry the assumption bill through Congress. Jefferson reports him as saying "that the President was the centre upon which all administrative questions ultimately rested, and that all of us should rally around him, and support with joint efforts measures approved by him."[1] It was from the same point of view that Rufus King, one of the framers of the constitution, criticised Jefferson's behavior in the presidential office. Commenting upon the political situation in 1806, King remarked : " It is scarcely credible that the public honor and safety, instead of being well guarded by well-concerted and prudent arrangements, should be suffered to become the sport of the casual, intemperate, and inefficient measures of inexperienced individuals ; and yet the several messages of the President look as if every subject were to be submitted to Congress, without the disclosure of the views of the executive, which by the letter and spirit of our government is charged with our foreign affairs."[2]

The growth of parliamentary control which

---

[1] Writings of Jefferson, Vol. I., p. 163.

[2] Life and Correspondence, Rufus King, Vol. IV., p. 481.

went on during the Virginia dynasty impaired
the original conception of presidential duty, but
did not extinguish it. It was still the usage for
Congress to respect the President's initiative and
provide for it. When this tradition of congressional behavior was ruptured by the violence of
party strife during the administration of John
Quincy Adams, there was a shock to conservative
sentiment. Benton, himself a leader of the Jacksonian party, whose work this was, said, "The
appointment of the majority of members in all
committees, and their chairmen, in both Houses,
adverse to the administration, was a regular consequence of the inflamed state of parties, although
the proper conducting of the public business
would demand for the administration the chairmen of several important committees as enabling
it to place its measures fairly before the House."[1]

The direct representative character imparted to
the presidential office, when the machinery of the
electoral college passed under the control of a
system of popular election, gave the office a much
firmer foundation than it originally possessed, and
invigorated all its functions, so far as the independent powers of the executive department sufficed to give them efficiency. This condition was
completely satisfied in the case of the veto power,
but the correlative function, the legislative initiative, still dependent as it is upon congressional

[1] Thirty Years' View, Vol. I., p. 92.

acquiescence, has shown no access of strength. It is complicated with the ordinary activities of Congress, and the operation of the presidential office in this respect has been obscure. Nevertheless, the fact is clear that the basis of administrative control is not Congress but the President. Possession of that office is the great object of party struggles. It is impossible for a party to carry out even a purely legislative programme unless it embodies a policy accepted by the President and sustained by the influence of his office.

The agency of the presidential office has been such a master force in shaping public policy that to give a detailed account of it would be equivalent to writing the political history of the United States. From Jackson's time to the present day it may be said that political issues have been decided by executive policy. The independent treasury system introduced during Van Buren's administration was a measure formulated by the President and forced upon Congress. Tyler, although his congressional following was so weak that it was known as "the corporal's guard," prostrated Whig plans for the reëstablishment of the Bank of the United States and controlled the tariff policy of Congress. The annexation of Texas, which was the issue of the election of 1844, originated as an executive proposal, and was consummated by Tyler before he retired from office. Polk's administration is associated

with tariff reform and the Mexican War, both
measures originating in executive policy. The
slavery agitation, whose growing intensity was
the chief feature of the administrations of Fill-
more, Pierce, and Buchanan, presented issues
which the executive department was, above all
things, anxious to avoid, so that presidential influence strongly supported a policy of adjustment
and compromise by negotiation among the congressional factions; but nevertheless the issues
which arose were shaped by executive policy, as
the inevitable result of its trenchant nature. In
the presence of emergency it is necessary to do
one thing or another, and the decision stands out
for condemnation or approval, thus furnishing a
dividing line for party formation. The election
of 1860 turned on issues raised by executive policy
in Kansas. The administration of President Lincoln saw the opening of a new arsenal of presidential authority in the war powers, whose extent
is still quite unmeasured. The President levied
an army without authority of Congress, and before
Congress had met. He assumed and exercised the
right of suspending the writ of *habeas corpus*.
The crowning event of his administration — the
emancipation of the slaves — did not take place in
pursuance of any act of Congress, but was done
on his own authority as President, and was as
absolute an exercise of power as the ukase of
the Czar which freed the serfs of Russia. Presi-

dent Lincoln was able to do these things by the direct support of public opinion, irrespective of the volition of Congress. Although in the case of his accidental successor, Congress was strong enough to enforce its own programme of reconstruction, it instinctively recognized the fact that it was not able to do so from its inherent authority. Senator Sherman put the case exactly when he said, "The recent acts of Congress, those acts upon which the President and Congress separated, were submitted to the people, and after a very full canvass and a very able one, in which great numbers of speeches were made on both sides, and documents were circulated, the people, who are the common masters of President and Congress, decided in favor of Congress."[1] That is to say, Congress prevailed not by virtue of its ordinary representative capacity, but by express delegation for that special purpose.

While all that a President can certainly accomplish is to force a submission of an issue to the people, yet such is the strength of the office that, if he makes a sincere and resolute use of its resources, at the same time cherishing his party connection, he can as a rule carry his party with him, because of the powerful interests which impel it to occupy ground taken for it by the administration. Many instances of this tendency may be

[1] *Congressional Globe*, January 8, 1867.

found in our political history. A noted case in our own times is the result of General Grant's veto in 1874 of the bill providing for an additional issue of legal tender notes. Later on, the same Congress passed an act providing for the redemption in coin of the outstanding issues.

On the other hand, unless a measure is made an administrative issue, Congress is unable to make it a party issue. Colonel W. R. Morrison, when the Democratic leader of the House, was unable to accomplish the passage of a tariff bill although there was a party majority. His explanation of his failure is that "my bills all lacked the influence of administration and party support and patronage." Colonel Morrison's successor, Mr. Mills, was more fortunate in his leadership of the House, because "when Mr. Cleveland took decided ground in favor of revision and reduction he represented the patronage of the administration, in consequence of which he was enabled to enforce party discipline, so that a man could no longer be a good Democrat and favor anything but the reform of the tariff."[1]

If, in default of a definite administrative policy vigorously asserted, Congress is left to its own devices, issues are compromised and emergencies are dealt with by makeshift expedients. The complex entanglements of the currency situation were brought about in this way. But even then, the

[1] New York Sun interview, September 12, 1893.

presidential authority, however passive its condition, continues to be a factor of great importance. The passage of the silver bullion purchase act of 1890, according to its framer, Senator Sherman, was thus the result of the President's attitude, although the President had nothing directly to do with it. Senator Sherman says : "A large majority of the Senate favored free silver ; and it was feared that the small majority against it in the other House might yield and agree to it. The silence of the President in the matter gave rise to an apprehension that if a free coinage bill should pass both Houses, he would not feel at liberty to veto it. Some action had to be taken to prevent a return to free silver coinage, and the measure evolved was the best obtainable." [1] The repeal of this law in November, 1893, after a memorable struggle in the Senate, affords a conspicuous example of the efficiency of the presidential office in influencing legislation when in earnest about the discharge of that duty.

The evidence which our history affords seems conclusive of the fact that the only power which can end party duplicity and define issues in such a way that public opinion can pass upon them decisively, is that which emanates from presidential authority. It is the rule of our politics that no vexed question is settled except by executive policy. Whatever may be the feeling of Congress

[1] Sherman's Memoirs, p. 1070.

towards the President, it cannot avoid an issue which he insists upon making. And this holds good of presidents who lose their party leadership as with those who retain it. Tyler, Johnson, and Cleveland, although repudiated by the parties which elected them, furnished the issues upon which party action turned.

The rise of presidential authority cannot be accounted for by the intention of presidents: it is the product of political conditions which dominate all the departments of government, so that Congress itself shows an unconscious disposition to aggrandize the presidential office. The existence of a separate responsible authority to which questions of public policy may be resigned opens to Congress an easy way out of difficulty when the exercise of its own jurisdiction would be troublesome. Its servitude to particular interests makes it chary of issues which may cause dissension. It goes only so far as it is compelled to go in obedience to a party mandate, and is apt to leave as much as possible to executive discretion. So it happens that important determinations of national policy are reached in ways that seem to ignore congressional authority, although the circumstances imply congressional acquiescence. A curious case in point is the well-known fact that the gold reserve fund, which became the base of the monetary system of the nation, was the creation of the executive department. There is no law on the statute

books which directed or authorized the establishment of a gold reserve fund. The act of 1875 for
the resumption of specie payments authorized the
Secretary of the Treasury to sell bonds to enable
him to redeem in coin the legal tender notes of
the United States. Under the authority of that
law Secretary Sherman collected $100,000,000 in
gold which was designated as the reserve fund,
and its existence has been only indirectly recognized by subsequent legislation.

When the reserve fund was depleted during the
panic of 1893–1894, the administration was reluctant to take the responsibility of selling bonds to
replenish the fund, and submitted to the Senate
Committee on Finance the draught of a bill,
specially authorizing the sale of bonds for that
purpose. The party leaders, however, advised the
executive department to proceed upon its own
responsibility, on the ground, as given by Senator Voorhees, chairman of the Finance Committee, that "it will be wiser, safer, and better for
the financial and business interests of the country
to rely upon existing law with which to meet the
present emergency rather than to encounter the
delays and uncertainties always incident to protracted discussion in the two Houses of Congress."[1] This confession of the incapacity of
Congress in the presence of an emergency, made
with such exquisite candor, gave no sting to par-

[1] Statement furnished to the Associated Press, January 16, 1894.

liamentary pride, and excited no comment. The opposition of course promptly denied the right of the administration to issue bonds, but it did not seem to occur to any one that the abased attitude assigned to Congress was at all unfitted to its dignity. The whole debate turned upon points of law.

The strong disposition of Congress to extend the scope of federal duty powerfully stimulates the development of presidential authority. That authority may emerge with startling vigor from the implications of laws enacted without any idea of producing such results. A memorable instance is the manner in which the last vestige of the old state sovereignty doctrine was obliterated from practical politics by the agency of the interstate commerce act. In assuming to regulate interstate commerce, Congress put upon the national administration the responsibility of maintaining interstate railroads as national highways. The significance of this never dawned upon the country until the railroad strikes of 1894 took place, when the arm of federal power was suddenly extended to suppress riot and quell disorder. The popular belief had always been that the national government could not act in such cases until requested by state authority, but now state authority was not only ignored, but its protests were unheeded. Time was when such action would have convulsed the nation and might have caused collision between

state and federal authority, but the act was hailed
with intense gratification both North and South;
the governors who took up the old cry of state
rights were loaded with derision, and a Congress,
Democratic in both branches, passed resolutions
by acclamation approving the action of the executive.

Such vigor, in an authority which the framers
of the constitution erected with painful misgivings
as to its stability, becomes the more impressive
when it is contrasted with the lot of the institution upon which it was patterned. The Federalist
makes a detailed comparison between the powers
of the President and the British crown, so as to
exhibit the more stringent limitations and the inferior authority of the presidency. Since then every
power ascribed to the king has withered; but there
is no authority conceded to the President, at the
time the duties of the office began, that is not
flourishing with unimpaired vigor. Moreover,
authority which the early Presidents would not
have ventured to assume is now regarded as belonging to the ordinary functions of the office.
This aggrandizement of presidential authority has
gone on under all parties since Jackson's time, and
in the hands of men of widely varying capacity.
The tendency is so powerful that it sustains itself
against the great weakness of the vice-presidency
in our constitutional system. That office, of such
small, ordinary importance that it is disposed of

as an incident in the struggle for the presidential nomination, serving as a make-weight on the ticket, or as a sop to faction, may at any time produce a President.   Men have been raised to the presidency who never would have been thought of as a candidate for that office ; but its powers have sustained no permanent loss thereby.   Although once executive power, in the hands of an accidental President, was bent and held down by the weight of a huge congressional majority, its springs were unbroken, and it sprang up unhurt when the abnormal pressure was removed.   Incidentally the history of Andrew Johnson's administration discloses the fact that the extraordinary check provided by the constitution — the process of impeachment — is practically worthless.   It remains in the armory of Congress, a rusted blunderbuss, that will probably never be taken in hand again.

Another check upon the power of the President, which has been made obsolete by the peculiar turn taken by our constitutional development, is the power of the House to refuse supplies.   Madison said : "The House of Representatives cannot only refuse, but they alone can propose the supplies requisite for the support of the government. . . . This power over the purse may, in fact, be regarded as the most effectual weapon with which any constitution can arm the immediate representatives of the people, for obtaining a redress of every grievance, and for carrying into effect every just and salutary measure."[1]   Such an opinion was fully warranted by English constitutional history, but it has been falsified by American experience. As a means of coercing the administration, control of supply failed so completely when the test was made that it is not likely that such an use of it will ever be made again.   Probably the attempt would not have been made at all had it not been for the extraordinary circumstances of the presidential election of 1876 and the moral weakness of President Hayes' position.   The House attempted to reduce federal control of elections by annexing conditions to appropriation bills ; but the demands of the House were baffled by a series of vetoes, and in the end Congress had to pass the appropriation bills without the extraneous legislation to which the President objected. It is now a fact recognized by all parties that the idea of stopping the government by withholding supplies cannot even be considered seriously.   As a practical expedient, such a check upon executive authority no longer exists.   The federal election laws that were attacked in 1876 were repealed in 1894, but that was not until the people had put a President in office who was favorable to the repeal.

Although the power of making appointments to office has been, to a large extent, practically taken over by the Senate, under the exercise of the au-

[1] The Federalist, No. 58.

U

thority to confirm or reject nominations, yet in this respect also, the executive department possesses abundant power for the protection of its constitutional rights. The President has power "to fill up all vacancies that may happen during the recess of the Senate, by granting commissions which shall expire at the end of their next session." As he has absolute power of removal, he can select his own time for making vacancies, and the commissions which he shall issue will hold good to the last day of the expiring session, whereupon, in case of a rejection, another commission may be issued of like duration. Precedents for such action go back to the early days of the republic. Robert Smith acted as Secretary of the Navy during the whole period of Jefferson's second administration without his appointment to that office being confirmed by the Senate, or any known authority except the verbal request or permission of the President.[1] The appointment of Taney to be the Secretary of the Treasury, in which office he carried out the financial policy of the administration, was never confirmed by the Senate. Jackson did not send in the nomination until the last week of the session, when Taney had finished all that he entered the office to do. There are numerous precedents for the appointment and retention of minor officials in the face of senatorial refusal to confirm the nominations. There

[1] Adams' History of the United States, Vol. III., p. 12.

were a number of such cases during President Cleveland's term of office.

The strongest and most unqualified statements of the powers of the presidential office come from experienced statesmen who have had the best opportunity of scrutinizing its operation. John Quincy Adams, at a time when presidential authority was less developed than now, said, " It has perhaps never been duly remarked that, under the constitution of the United States, the powers of the executive department, explicitly and emphatically concentrated in one person, are vastly more extensive and complicated than those of the legislature."[1] Secretary Seward told a *London Times* correspondent, who was interrogating him as to the nature of our government, " We elect a king for four years, and give him absolute power within certain limits, which after all he can interpret for himself."[2] Quite as strong were the expressions used by ex-President Hayes to a publicist who applied for information on the subject. "Practically the President holds the nation in his hand."[3] Hare, the leading legal authority on this subject, sums up the case as follows : —

" A chief magistrate who wields the whole military and no inconsiderable share of the civil power of the state, who can incline the scale to war and

---

[1] Discourse on the Jubilee of the Constitution.

[2] Jennings' Republican Government in the United States, p. 36.

[3] Stevens' Sources of the Constitution, pp. 167–170.

forbid the return of peace, whose veto will stay the force of legislation, who is the source of the enormous patronage which is the main lever in the politics of the United States, exercises functions which are more truly regal than those of an English monarch." [1]

It should be carefully noted, however, that this power of the presidential office does not proceed from its strength as an embodiment of royal prerogative as conceived by the framers of the constitution. Their expectation was that in the ordinary working of the machinery of election they had devised, there would be numbers of candidates in various states — "favorite sons," to use the modern phrase. Therefore the electoral college of each state was to vote for two persons, one of whom should not be an inhabitant of that state, so that, at least in one instance, the vote of each state would be likely to "fall on characters eminent and generally known." [2] The Federalist speaks of this scheme with a complacency rare in that sombre treatise ; but it was a complete failure. It never worked according to the design, except in the election of Washington, when the work of the electoral college was really done for it in advance, and it had simply to register an unanimous consent. The greatness of the presidency is the work

---

[1] American Constitutional Law, p. 173.
[2] Madison's Journal, September 5.

of the people, breaking through the constitutional form.

The truth is that in the presidential office, as it has been constituted since Jackson's time, American democracy has revived the oldest political institution of the race, the elective kingship. It is all there : the precognition of the notables and the tumultuous choice of the freemen, only conformed to modern conditions. That the people have been able to accomplish this with such defective apparatus, and have been able to make good a principle which no other people have been able to reconcile with the safety of the state, indicates the highest degree of constitutional morality yet attained by any race.

CHAPTER XXIII

PARTY is as old as politics, and the operation of party in working the machinery of government is seen in all countries having free institutions ; but of party as an external authority, expressing its determinations through its own peculiar organs, the United States as yet offers to the world the only distinct example, although tendencies in that direction are showing themselves in England. There is still, however, nothing of which the British Parliament is more intolerant than an assumption that there exists any constitution of authority exterior to its own, which can claim to give expression to the will of the people. No less keen a jealousy might have been expected from the Congress of the United States, which, according to the constitution, directly represents both the people and their state governments. Assuredly nothing would have been more incomprehensible and astonishing to the framers of the constitution than to have been informed that a political jurisdiction would be established, unknown to the constitution and without warrant of law, whose determinations would be recognized as entitled to delineate the policy of the administration and bind the proceedings of Congress. Such obligation, though constantly paltered with by faction interests and continually evaded by tricky politicians, is nevertheless unreservedly admitted. To such an extent is this submission carried that it is not an uncommon thing for members of Congress to admit that they are acting under the compulsion of such obligation against their own judgment.[1]

Although party organization asserts jurisdiction over the constitutional organs of government, its own pretensions to a representative character have a very slight basis. The theory of party organization is that its power emanates directly from the people, by means of a system according to which the party membership, at primary elections, choose delegates who meet to state the party principles and name the party candidates. In practice, few people besides the politicians have any share in the transaction. As a rule, the vote at primary elections is very small, and even when exceptional

---

[1] *Mr. Gorman.*—The senator from Wisconsin says that both parties were somewhat intimidated by the people who were the special advocates of this law. For one, I do not believe we can shirk our duty in this matter.

Mr. Spooner. — All I said was this, and I repeat it, that both the political parties were committed to the principle of the civil service law and its maintenance.

Mr. Gorman. — To that I agree.

—Congressional Record, February 24, 1891, p. 3395.

circumstances bring out a large vote, it is still small as compared with that polled at a regular election. In many cases there is hardly the pretence of an election by the party membership, but the politicians frankly bargain among themselves who shall attend the conventions and figure as party representatives. The total vote polled for the members of a national convention, which nominates the President and declares the policy to be pursued by the government, is but a small percentage of the vote polled at a congressional election.

What is still more significant is the fact that there appears to be no connection between the extent to which a constituent quality has been imparted to a convention, and the force with which its decisions appeal to public confidence and support. So far as the appearance of representative character in party organization is concerned, it is generally greatest when its subjection to professional management is most complete. In an old party, which has acquired a valuable stock of traditional sentiment and popular attachment, the reciprocal efforts of struggling factions have evolved a stringent code of regulations to prevent unfair advantages, and their mutual jealousies insure vigilant attention to regularity of procedure. A spontaneous movement, issuing from popular enthusiasm, is tolerant of irregularity in method. It welcomes without question those whose heart is in the cause. The convention of a new party has largely the character of a mass-meeting. Established usage requires some observance of the form of delegation, but practically any one of respectability and standing, who is in sympathy with the movement, may take part in the proceedings. A reform movement will eagerly cluster around a self-constituted leadership, while the regular political boss in selecting candidates must carefully respect the form of nomination by delegates from the people. The Committee of Seventy, appointed by some citizens' associations, nominated a ticket which swept New York City in the election of 1894, while the Tammany ticket, regularly nominated by a body of genuine constituent character, was defeated.

Such considerations make it plain that the true office of party organization is that of a factor. It carries on a self-assumed procuration in the name of the people and by their acquiescence, but not by their desire. The appearance of a representative character is· the result of arrangements gradually effected under pressure of a demand that the emoluments and opportunities of this business of factorship should be open to competition. This view of the case is fully confirmed by the history of party organization sketched in the preceding chapters. The occasion for it was the need of means of concentration so as to establish a control over the divided powers of government. Party machinery was devised under the stimulus of necessity and has been submitted to because there was no help for it. A paradoxical phrase, often used in regard to this very matter, puts the case exactly as the people regard it. It is a necessary evil.

The development of party organization has been elaborate and extensive in keeping with the vast expansion of the nation and the multifarious political activities of our complicated system of government. The struggles of the people to convert the government to democratic uses have introduced complications which have greatly enlarged the functions of party organization and intensified their energy. The movement towards the multiplication of elective offices originated in popular revolt against class rule. The constitutional framework of the national government was so unyielding that effort was expended upon it in vain ; but plastic material was found in the state constitutions. The democratic movement which raised Jackson to the presidency, although baffled in all its designs of amending the constitution of the United States, has left a deep influence upon state constitutions. A sentiment of popular hostility to aristocratic control was the force that sustained the movement of constitutional reform, and, as a means of diminishing the sphere of such control and admitting new interests to power, there was no expedient so effective as turning appointive into elective offices. The powers of the governor were reduced by converting local agencies of government into elective offices. Heads of state departments, that had been appointed by the governor or by the legislature, were also cut loose to be filled under the form of popular election. Even the judiciary did not escape, and in most of the states the office of judge was abandoned to party politics by making it elective. The practical effect of the change was to convert a system of responsible appointment into a system of irresponsible appointment. It is obviously impossible for the people to select officers for innumerable places except by some means of agreement and coöperation, which means is ordinarily supplied by the activity of the political class. It may be laid down as a political maxim, that whatever assigns to the people a power which they are naturally incapable of wielding takes it away from them. It may be argued that this principle carried to its logical conclusion implies that the people are unable to select their own rulers in any case. This is perfectly true. The actual selection will be always made by the few, no matter how many may seem to participate. The only value of popular elections is to establish accountability to the people, but this rightly used is quite enough to constitute a free government.

The multiplication of elective offices and the distribution of the responsibilities of government

among independent authorities, dissipates accountability so that practically it ceases to exist. It
puzzles foreign observers to understand how any
public responsibility can be enforced under such
a system.   Mr. Bryce remarks: "Will not a
scheme, in which the executive officers are all
independent of one another, yet not subject to
the legislature, want every condition needed for
harmonious and efficient action? They obey nobody.   They are responsible to nobody, except a
people which only exists in concrete activity for
one election day every two years, when it is drop-
ping papers into the ballot-box. Such a system
seems the negation of a system, and more akin
to chaos."[1]   The explanation of this mystery is
that the scattered powers of government are resumed by party organization, and this concentration of power carries with it a public responsibility
which may be enforced. The soundness of the
popular instinct on this point is shown by the
indifference of voters to the personal merits of
candidates, when moved by resentment against
party organization.   One of the peculiarities of the
great revulsions of feeling, which have obtained
the name of "tidal-waves," is the way in which
they toss into prominence, grotesque nonentities
and incapables who never could have obtained
important office by the ordinary gradation of
political preferment.

[1] American Commonwealth, Vol. I., p. 530.

The interdependence of political interests is such that local transactions cannot be separated from state and national concerns. If the party is hurt anywhere, it feels it everywhere.[1] Needs of adjustment between local and general political interests have thus been created, which have gradually evolved a hierarchy of political control, with respective rights and privileges that are tenaciously insisted upon. In this respect party organization curiously resembles feudalism. The city boss and the state boss are the grand feudatories of the system. The city boss is the nexus of municipal administration, — a centre of control outside of the partitions of authority which public prejudice and traditional opinion insist upon in the formal constitution of city government. The boss system is enormously expensive, but so great is the value of concentrated authority in business management that one may hear it said among practical men of affairs that a city needs a political boss in order to be progressive. The fact is well known that it was due to authority of this kind that the national capital was transformed from an area of swamps and mud-banks into the beautiful city it is now. The state boss is the

---

[1] At the New York City election of 1897, the Low movement confined itself to local purposes, and offered its adherents no candidate for the state office voted for at the same election. As a result, 67,677 votes that were cast for local candidates were not cast at all for judge of the Court of Appeals.

natural complement of the situation produced by
the dissolution of executive authority in state
government. The office restores outside of the
formal constitution what is lost inside of it —
efficient control. In the national government no
such dissolution having taken place, the case is
different. There is no national boss but the
President, and that is what the people put him
there to be. If he does not boss the situation, he
is a political failure, no matter what else he may
be.

Thus by a perfectly natural process of evolution,
the structure and functions of party organization
have been elaborated, so as to comprehend the
political activity of American citizenship from the
minutest subdivision of local government up to
the formation of a national administration. Party
organization selects candidates for innumerable
offices; it superintends the perpetual succession
of elections; its operation is continuous. Since
politics in all their gradations have their connections with trade and society, the activities of
politics permeate the whole sphere of civic life.

The community of interest thus established
causes party organization to exercise a moderating influence of immense importance. When the
convention system was established, its direct appeal to the people, followed by numerous mass-
meetings and floods of oratory, excited a violence
of party feeling that horrified statesmen of the

old school. "Here is a revolution in the habits
and manners of the people," wrote John Quincy
Adams in his diary. "These meetings cannot be
multiplied in number and frequency without result-
ing in deeper tragedies. Their manifest tendency
is to civil war."[1] Calhoun had no doubt that
"the appeal to force will be made whenever the
violence of the struggle and the corruption of
parties will no longer submit to the decision of
the ballot-box."[2]

But history plainly shows that party spirit has
not had any such tendency. On the contrary,
party organization long repressed the operation of
the forces which did indeed eventually produce
civil war. Before the slavery question could be
brought to the front as the decisive issue of
national politics, an entirely new and purely sectional party had to be formed. National party
organization held the Union together long after
the South had become at heart a separate nation,
from the distinct interests and purposes developed
by slavery. As early as the forties, great religious
denominations split into Northern and Southern
divisions. Calhoun, in his last speech, called attention to the manner in which tie after tie was
snapping. But still party organization continued
to bear the strain, and it was the last bond of union
to give way. Then war or disunion became inevi-

---

[1] Memoirs, Vol. X., p. 352.
[2] Calhoun's Works, Vol. I., pp. 378, 379.

table.   After the war, the powerful agency of
party organization was again displayed in the
rapidity with which the revolted section was re-
incorporated into the life of the nation.

The truth is that a remarkable nonchalance
underlies the sound and fury of partisan politics.
The passionate recrimination that goes on is like
the disputes of counsel over the trial table.   Back
of it all is a substantial community of interest.
The violence of politicians does not usually go
higher than their lips.   The antagonists of the
stump often have a really friendly feeling for one
another.   It is not an uncommon thing for professional politicians of opposing parties to display a
spirit of mutual good will and helpfulness in promoting the personal political interests of one another.   The extraordinary thing about American
party politics is really their amenity.   Public sentiment, while permitting great license of speech,
exacts a decorum of behavior that is surprising to
English visitors, accustomed as they are to popular turbulence — the howling down of speakers,
storming of platforms, and scuffling of excited
partisans.[1]   There is in this country an immense
business preparation for a campaign, an enormous

---

[1] A letter in the *New York Evening Post*, November 13, 1897,
makes an interesting comparison of electioneering in the two countries.   The writer concludes that "an American public meeting is
one of the quietest and most decorous forms of entertainment yet
invented."

investment in spectacular effects and stage properties, and a prodigious display of enthusiasm, culminating in the thrilling scenes of election night; but as soon as the result is fully known, it is good-humoredly accepted and the people eagerly return to their ordinary business pursuits.

This curious circumspection that attends the periodical national mood of party frenzy is traceable to the same moderating influence that developed a constitutional system of party government in England — the succession of opportunity in enjoyment of the offices of government. Burke's expressive metaphor fits the case exactly. "The parties are the gamesters; but government keeps the table." No matter how passionately they contend, they will take care that they do not kick over the table and lose the stakes. The same influence is seen in the way in which party spirit reacts against mob spirit. By its habit of consulting and flattering all interests, party spirit may encourage mob spirit up to a certain point; but when the limits of fair accommodation are overpassed, there is a sudden change of attitude and a fierce energy is shown in repressing disorder.

The true office of the elaborate apparatus used to work up popular excitement over party issues is to energize the mass of citizenship into political activity. Although so dissimilar in character, national party organization fulfils a function similar to that indirectly accomplished in England by royal

X

prerogative during the period when it was really massive; but with the important difference that, whereas then the various classes of the population were fused into political community by the weight of royalty, party spirit now draws them together by ardent sympathies which elicit a copious and constant supply of political force. Their operation extends far beyond the sphere of the intelligence, for they thrill and penetrate the bottom strata of character, — the inheritance of ancestral habit moulded by tribal discipline, the deposits of race experience throughout the ages, — bringing into play those deep instincts of which we are unconscious, but which constitute the wisest part of us.

This nationalizing influence continues to produce results of the greatest social value, for in coördinating the various elements of the population for political purposes, party organization at the same time tends to fuse them into one mass of citizenship, pervaded by a common order of ideas and sentiments, and actuated by the same class of motives. This is probably the secret of the powerful solvent influence which American civilization exerts upon the enormous deposits of alien populations thrown upon this country by the torrent of emigration. Racial and religious antipathies, which present the most threatening problems to countries governed upon parliamentary principles, melt with amazing rapidity in the warm flow of a party spirit which is constantly demanding, and is able to reward, the subordination of local and particular interests to national purposes. The extent to which accidents of foreign nativity or extraction are made use of, to constitute what is known in politics as "a vote," is generally regarded as the great weakness of American politics, but it is really a stage in the process of fusion. In order that "the Irish vote," "the German vote," "the Italian vote," etc., shall be recognized as such, they must display a spirit of mutual accommodation and enter into amicable relations. It is a matter of common observation in the politics of our great cities that a surprising amount of intimacy and association between people of different nationalities is thereby brought about. In the district headquarters of a party organization, one may perchance see an Irish ward captain patting on the back some Italian ward worker who can hardly speak intelligible English, but whose pride and zeal in the success of his efforts to bring his compatriots "in line with the party" are blazoned upon his face. American politics seem able to digest and assimilate any race of the Aryan stock, but it fails with the negro race, so that where the negro vote is large enough to be a controlling factor, the tendency is to suppress it by the direct resistance of the community or else reduce it to manageable dimensions by special contrivance of law.

The extensive business of political factorship,

created by the peculiar circumstances of American politics, naturally attracts to its various employments men of congenial aptitudes. Energy, address, and opportunity tell in this just as in other pursuits. The power exercised by the political class is certainly the most striking characteristic of American public affairs, but there is nothing mysterious about it. Burke gave the explanation long ago when he remarked that "nations are governed by the same methods and on the same principles by which an individual without authority is often able to govern those who are his equals or superiors : by a knowledge of their temper and a judicious management of it."[1]

It is the fashion to regard American politicians as a peculiar class, who as individuals are addicted to envy, hatred, and all uncharitableness, and whose machinations as a body are responsible for the wide disagreement between the accepted theory and the actual practice of our politics ; but this is a mistaken view of the case. Whenever people come in contact in the struggles of life, there is friction. People in the same line of business, of whatever sort, have their feuds as well as their friendships, and if the public heard all that goes on in the business world, it would be found that envy, selfishness, and bickering abound there too. The public business being everybody's business, stuff which, if it concerned the transactions

[1] The Present Discontents.

of ordinary business, would be considered as mere scandalous gossip and backbiting, in politics assumes the rank of public discussion and criticism, and the vast reverberation of the press swells the murmur into clamor. Intimate knowledge and good understanding, however, reveal an extent of toleration, charity, and downright generosity in politics that raises one's esteem for human nature. The consideration shown by professional politicians for the poor and unfortunate is a beautiful trait in their character. The relations between them and their constituents in many cases embrace sympathies far deeper and stronger than any connection, founded merely upon community of political ideas, could excite.

There is really nothing peculiar in the character of American politicians; but the circumstances which condition their activity are very peculiar. Their demerits are those which pertain to their period, and find abundant parallels in the history of English politics. On the other hand they have displayed, in meeting the peculiar exigencies of their situation, a readiness of invention and an adaptability of method which are characteristically American. Not even the great industrial development of the nation affords so striking an exhibition of American inventive genius and faculty for organization as that huge, complicated mechanism which, in default of any provision for direct party control of legislative procedure, has been extended

to every part of the government — national, state,
and municipal — so as to reach and subject to some
degree of public responsibility the political activities finding expression in the various state legislatures and in Congress.   Nowhere else in the world,
at any period, has party organization had to cope
with such enormous tasks as in this country, and
its efficiency in dealing with them is the true
glory of our political system.   As to this, the
testimony of so competent and unbiassed a critic
as Mr. Bagehot may be cited.   He says : " The
Americans now extol their institutions, and so
defraud themselves of their due praise ; but if
they had not a genius for politics, if they had not
a moderation in action singularly curious where
superficial speech is so violent, if they had not a
regard for laws such as no great people have yet
evinced, and infinitely surpassing ours — the mul-
tiplicity of authorities in the American constitution would long ago have brought it to a bad end.[1]

All these characteristics are phases of that
genius for politics of which party organization is
the expression and the organ.   The conclusion
may be distasteful, since it is the habit of the
times to pursue public men with calumny and
detraction ; but it follows that when history comes
to reckon the achievements of our age, great party
managers will receive an appreciation very different
from what is now accorded to them.

[1] Bagehot's English Constitution, Chap. VII.

CHAPTER XXIV

PARTY SUBSISTENCE

HAVING so much to do, party organization provides employment for an enormous staff of managers, agents, and servants. Their number exceeds immensely the number of those connected with politics in any country in which unity of administrative control is provided by the constitution. In England the class of professional politicians is comparatively small. Mr. Bryce makes an interesting comparison on this point. He says that by the most liberal computation — one that includes the members of Parliament and expectant candidates; editors, managers, and chief writers on leading newspapers; and party agents in the various constituencies — he reached a total of 3500 in all England. Of their number in this country he says, " I can form no estimate, save that it must be counted by hundreds of thousands, inasmuch as it practically includes nearly all office-holders and most expectants of public office." [1] This estimate, although large, is very moderate, since it includes besides federal office-holders the numerous officials holding office under state and local authority. To

[1] American Commonwealth, Chap. LVII.

these should be added the large class of men who find the gains of their political activity, not in office-holding, but in the exercise of political influence.   The probability is that the machinery of control in American government requires more people to tend and work it than all other political machinery in the rest of the civilized world.

So huge an organism necessarily requires provision of corresponding magnitude for its subsistence.   It is notorious that party demands possession of all the offices of government for its support, but only a part of its maintenance can be provided in this way.   The public service furnishes pay and quarters for what may be called the office staff of the business of party management, and the compensation attached to official employment may be squeezed for party purposes, but the direct emoluments of office-holding certainly do not sustain the management nor can they supply funds in amounts large enough to finance the large transactions of the business.   It is a matter of observation that as politicians get into the first rank in influence and control their inclination is to seek office for their followers rather than for themselves. Often when they do hold office the expenses they have to assume are notoriously in excess of the compensation provided by law, and the real value of the office must lie in some advantages of position facilitating their management of politics. Many of the men who are recognized chiefs of party management, "the bosses," do not hold office at all. Indeed, this avoidance of direct official responsibility may almost be said to be the distinguishing characteristic of the boss in a large city. Such men must find their account in politics in other ways than in the emoluments of office-holding.

It is also to be observed that the revenues required by party management are much too large to be raised by assessments upon office-holders or candidates. Although large sums are raised in this way, they form only what may be called the ordinary revenues of party organization, and are quite inadequate for the extraordinary expenditures of an important campaign. Vast sums are then expended in party agitation — public addresses, circulation of documents, mass-meetings, barbecues, picnics, and parades. Then, too, large expenditures are made in qualifying voters by getting out naturalization papers, or paying their taxes when the exercise of the franchise is so conditioned. Moreover, on election day the captain of every election district expects to be supplied with funds so as to be able to meet the expense of getting voters to the polls or to offer inducements to the wavering or indifferent. While it is impossible to get exact figures, yet the way in which money is poured out to carry elections shows that copious sources of supply are open to party managers.

It has been the experience of other countries,

having representative institutions, that the gratifications which political distinction offer to people of means are such as to make them willing to bear the burden and expense of party management. But in such countries political activity is a department of the general activities of good society, and hence may confer a social distinction which affords a powerful incentive to effort, while the work required makes only occasional demands upon the time and attention of those taking it up, and can be done under simple forms of organization. If American party organization meant only the existence of such regular machinery as the congressional committee, supplemented by the organization in each district of a committee of citizens to bring out a candidate in the party interest and to canvass votes in his behalf, party management in America would then mean something like what it does in England. The far more extensive duties assumed by party organization in this country make it so intricate in its nature and so absorbing in its demands that it can be managed only by those who are trained to it as a business, and in becoming a trade politics cease to offer the inducements which in other countries commend them as a social duty. There may be political prominence so great as to compel a certain amount of social recognition ; but it is given with reserve, and no one would think of taking to party management as a road to social distinction.

There is no lack of public spirit in the American character. The spontaneous vigor and multitudinous variety of ecclesiastical organization, for which the United States is a wonder among nations, alone afford sufficient proof that the American people possess extraordinary powers of gratuitous voluntary effort in behalf of public interests. In this country, more perhaps than elsewhere, public service exerts an attraction upon the mass of society which elicits a vast amount of activity ; but in order to obtain a field in which to operate, it must as a rule avoid an occupation which established conditions reserve so exclusively to professional control as party management. The public spirit, which under simpler forms of government includes in its operation the direction and maintenance of party activity, in the United States confines itself to the administration of charities, to unpaid service upon the directories of public institutions, or to service upon public commissions whose duties and objects put them out of the sphere of partisanship, or else are shielded by a consensus of public opinion which the politicians feel compelled to respect. To service of such character public esteem attaches, and to mark this it is the practice of common speech to designate such employment as "outside of politics." Distinctions of this sort have impressed a narrow meaning on the word "politics." In Europe the politicians are those who in one capacity or another are engaged in directing the administration of public affairs. In the United States the politicians are the class of men who attend to the working of party machinery. If it is desired to indicate that the reputation of a public man has been gained in service to administration rather than in party management, the word "politician" is avoided, and he is spoken of as a statesman. The late Mr. Tilden was spoken of as both a great politician and a great statesman, because of his eminence in both respects.

Motives of public spirit and honorable ambition doubtless enter into the direct work of party management to a far greater extent than is generally supposed, and their influence retains in party service capacities which would command far larger remuneration if exercised in other employments; but nevertheless politics are regarded as a business, and as a rule those who follow it expect to live by it. The political class must in one way or another extract from their occupation the remuneration of their labor as well as obtain funds for party undertakings, and in so doing they have to encounter a state of popular feeling disposed to grudge reward and envy acquisition. This being so, it is the more inconceivable that the attachment of the people to their party principles should prompt the contribution of such enormous sums of money as are handled by the politicians without account or audit.

The matter does not become comprehensible

until the nature of the opportunities which accompany the power of party organization over the conduct of government is considered. It is then easy to see that a potentate whose sway extends over the administration of state governments and innumerable subordinate governments, controlling franchises of immense value and extent, and able to affect the welfare of a myriad of wealthy interests, will not be without an ample retinue of courtiers, nor lack obliging friends willing to relieve his necessities by princely gifts, and thus enjoy his favor. Party organization is able to command more generous benevolences from rich subjects than were ever the Tudor kings. Thus in indirect ways party organization is able to give its chiefs rich opportunities of money-making, and is able to levy enormous sums from wealthy interests for political purposes.

Public spirit, party attachment, and personal good will towards party managers in numerous cases conspire to elicit contributions which are very large in the aggregate, but it is unlikely that the supply would be so copious were it not that extensive interests find it to their advantage to lay party organization under obligations. The business calculation of the system is shown by the non-partisan spirit of its beneficence. In testifying before a committee of the United States Senate, the president of the American Sugar Refining Company said, "It is my impression that wherever there is a dominant party, wherever the majority is large, that is the party that gets the contribution, because that is the party which controls the local matters." He explained that this system of contribution was carried on because the company had large interests which needed protection, and he added, "Every individual and corporation and firm, trust, or whatever you call it, does these things, and we do them."[1]

But even this source of revenue must be inadequate to the needs of party organization. It is a tribute to an established control, but it neither creates nor maintains that control. The main resource of party management — the working capital of the business — is the negotiation of the value of its good will that in one way or another is being constantly carried on. Franchises to the use of streets and highways, the grant of rights of way, concessions of charter privileges, legislative sanctions to corporate undertakings, lucrative usufructs of various species of public wealth, real estate development in connection with municipal improvements, etc., are fields of investment for many millions of private capital, an obvious policy with whose representatives is to confederate their interests with political influence.[2] Probably more

[1] Senate Report, No. 606, Fifty-third Congress, second session, pp. 351, 352.

[2] The financial statement of Berlin for 1893–1894 showed that the profits from the city gas and water-works and revenues from

money is lost than is made in politics, but when, as is sometimes the case, a high degree of business capacity is united with great political influence, a splendid fortune may be accumulated by cultivating the opportunities of a political career.

This connection of business opportunity with political position is at the bottom of many of the fierce faction fights that go on inside of party organization. They usually originate in conflicts over the apportionment of respective privileges in the adjustment of party interests, and are in their nature essentially like the hostilities that sometimes break out among competitive interests in the business world, lasting until the strength and resources of rival interests are thoroughly tested, when the stage of business combination is reached. In the same way political interests measure strength in the primary elections, and then reach an adjustment in accordance with the developments. Thus it so often comes about that factions, which at one time seem bent on tearing each other to pieces, may at another time be seen snuggled together cheek by jowl. These adjustments of interest are sometimes entered

franchises amounted to more than $5,000,000 a year. With comparatively small exception, such sources of revenue are in this country exploited on private account. The enormous increase in the value of street railway franchises, attending the introduction of electric power, went nearly all to the enrichment of private interests able to enlist the needful amount of political influence, which of course was duly rewarded.

into under written covenants as formal as in regular business negotiation. Of course such instruments rarely see the light of day, for even faction fury is slow to commit such an imprudence, yet such a thing has happened. A quarrel of Pennsylvania factions made public a remarkable draught of a treaty between state and local political interests, the preamble of which set forth that it was for "mutual political, and business advantage."[1]

The process will be misunderstood if it is regarded as altogether mere venality. Bargain and sale of legislation and downright blackmail go on to a large extent, but such abuse of trust always bears the distinct brand of corruption. The political class, like every class of business men, includes great variety of talent and character. Vulgar cheats and ordinary rogues get into politics and use their opportunities for their own pelf with as little regard for the interests of their party as they dare reveal. This class of politicians sometimes invade city councils and state legislatures to such an extent as to stamp those bodies with their character. Indeed, it may be said to be the rule that lobby influence, which within its legitimate field of advocacy is a valuable and a really necessary adjunct of legislation, is compelled to assume a corrupt character, and it must select for its principal service agents skilled in systematic bribery. It is also true that blackmail purposes inspire many

[1] The Pittsburgh newspapers of March 16, 1896.

legislative proposals, and operate to a vast extent
under cover of the police power and the punishment
of misdemeanors. The maximum of the latter
species of corruption was probably reached under
the bi-partisan police administration of New York
City, when the responsibility was divided between
the two parties, and was the full risk of neither.
But such practices are regarded as antagonistic to
party interests, and the tendency of party management is to go as far as its strength permits in
stopping them. They excite resentments and
accumulate odium, which injure the party and
at times provoke popular revolts. The political
consequences of the disclosures made by the
Lexow committee are still fresh in public recollection. Moreover, the revenues of downright
venality and blackmail are personal plunder and
probably yield little to party resources. In restraining such abuses, party managers are hindered
by the fact that they can retain command only on
condition of service to the interests in possession
of the field. For every boss in power, there are
plenty of would-be bosses, and his success in maintaining his position is contingent upon his ability
to satisfy inexorable conditions of efficiency. The
baser sort of politicians are generally dexterous in
securing to themselves a certain amount of influence, so that they are in a position to compel recognition and secure toleration of their practices
unless carried to excesses which plainly jeopard

Y

party interests. Even then the task of curbing them is difficult and dangerous, owing to a state of public sentiment which fosters a spirit of insubordination. The traditional spirit of hostility to all regular party organization is so strong that the appearance of a breach invites a raid of forces collected from all quarters for the special attack. There is always a great risk that the enforcement of too strict a discipline may provoke a mutiny in the camp which will furnish to some casual aggregate of opposition the services of a band of experts to give force and direction to the assault. The professional gambler, John Morrissey, once effected a political revolution in New York City by going over to the opposition in his rage at pretensions on the part of the municipal administration which he regarded as being rather too high and supercilious to be endured.

The close association of partisanship with corruption in our political system is the result of circumstances, not of affinity. They are really antagonistic principles. Partisanship tends to establish a connection based upon an avowed public obligation, while corruption consults private and individual interests which secrete themselves from view and avoid accountability of any kind. The weakness of party organization is the opportunity of corruption. Party organization undertakes to supervise the conduct of legislative bodies only so far as party interests distinctly require, and it has no warrant to go further. This permits a latitude of action in regard to general legislation which abounds in pernicious reactions throughout the business world. In proportion as party control is strengthened, a counteracting force is brought to bear. The way in which, in some of the large states, the development of the state boss has systematized the relations between corporations and politics, has therefore caused a marked improvement in legislative behavior. The boss, being supplied with resources which enable him to finance the details of party management, — the running of primaries, the setting-up of delegates, the selection of candidates, etc., — is in a position to interpose a party obligation between legislative marauders and their prey.

The cost of party subsistence cannot be computed. Exact data are unattainable. Although various estimates have been made, they are all worthless and are all probably below the mark, although some of them mount into many millions of dollars. It is quite probable that party organization costs more than any one of the regular departments of government. It is a fond delusion of the people that our republican form of government is less expensive than the monarchical forms which obtain in Europe. The truth is that ours is the costliest government in the world, and none save a nation so industrious and energetic, and which possesses such great natural resources as our own, could possibly sustain it. No other nation in the world is rich enough for the political experimentation which the United States is carrying on; but when the end crowns the work, its cost may be found to have been small in comparison with the value of the recompense.

CHAPTER XXV

SINCE it lacks a true representative character, and its concern in public affairs is at bottom a business pursuit carried on for personal gain and emolument, the service which party performs in executing the behests of public opinion and in carrying on political development must be an incident of its ordinary activity. That this is the case all observation confirms. It is a common remark, that all political parties seem to care for is the possession of the offices, and that they are willing to shift and change their principles as much as need be in order to win. Talleyrand's cynical remark, that a man who is always true to his party must be prepared to change his principles frequently, is peculiarly applicable to American politics. Party effrontery is carried to such a pitch that in one state a party may take up and energetically advocate doctrines, which the same party in another state will be just as actively engaged in denouncing and opposing. So accommodating is party policy in this respect, that state political campaigns have become tests of the public disposition, and the results of such experimentation are studied for data upon which to base plans for the grand quadrennial adventure of the presidential election.

It therefore appears that wherein party serves public interests is in the catering to public wants and desires which every party organization must carry on to get and hold business in competition with opposing party organization. Hence party is obliged to consult public opinion and assume engagements to be carried out in the administration of public affairs. American politics are not peculiar in this respect, for that is the way in which party discharges its function wherever it carries on the government. What is peculiar to American politics is that party organization is so situated that it cannot negotiate as a principal, but as a go-between. Unlike an English party, it cannot itself formulate measures, direct the course of legislation, and assume the direct responsibility of administration. All that it can do is to certify the political complexion of candidates, leaving it to be inferred that their common purpose will effect such unity of action as will control legislation and direct administration in accordance with party professions. The peculiarities of American party government are all due to this separation of party management from direct and immediate responsibility for the administration of government. Party organization is compelled to act through executive and legislative deputies, who,

while always far from disavowing their party
obligations, are quite free to use their own discretion as to the way in which they shall interpret
and fulfil the party pledges. Meanwhile they
are shielded, by the constitutional partitions of
privilege and distributions of authority, from any
direct and specific responsibility for delay or failure in coming to an agreement for the accomplishment of party purposes. Authority being divided,
responsibility is uncertain and confused, and the
accountability of the government to the people is
not at all definite or precise. When a party meets
with disaster at the polls, every one may form his
own opinion as to the cause. It is purely a matter
of speculation. The situation of affairs is one
which was accurately foretold in The Federalist.

" It is often impossible," said Hamilton, "amidst
mutual accusations, to determine on whom the
blame or the punishment of a pernicious measure,
or series of pernicious measures, ought really to
fall. It is shifted from one to another with so
much dexterity, and under such plausible appearances, that the public opinion is left in suspense
about the real author. The circumstances which
may have led to any national miscarriage or misfortune are sometimes so complicated that where
there are a number of actors who may have had
different degrees and kinds of agency, though we
may clearly see upon the whole that there has been
mismanagement, yet it may be impracticable to

pronounce to whose account the evil which may have been incurred is truly chargeable." [1]

As a natural consequence of the detached and subordinate position of party organization in the conduct of the government, public opinion is not concentrated upon its acts with steady scrutiny and vigilant supervision. The activity of party is largely concerned with details of its own business management, not possessing much interest for the mass of the people who have their own affairs to attend to. Its contentions are largely personal squabbles, whose political results may be very important, but which do not themselves present political issues. They are like the intrigues which used to go on among the English gentry, over court honors and official emoluments, in the Georgian era of English politics, the mass of the electorate but dimly comprehending what was going on and regarding the strife with disgust and aversion, although quickly roused to activity by issues appealing to their political instincts. The true public opinion of the nation is ordinarily in a state of suspense. The minds of people are preoccupied by too many interests to attend closely to the transactions of the politicians, and not until the issue is thrust upon the public in a definite form by some pressing emergency is the genuine expression of public opinion evoked. Meanwhile the political opinion with which party organization is concerned, and to

[1] The Federalist, No. 70.

which it defers, is that with which it comes in contact in soliciting business. The acrid and fretting humors of the body politic exert a more direct and active influence upon party behavior than the judgment and intelligence of the nation, because elements of unrest and dissatisfaction are importunate in their demands and therefore receive attention, while social interests of incomparably greater magnitude are ignored.

The readiness with which party organization lends itself to the service of temporary manias and recognized delusions proceeds from an instinct of self-preservation. Everywhere the ins are menaced by the activity of the outs, prompt to seize upon any whim, passion, or prejudice, no matter how foolish or noxious, if it can be turned to present account. Party organization, therefore, exploits outbreaks of popular folly and knavery, and caters to the prejudices of ignorance and fanaticism in a way that invests them with factitious importance, and confers upon them inordinate legislative influence. This feature of American politics, more than any other, causes the national character to be misunderstood, and the worth of democratic institutions to be undervalued. It is inferred that public opinion in this country is subject to periodical hallucinations, that there is a popular contempt of authority, and a frequent recurrence of reckless desires to try over again the old failures, heedless of the abundant instructions of history and the warnings of our own national experience. This is a mistake. Folly does not more abound, but it is magnified in force and effect by the peculiar conditions of American politics. American citizenship is probably superior in average intelligence to that of any other country. The public press, although considerate of the value of party good will to an extent that unfits it for fairly representing public opinion, must nevertheless keep that in view, since it caters to the public at large, and not merely to the fraction which busies itself with politics.; and it is well known that the voice of the press is different from the voice of party on questions of public policy. Sanity and conservatism prevail in the tone of the press, even when party organization is most supple and accommodating to the folly of the hour.

Party organization not being directly burdened by the difficulties and necessities of government feels at liberty to court public opinion in all its vagaries. Great art is employed in framing platforms so as to be susceptible to various interpretations. Concerning issues which are settled, party speaks in a clear, sonorous voice. But on new issues it mumbles and quibbles. Subdivisions of the party organization make such professions as will pay the best in their respective fields of activity. If the issue cannot be dodged, straddling may be resorted to. Declarations really incongruous in their nature are coupled, and their inconsistency is cloaked by rhetorical artifice. Sometimes such expedients are employed as making the platform lean one way and putting on it a candidate who leans the other way, or candidates representing opposing ideas and tendencies are put upon the same ticket. Such practices are results of the ordinary instincts of party in all countries, and obtain such monstrous growth in America because of extraordinarily favorable conditions. Party never commits itself to any new undertaking until it has to. In England there must be a long period of agitation and education of public sentiment before a new issue is raised to the rank of what is known as a cabinet question, but when that time arrives, party is in a position to enter into exact and specific engagements as to the disposition which will be made of it. In this country the only way in which party can be forced into such a position is through the exigencies of the national administration. Whatever may be the policy then adopted, it puts upon party the necessity of acquiescence or dissent in a way that requires a categorical response to the demands of public opinion.

In the discharge of this function national party organization claims and exercises supreme jurisdiction. When it reaches its decision, all indulgence of local heterodoxy disappears and is succeeded by a ferocious intolerance. State and local party leaders must submit on penalty of excommunication. The coercive force which party organization then develops was strikingly manifested by the way in which the Democratic platform of 1896 was forced upon dissenting state party organizations. Some, which had adopted platforms antagonistic to the platform of the national party, were compelled to meet and eat their words. It is the established principle of American politics that fidelity to the national platform is the crucial test of party orthodoxy. Hence national issues are the controlling force in politics. Attempting to reform state or local politics, while ignoring national politics, is like expecting to accomplish a local purification of the atmosphere by palisading a patch of ground in a swamp. A little may be done, but not much. It follows that, in this country, — as was the case in England, — the effectual purification of our politics will begin with national politics and will spread from them to local politics.

The pliable and time-serving disposition of party, which is the natural consequence of its own anxious calculation of its business interests, prepares for it tremendous reverses. It becomes committed to methods of administration and courses of policy inimical to the public interest, so that there comes a time when genuine public opinion is roused to action with a vigor which nothing can withstand. The shelters of falsehood and the refuges of deceit are swept away, as by the blast of a hurricane, and the discomfited party managers lie choking and dumfounded in the dust and the wreckage. The readiness of the people to treat their great national parties in this way must eventually beat those parties into serviceable tools of government or break them up to make room for better material. The situation confronts political leaders with problems of party control and discipline, whose solution tends to improve the apparatus of government. The results of this tendency are already very plainly marked in the improvement of the House of Representatives; but far more extensive changes must take place in all the organs of government before the rule of public opinion is definitely established. The present inadequacy of party organization for a true representation of public opinion is so exasperating to impatient reformers that they would like to shatter it to bits; but that is not the way to better the state of affairs. Party rises to new occasions by consulting its own interests. This consultative faculty in party organization, mischievous as seems to be its irregular and irresponsible operation, is that which sustains political development, and eventually it will perfect the democratic type of government.

PART IV

TENDENCIES AND PROSPECTS OF AMER-
ICAN POLITICS

—◆—

CHAPTER XXVI

POLITICAL IDEAS OF OUR TIMES

In attempting to forecast the future of our politics, the ideas of our times must first be considered, since ideas are the sap from which institutions obtain their growth. Examination discloses the remarkable fact that there is as yet little change in political ideas. The doctrine of a distribution of authority, so that the various branches of the government shall check and balance one another to protect the public welfare, still possesses the public mind. Although the working of the constitution has undergone profound change, the theory has remained almost intact. That the constitution does not work well in practice is freely admitted; but of course that is not its fault. The constitutional ideal is noble; but the politicians are vile. If only the checks could be made more effective, if only a just balance of power could be established beyond the strength of the politicians to disarrange, — or, above all, if some barriers could be erected, so tight and strong as to shut the politicians out altogether, — the constitution would work perfectly. Therefore, more checks upon the abuse of power; more contrivances to baffle the politicians, whose machinations pervert the constitution and corrupt the government!

These ideas are products of the Whig theory of government. They abound in the voluminous reform literature of the eighteenth century, when England, too, was under a system of government in which authority was distributed and responsibility confused, and the resultant corruption tormented the conscience of the nation. In Macaulay's brilliant essays, [1] Trevelyan's fine work on the "Early History of Charles James Fox," and in Lecky's great "History of England in the Eighteenth Century" we have vivid pictures and abundant details of the state of politics in that age. As Burke remarked, "Every age has its own manners, and its politics dependent upon them." There are many differences between the politics of England in the eighteenth century and the politics of the United States in the nineteenth century; but such is the fundamental identity in the cause of the disease that it is impossible to read any description of English politics in that age without recognizing

[1] In particular, those on Horace Walpole and The Earl of Chatham.

traits of American politics of the present day. On
the other hand, so great a change has taken place in
English politics that men of this generation in that
country can hardly imagine such a state of affairs
as existed in the past.   Mr. Trevelyan, himself
an English statesman of high rank, says, " We,
who look upon politics as a barren career by
which few people hope to make money and none
to save it, and who would expect a poet to found
a family as soon as a prime minister, can with
difficulty form a just conception of a period when
people entered Parliament, not because they were
rich, but because they wanted to be rich, and when
it was more profitable to be a member of a Cabinet
than a partner in a brewery." His American readers have no difficulty in forming such a conception :
the difficulty with them is to conceive of a state
of politics in which private gain is not the main-
spring of activity.   The political characteristics
which Mr. Trevelyan locates in the past are familiar features of the present in this country.   What
observations could be more commonplace than such
as these ?   The legislative party hack "cared nothing whatever for the disapproval of any one outside
the House . . . who did not happen to be a free-
man (voter) in his own borough ; and among those
with whom he lived, and whose esteem he valued,
public employment was looked upon as a sort of
personalty of which everybody had a clear right
to scrape together as much as he could without

inquiring whether the particular post he coveted ought to exist at all, or whether he himself was the proper man to hold it." In deciding contested elections " even exceptionally high-minded men were not ashamed of allowing that they had voted on party grounds ; and an appeal to any other motive would have been scouted by the lower class of parliamentary tacticians as clap-trap." Talk about disinterestedness inspired disgust. Lord Shelburne, when a young man, once made a remark to Henry Fox to the effect that gentlemen of independent position, in their political conduct, should act as the trustees of public interests. The veteran bade him get "rid of such puerile notions " and push for the offices if he wanted to get on in politics. Aptitude for cabal and intrigue rather than capacity for the administration of public affairs was the source of political influence. "Power went to such as had the strength to seize and hold it." There was "a profound distrust of public men." [1]

During this stage of English politics, as now in this country, the attitude respectively of literature and politics, which should be as reciprocal as thought and action, was characterized on the one side by disgust and aversion ; on the other by contempt. The tone of newspaper comment was one of calumny and abuse. Serious criticism must

[1] Trevelyan's Early History of Charles James Fox, Chap. III.

z

have definite grounds; when discussion of responsibility must proceed by guess-work and inference, it inevitably degenerates into slander, and journalism so circumstanced is prone to develop levity, recklessness, and sensationalism as its prevailing characteristics.

In respectable literature, the tone of thought was pessimistic. Browne's "Estimate of the Manners and Principles of the Times," which appeared in 1757 and had a wide popularity, argued that virtue was rotting out of the English stock from the development of a commercial spirit, which was corroding patriotism and all the moral elements that are the true sources of national greatness. He eloquently insisted that no increase of material resources could compensate for the moral deterioration which had come upon the English people. This once famous treatise is now preserved from oblivion only by casual references to it made by Burke and Macaulay; but the melancholy which clouded the thought of the age produced a durable literary monument in Samuel Johnson's noble poem on "The Vanity of Human Wishes." All its political allusions are scornful.

> "Through freedom's sons no more remonstrance rings,
> Degrading nobles and controlling kings;
> Our supple tribes repress their patriot throats
> And ask no questions but the price of votes;
> With weekly libels and septennial ale,
> Their wish is full to riot and to rail."

The deceits of the world and the general depravity of mankind present a scene of gloom which no ray of hope illumines. The only peace for the soul is in resignation.

> " Must helpless man, in ignorance sedate,
>   Roll darkling down the torrent of his fate?
>   Must no dislike alarm, no wishes rise,
>   No cries evoke the mercies of the skies?
>   Inquirer cease ; petitions yet remain
>   Which heaven may hear, nor deem religion vain.
>   Still raise for good the supplicating voice,
>   But leave to heaven the measure and the choice."

Then as now the existence of corruption was the theme of an insincere party recrimination. Says Macaulay : " The outs were constantly talking in magnificent language about tyranny, corruption, wicked ministers, servile courtiers, the liberty of Englishmen, the great charter, the rights for which the fathers bled. . . . They excited a vague craving for change by which they profited for a single moment, and of which, as they well deserved, they were soon the victims." Even in particular details there are striking resemblances of practical politics between that age and our own. "The undertakers" who figured prominently in the government of Ireland had political functions like those of our bosses. Mr. Lecky describes them as great Irish borough owners "who, in consideration of a large share of the patronage of the crown, 'undertook' to carry the king's business through (the Irish)

Parliament." In other words, the method was that of boss rule founded on the spoils system. Mr. Lecky remarks that "more corruption was employed to overturn their ascendency than had ever been required to maintain it," and he thinks that "the formation of a connected influence . . . binding many isolated and individual interests into a coherent and powerful organization, was a real step towards parliamentary government."[1]

Disgust and irritation at the degradation and corruption of politics produced phases of public sentiment like those with which we are familiar. Non-partisanship was continually preached. Honest men should "enter into an association for the support of one another against the endeavors of those whom they ought to look upon as their common enemies, whatsoever side they may belong to. Were there such an honest body of neutral forces, we should never see the worst of men in the great figures of life, because they are useful to a party; nor the best unregarded because they are above practising those methods which would be grateful to their factions. We should then single every criminal out of the herd and hunt him down, however formidable and overgrown he might appear." This is not an extract from a recent appeal to the public in behalf of the formation of good gov-

[1] Lecky's History of England, Vol. II., p. 443 ; Vol. IV., pp. 383-384.

ernment clubs, but is an extract from Addison, in the Spectator, No. 125, Tuesday, July 24, 1711.

A memorable experiment of this sort was made. The revolt against Walpole was a magnificent independent movement. Whigs and Tories coalesced to overthrow corruption. All the leading men of letters supported the movement. Macaulay said, " The downfall of Walpole was to be the beginning of a political millennium ; and every enthusiast had figured to himself that millennium according to his own wishes." Akenside's best poem was called forth by this movement, and, expatiating upon what was to be expected from the overthrow of the great master of corruption, he exclaimed : —

> "See private life by wisest arts reclaimed,
> See ardent youth to noblest manners framed."

The victory of the Patriots, as they were called, was not only complete, but the man who was raised to power in Walpole's place realized in his conduct their professions of contempt for Walpole's methods. Carteret despised office-mongering and would have nothing to do with it. He neglected, says Macaulay, "all those means by which the power of Walpole had been created and maintained." Chief-Justice Willes once went to him to beg some office for a friend. Carteret replied that he was too much occupied with Continental politics to think about the disposal of places and benefices. "You may rely on it, then," said the justice, "that people who want places and benefices will go to those who have more leisure." [1] The prediction was fulfilled. Carteret's parliamentary support fell away, and before long he had to retire from an office in which he could not sustain himself. With Walpole's downfall had disappeared the sole point of policy on which the Patriots were united. To form an efficient administration, party connection had to be established, and for this purpose the usual arts of political management were found necessary. The nation soon found that a change of men had made no change of method. The popular disgust was intense. The very name of Patriot became a by-word. Samuel Johnson was so completely cured of enthusiasm that he declared that patriotism was the last refuge of a scoundrel.

Still another phase of popular sentiment in our own times that has its prototype in English politics of the eighteenth century is that which may be described as the Messianic hope of politics — expectation of the advent of some strong deliverer. The ideal president or governor who rises superior to party, and calls all good citizens to his support, is Bolingbroke's "Patriot King" in republican dress. Although the political philosophy of Bolingbroke is long since obsolete, it powerfully impressed the thought of his age and was in high repute with the fathers of the republic. There was nothing servile

[1] Macaulay's Essay on Horace Walpole.

in Bolingbroke's attitude towards kingship. He ridiculed the idea that a king ruled by divine right, and, laying down the principle that "the ultimate end of all governments is the good of the people," he upheld monarchy as the most feasible system by which social order might be preserved and civil liberty protected. The great advantage which monarchical government possessed over every other kind of government was its power of reform by the accession of a patriot king. "A corrupt commonwealth remains without remedy, though all the orders and forms of it subsist; a free monarchical government cannot remain absolutely so, so long as the orders and forms of the constitution subsist." He based this opinion on the ground that no matter how bad public men may have become, the king in the normal exercise of his sovereignty can elevate the standard of public service so that every part of the constitution will experience a purgation which will restore it to its proper functions. "By rendering public virtue and real capacity the sole means of acquiring any degree of power or profit in the state, he will set the passions of their hearts on the side of liberty and good government." The essential thing was to uproot partisanship. "To espouse no party, but to govern like the common father of his people, is so essential to the character of a patriot king that he who does otherwise forfeits the title. . . . Instead of abetting the divisions of his people, he will endeavor to unite them and to be himself the centre of their union; instead of putting himself at the head of one party in order to govern his people, he will put himself at the head of his people in order to govern, or more properly to subdue, all parties."

This was the theory which produced George III. In his private life he exactly fulfilled the popular ideal of the good ruler. In an age when fashionable society was recklessly dissolute, he was chaste in his conduct, temperate in his diet, and simple in his manners. While irreligion abounded, he kept a virtuous home whose days, beginning at dawn with family prayer, were passed in laborious performance of duty. He modelled his political conduct precisely in accord with Bolingbroke's instructions. Writing of the beginning of his reign, Macaulay says: "The watchwords of the new government were prerogative and purity. The sovereign was no longer to be a puppet in the hands of any subject or combinations of subjects. . . . The system of bribery which had grown up during the late reigns was to cease." Britain was to be freed from corruption and oligarchical cabals. But in separating himself from existing parties, he still had to secure to himself legislative support, and this practically meant the organization of a personal faction. "Thus sprang into existence and into note," Macaulay says, "a reptile species of politicians never before and never since known in our country."[1] They were known as " The King's Friends." By their aid the king was temporarily able to overthrow party government. As a result, corruption soon abounded more than ever before, and every evil in the state was aggravated. In wrecking party discipline and control, he dissolved restraint upon faction violence and brought on an anarchic condition of politics which menaced all social interests.

Burke's famous " Thoughts on the Cause of the Present Discontents," written in 1770, made a diagnosis of the malady from which politics were then suffering ; and since our government has preserved the essential characteristics of the English constitution of that period, that diagnosis, in all its general observations, is still pertinent to the condition of American politics. Then as now it was the popular disposition to account for evils by the predominance in administration of some obnoxious person. Lord Bute was then the target of obloquy. Burke disdained to join in the clamor, remarking that, "where there is a regular scheme of operations carried on, it is the system, and not any individual person who acts in it, that is truly dangerous." He went directly to the source of the disease by pointing out that it arose from the separation between administration and responsibility. There was a double ministry : the one a sham set up before the public ; while the real

[1] Essay on The Earl of Chatham.

power of administration was controlled by a cabal working behind the scenes. The interests in control behind the scenes "contrived to form in the outward administration two parties at least, which, whilst they are tearing one another to pieces, are both competitors for the favor and protection of the cabal; and by their emulation contribute to throw everything more and more into the hands of the interior managers." The principle of the double ministry is still in full force in American politics. Back of the apparent administration stands the political ring, and the powers of government are wielded by irresponsible managers behind the scenes. Burke made an observation, whose justness is strikingly illustrated by the way in which every now and then in our politics the people in a frenzy of rage crush the boss's candidate while the boss remains, when he said that "they have so contrived matters that the people have a greater hatred to the subordinate instrument than to the principal movers."

Speaking of the evils caused by the lack of direct responsibility for the management of public affairs, Burke said that it "not only strikes a palsy into every nerve of our free constitution, but in the same degree benumbs and stupefies the whole executive power; rendering government in all its grand operations languid, uncertain, ineffective; making ministers fearful of attempting, and incapable of executing, any useful plan of domestic arrangement or of foreign politics." As regards the effects upon the temper of the people he said, with striking appositeness to the present condition of American politics : "When the people conceive that laws and tribunals, and even popular assemblies, are perverted from the ends of their institution, they find in those names of degenerated establishments only new motives to discontent. . . . A sullen gloom and furious disorder prevail by fits. . . . A species of men, to whom a state of order would become a sentence of obscurity, are nourished into a dangerous magnitude by the heat of intestine disturbances ; and it is no wonder that, by a sort of sinister piety, they cherish in their turn the disorders which are the parents of all their consequence. Superficial observers consider such persons as the cause of the public uneasiness, when in fact they are nothing more than the effect of it."

Burke dismissed somewhat contemptuously the various projects in the way of new checks and prohibitions. A favorite reform proposal then was a bill to exclude office-holders from Parliament. He remarked, " It were better, perhaps, that they should have a corrupt interest in the forms of the constitution than that they should have none at all." He did not share in belief "of the infallibility of laws and regulations, in the cure of public distempers." Whatever they might be, the politicians would get around them. " The science of evasion, already tolerably understood, would then be brought to the greatest perfection." The doctrine "that all political connections are in their nature factitious, and as such ought to be dissipated and destroyed," and that "the rule for forming administration is mere personal ability," he energetically denounced as pernicious counsel. "Every honorable connection will avow it is their first purpose to pursue every just method to put the men who hold their opinions into such a condition as may enable them to carry their common plans into execution, with all the power and authority of the state. As this power is attached to certain situations, it is their duty to contend for these situations. Without a proscription of others, they are bound to give to their own party the preference in all things." In fine, Burke's remedy for factious strife and abounding corruption was frankly to adopt party rule by conferring upon party full power to act, coupled with complete responsibility for what was done. It was from partisanship, thus strengthened and steadied, that the nation might hope "to see public and private virtues, not dissonant and jarring and mutually destructive, but harmoniously combined, growing out of one another in a noble and orderly gradation, reciprocally supporting and supported."

The event has shown that just by such partisanship the regeneration of English politics was accomplished. The corruption of English politics seems to have been accompanied by a more general infection of society than has taken place in this country, and the conditions of public life were more degraded than at any period of our history. We read with amazement of the torrent of bribery flowing through English constituencies, of candidates going to the polls surrounded by gangs of hired pugilists, and of the savage rioting or sodden drunkenness that invested the polling booths. And yet it was from material furnished by such an electorate that the workings of public opinion wrought great party leaders and statesmen of shining integrity.

" Responsibility is a tremendous engine in a free government," said Jefferson. [1] " Responsibility, in order to be reasonable," said Madison, " must be limited to objects within the power of the responsible party ; and in order to be effectual must relate to the operations of that power, of which a ready and proper judgment can be formed by the constituents." [2] These conditions were established in England when the cabinet system became definitely converted into a party agency, uniting administration with the initiative of legislation. All that was then needed to establish accountability was the overthrow of the privacy of debate and voting, anciently regarded as a most sacred privilege for the protection of Parliament. This barrier

[1] Writings of Jefferson, Vol. V., p. 410.
[2] The Federalist, No. 63.

was broken down after violent struggles, and then the reign of public opinion began. The new conditions developed a new type of statesmanship. The ability preferred by the situation was no longer that which excelled in the manipulation of the individual interests of members so as to obtain their coöperation in the transaction of public business. That was attended to by the constituencies themselves in fixing the party obligations of their representatives. The ability now ascendant was that which appealed to the support and confidence of the nation, and which was able to sustain the high responsibilities of public office.

In meeting these responsibilities, English statesmen have devised various instruments for correcting abuses and arresting corruption, the adoption of which, in this country, is now the great object of reformers. The idea seems to be that if similar machinery is forced upon our politicians, a proper and effective use of it must necessarily follow ; but so far such expectations have been disappointed. What has been introduced in this country as civil service reform, was established in England by the Aberdeen ministry in 1853 as a barrier against the selfish importunity of aristocratic influence. The reports of reform associations and the disclosures of congressional investigations afford ample testimony of the fact that a device adopted by English party leaders to relieve them of pressure to do what they did not want to do, does not serve so well to prevent American party leaders from doing what circumstances incline them to do, whether they like it or not. The Corrupt Practices Prevention law, which also is being introduced in this country, with high hopes of its utility as a reform measure, is the product of a series of English statutes, the first of which was passed in 1854. It is not very difficult for our clever politicians to evade such laws, but they have been effective in England because they are regarded as a protection for candidates against blackmail and corruption, and because they are useful as a handy club to knock out of public life men mean enough to resort to cheating. Far from desiring to evade such legislation, the tendency among English party leaders is to tighten its restraint so as to keep down election expenses. Before the creation of a regenerative force to give life and vigor to statutes, such legislation was as great a failure in England as in this country. In 1705, De Foe, after adverting to some acts passed against bribery, remarked, "Never was treating, buying of voices, freedoms and freeholds, and all the corrupt practices in the world, so open and barefaced as since these severe laws were enacted." Lecky states that "by an act of 1729, any elector might be compelled on demand to take an oath swearing that he had received no bribe to influence his vote, and any person who was convicted of either giving or receiving a bribe at election was deprived forever of either giving or receiving the franchise and fined £500, unless he purchased indemnity by discovering another offender of the same kind"; but the historian remarks that so long as it was to the interest of politicians to shelter corruption, laws against it were a dead letter. On the other hand, even without specific legislation against corruption, the operation of public opinion, addressing a responsible control, exerted a purifying influence. Writing in 1833, Macaulay remarked that whereas, formerly, nobody thought worse of a man because he had bought votes, the practice had become dishonorable. The remedial process was a gradual one, effecting not a sudden cure, but a steady improvement. Mr. Bagehot, in his famous work which finally disposed of the old Whig theory of the English constitution, pointed out that the really valuable reforms were instituted and made effectual by the politicians themselves. "The statesmen who worked the system that was put up had themselves been educated under the system that was pulled down."

There is no reason for thinking that American politicians will be any less amenable to public opinion or less capable in obeying its requirements. But so long as our constitutional system provides that an administration chosen to carry out a party policy shall be debarred from initiating and directing that policy in legislation, just so long is the party machine a necessary intermediary between the people and their government, and just so long will party management constitute a trade which those which have a vocation for politics cannot neglect, and those who make a business of politics will make as profitable as they can.   As Burke ⌣ wisely said, "Whatever be the road to power, that is the road which will be trod."

2 A

CHAPTER XXVII

THE POLITICAL PROSPECT

ALTHOUGH "the Cause of the Present Discontents" has taken rank as a classic, it does not appear to have had any marked effect upon contemporaneous thought. The general current of political speculation continued to be deeply tinctured by the fallacies of the old Whig theory. John Adams probably expressed the prevailing opinion when he wrote that Burke was far inferior to Bolingbroke as a thinker. Burke's essay gave great umbrage to reformers and called forth counter manifestoes. What the age admired was Churchill's satire, the invectives of Junius, and Mrs. Catherine Macaulay's [1] dissertations proving to the satisfaction of every one not a dolt or a knave that the corruptions of politics were due to

[1] Mrs. Macaulay was in high repute as the "celebrated female historian." She is referred to by John Adams as a recognized authority. A poet of the age declared: —

> "Macaulay shall in nervous prose relate
> Whence flows the venom that distracts the state."

The prophecy was exactly fulfilled by a Macaulay whose fame has obliterated that of his predecessor, whose name is now preserved from oblivion mainly by some ungallant remarks at her expense by old Dr. Johnson, duly recorded by Boswell.

the disturbance of the constitution caused by the growth of partisanship.

The belief that the constitution could be tinkered into some sort of mechanical excellence possessed reformers too strongly to be disturbed. An elaborate presentation of their ideas was made in Burgh's " Political Disquisitions, an Inquiry into Public Errors, Defects, and Abuses," published in 1774. John Adams mentions that it was favorite reading in the colonies, and Jefferson recommended it to a friend as a good work on politics. It is cited in The Federalist as a standard authority. In its three stout volumes one finds all the familiar nostrums for remedying the ills of the body politic — such as annual elections, rotation in office, the ballot, the extension of the suffrage, the requirement of residence in the constituency as a qualification for election, and above all things the suppression of partisanship. In England the course of practical politics would not budge for such reforms, but they have had a grand field in this country. New nostrums are now in favor, but the spirit of reform is unchanged. The great object is still, as in Burgh's time, "not to set up one party against another, the one to battle against the other; but to take away the fuel of parties, the emolumentary invitations to the fatal and mischievous strife, in which every victory is a loss to the country." [1]

[1] Burgh's Disquisitions, Vol. III., p. 332.

Legislation conceived in this spirit has had grave consequences; but for the present purpose it is sufficient to remark that there is nothing in the present condition of our politics to indicate that constitutional development is taking any different course than it has followed hitherto, as described in the second part of this work. On the contrary, there is abundant evidence to confirm the opinion that party organization continues to be the sole efficient means of administrative union between the executive and legislative branches of the government, and that whatever tends to maintain and perfect that union makes for orderly politics and constitutional progress; while whatever tends to impair that union, disturbs the constitutional poise of the government, obstructs its functions, and introduces an anarchic condition of affairs full of danger to all social interests. This is the cardinal principle of American politics.

The situation is such that the extension of executive authority is still the only practical method of advancing popular rule. This disposition of American politics to exalt executive authority causes some critics of our institutions to infer that democracy tends towards personal rule. Appearances seem to corroborate this theory; but all that it really amounts to is that at the present stage of our political development American democracy, confronted by the old embarrassments of feudalism, compounded from new ingredients, in-

stinctively resorts to the historic agency for the
extrication of public authority from the control
of particular interests — the plenitude of executive
power. The circumstances are such as are likely
to put increasing emphasis upon this tendency.

The actual situation as regards the practical
work of government assigns real control to two
systems of authority : one the power of the
Speaker of the House over the opportunities
of legislation ; the other the power of senators
over the details of legislation. The latter is by
far the more important, as it is the positive force;
the former operating simply as a check or inhibi-
tion at large, and, from its gross and massive nature, incapable of discrimination. The senatorial
control is supple, insinuating, and under existing
conditions it is ordinarily incontestable. By so
much as particular interests are brought under a
general control in the House, the more they value
the opportunities afforded by senatorial prerogative; and thus there is created in the membership
of the House a sense of dependence upon the offices of senators, which greatly weakens the House
as a body in any controversies with the Senate.
There are always a large number of members who
are fearful of injuring some special interests which
they are pursuing by the aid of senators, so that
they have no stomach for a conflict, and are quite
willing to sacrifice the dignity of the House for
their individual advantage.

The possibility that the constitutional privileges of the Senate might be abused, so as to erect oligarchical power, was foreseen by the framers of the constitution, and the representatives of the larger states would never have agreed to equality of senatorial representation with the smaller states had it not been supposed that the House of Representatives would dominate the legislative branch of the government. Speaking of that equality, Madison remarked : —

"The peculiar defence which it involves in favor of the smaller states would be more rational if any interests common to them, and distinct from those of the other states, would otherwise be exposed to peculiar dangers. But as the larger states would always be able, by their power over the supplies, to defeat unreasonable exertions of this prerogative of the lesser states ; and as the facility and excess of law-making seem to be the diseases to which our governments are most liable, it is not impossible that this part of the constitution may be more convenient in practice than it appears to many in contemplation."[1]

In this, as in all their estimates of the practical working of the constitution, the fathers were misled by deceptive analogies drawn from the English constitution. All the checks upon which they relied for the control of the Senate, by means of the superior weight and influence of the House,

---

[1] The Federalist, No. 62.

have failed in practice. Events have shown that the House is so little jealous of its power and consequence that members quietly permit the will of the nation, as declared in the election of the President and an overwhelming majority of the House of Representatives, to be thwarted by an accidental preponderance of minority representation in the Senate, rather than risk the trouble and annoyance of combating senatorial usurpation. Nay, it has been shown that members of the House are so absorbed in the service of their local interests that they eagerly seize the fact of an adverse majority in the Senate as an excuse for abandoning any effort to fulfil national party pledges, preferring to await the chances of political adjustments which may establish an accidental coincidence between the purposes of the Senate and the will of the nation.

It was very natural to suppose that the superior weight and controlling authority of the House of Commons in the British legislature was due to the fact that it was the body immediately representing the people, but such was not the case. The ascendency of the House of Commons dates no farther back than to the period when the seven years' term of membership was fixed. Mr. Lecky points out that "during the triennial period the frequency of elections made the members to a great extent subservient to the people who elected or to the noblemen who nominated them, and gave each Parliament scarcely time to acquire much self-confidence, fixity of purpose, or consistency of organization. The Septennial Act, and the presence of Walpole in the House of Commons during the whole of his long ministry, gradually made that body the undoubted centre of authority."[1] The parallel between the present condition of our House of Representatives, and the House of Commons before it obtained stability of position and became the seat of executive authority, is obvious. Although fresh from the people, and just at the beginning of their term, it was with great difficulty that Speaker Reed was able to hold the majority of the House to their shrewd and effective policy, at the extra session of 1897, of refusing to take up general legislation until the Senate had passed the tariff bill to enact which Congress had been specially convoked.

At present, however, the government is subject to the rule of an oligarchy intrenched in the Senate. Senator Hoar, a zealous defender of the dignity and privileges of the body of which he is a member, in a review article stated : —

" We choose our chief magistrate every four years, and the members of one House of Congress every two years. One-third of the senators go out of office every two years. The term of office of an individual senator is six years. The Senate is controlled by a majority of the states. A majority of

[1] History of England, Vol. I., p. 472.

the people cannot change the policy of the country unless a majority of the states also consent. A senator must be a citizen of the state from which he is chosen. Thus no change in the popular opinion can compel a change of policy during the four years of the President's term, nor can it compel a change of policy in a body where great and small states meet as equals, unless a majority of the states agree to the change. But the purpose and desire of the numerical majority of the American people may be baffled for twenty years by the local interests and feeling of a majority of the states, and those, perhaps, the smallest in population." [1]

This is a revival of the state sovereignty doctrine without any historical basis. It is bottomed wholly upon usurpation. But there is no likelihood that the House of Representatives, out of its own resources, will be able to make the effective resistance upon which the framers of the constitution relied as a means of preventing the Senate from turning the government into an oligarchy. The remedy must come, as in England, by the coöperation of executive power with representative authority. How potent is such a union of force is shown by the fact that in England it was able to reduce even a body of hereditary legislators into subordination to the will of the people, as expressed through their direct representatives by majority

[1] The Forum, August, 1897.

rule. Legally, the position of the British House of Lords seems impregnable. There is no way of getting any one of them out of office, and theoretically nothing can be done without their consent. But, practically, they must agree to anything on which the House of Commons is resolutely determined. Of late years, since the functions of the Commons, as a college of electors, are somewhat impaired by the degeneracy of party government, the Lords have plucked up more spirit in opposing the Commons; but in defeating a bill, they do it on the ground that their action is a method of invoking a referendum. If the appeal to the people goes against the Lords, they have nothing to do but to submit.

It is no longer possible for any institution of government, no matter what paper safeguards it may possess, to have any genuine strength, unless it is invigorated by democratic influence. One need only consider the real extent of the presidential authority in appointments to office, and the control over details of legislation inherent in the veto power when fully brought into play, to be convinced that the presidential office still retains its efficiency as an agency of popular control over the government, and that the power and influence of the office afford ample resources for the redress of grievances as soon as the determination to use them for that purpose shall have been developed. It is hardly too much to say that the President and the House of Representatives, acting in accord, are constitutionally omnipotent ; but the vast reserves of power which they together possess would not have to be drawn upon to any great extent. The influence of party connection would make its influence felt in the Senate, just as it has done in its prototype, the House of Lords, long before any controversy could reach an acute stage ; but it is altogether probable that some very forcible interposition of the authority of the two representative branches of the government will have to be made before the oligarchical power of the Senate is curbed, and its authority reduced to constitutional dimensions. The only way in which the Senate will ever be reformed is by divesting it of all power to domineer. When it is out of the question for the Senate to oppose its will to the will of the nation, and its influence becomes wholly dependent upon the worth and dignity of its membership, then it will assume the characteristics which the fathers hoped to secure by its constitution. Party interest will then inspire the selection of the ablest men that can be found for service in the Senate, so that in the discharge of the purely advisory functions, which are all that senators should be permitted to exercise, their action will have the weight and influence which belong to wisdom and experience.

Although the main instrument for the destruction of the feudal characteristics which deface our form of government will be executive authority, yet in performing that service the presidential office will be surrounded by influences which will tend to preclude the subversion of its representative character by the caprice or presumption of the individual who may chance to hold the office. The situation is such that only by entire accord and close association with a majority in the House of Representatives can such an exaltation of presidential authority be sustained, so that the aggrandizement of the office can be accomplished only under conditions insuring democratic control.

CHAPTER XXVIII

THE ULTIMATE TYPE

THE principle of elective kingship, — as represented by the masterful Mayor, Governor, or President, — in which democracy puts its trust, does not tend to a suppression of parliamentary agencies of government, such as took place in Europe during its period of emergence from feudalism; but it tends rather to subordinate their action to general requirements, as in England, so that all that there is in them of public utility will be preserved for the use of the new type of government which American democracy is perfecting. The greatest curtailments of the authority of legislative bodies are those which have taken place in municipal charters and in various state constitutions; but even at their lowest point of authority such bodies are retained as an indispensable part of the apparatus of government, open to an invigoration of their functions when political conditions correspond to such development. In national politics, the form of the legislative agencies of government has remained intact, and changes that have taken place in their functions have been sustained by their own activities. The House of Representatives has practically subjugated its elaborate organization for the representation of local interests, by developing a collective authority, which needs only direct association with executive policy to become an effective organ of responsible national control. The monstrous list of committees may very well continue, as now, to serve as convenient cemeteries for undesired legislation ; the complicated system of rules may still serve a useful purpose in controlling the moblike characteristics naturally appertaining to so large a body ; and it will quite suffice for all the purposes of a responsible administration of public affairs under representative institutions if that resistless engine of control, forged by the development of the Speaker's authority and by the creation of the mandatory powers of the Committee on Rules, is made part of the apparatus of executive authority. So far as the constitution of the House of Representatives is concerned, party organization has very little left to do in completing the means of administrative union between the executive department and the legislative branch.

The uniform experience of other countries has shown that when the executive power has been directly connected with the legislative branch, the tendency is not towards an increasing subordination of the legislative branch, but is just the other way — the legislature is apt to annex the functions of the executive department. The invigoration of legislative control by direct association with executive authority is the ground upon which some of our wisest statesmen have urged the deliberate adoption of measures to bring the administration face to face with Congress. The subject has been considered by a Senate committee of exceptional ability, whose report is so important a document that the main portion is given as an appendix to this work. The measure recommended has never developed any practical strength, as it was not appreciated by public sentiment, nor did it meet with any favor in Congress, where it encountered the latent opposition of particular interests naturally conservative of the opportunities which they now derive from representative institutions unaccompanied by responsible government.

The development of executive authority, as an agency of popular control over the government, may, however, transform political conditions in a way that will promote a direct administrative union between the executive and legislative branches. [Such an association between the presidential office and the House of Representatives, as must sooner or later ensue from their coöperation in suppressing the oligarchical power of the Senate, will have the result of making the House the real base of administration]— not, as in the early days of the republic, by a transient location of support, but by firm establishment, fortified by party interests, and garrisoned by the activities of practical politics.

The relations of particular interests to the general control, which then will have been established, will be such that the same inclinations which now conspire to make the House membership deferential to the senatorial oligarchy, will then tend to favor the most extensive contact possible between the House and the administration. Members now run after senators because senators have arbitrary powers of control over offices, imposts, and appropriations; when the administration obtains control of the situation, particular demands will be no less avid, but they must then operate under new conditions. It is not likely that the mass of the members will be satisfied to allow privileges of effective access to the government to be monopolized by committee chairmen, and they will find that their best opportunity, under the circumstances, will be obtained by embodying the administration directly in the House, where it will be open to direct negotiation and engagements. The ultimate type of democratic government will be reached by a natural development, promoted by the political opportunism which affords the only safe process, as it always keeps in touch with practical expediency.

Much more extensive in character and radical in nature are the changes which are likely to take place in the executive department under such conditions. The presidency now combines two distinct functions — one ceremonial; the other practical — which advancing civilization makes

incongruous, so that, as history shows, they tend
to severance. The President is the head of the
nation, the chief magistrate, the common father
of the people, to whom they write when in trouble
or deeply moved, to whom they feel they have
a right of personal access as primitive in its
simplicity as if the office were still a tribal
chieftainship; but he is also the premier of the
administration, a busy man of affairs, with so
many things to attend to that there do not seem
to be hours enough in the day for them all. The
attempt to compass these two functions is a killing
task, fraught with great perils to the individual
incumbent and to the public welfare. With the
establishment of a direct parliamentary basis for
the government, the actual management of affairs
will naturally tend to pass into the hands of groups
of statesmen trained to their work by gradations
of public service, their fitness attested by success in coping with their responsibilities under
the direct and continuous scrutiny and criticism of
Congress. The presidency will tend to assume
an honorary and a ceremonial character, and will
find therein its most satisfactory conditions of
dignity and usefulness.

This ultimate type of government, while it will
have a parliamentary forum and will follow parliamentary usages in its ordinary mode of expression,
will not be parliamentary in its nature. The limitations of the constitution, and the direction taken

by constitutional development, provide an exclusively executive structure for the administration, and it will be independent of parliamentary vicissitudes. The government will represent the will of the nation, as expressed at the presidential election. Congress will have no power to suppress national volition, but it will possess the independent, but no less important, function of serving as the agency of the moral inhibitions which should attend the exercise of the will, insuring due consideration of all interests, and circumspection of procedure. Congress will retain the power to inhibit altogether any determination of the government requiring legislative assent, but will have no power to prevent the government from shaping its proposals, defining exactly its position, and confronting the opposition with an explicit responsibility for which it must answer to the people. Having reached such a position, the administration of the government will have nothing to ask of party but the cultivation of public sentiment and the propagation of opinion. Party organization will therefore tend to revert to more simple structure and to become dependent upon spontaneous effort, while its present violence will disappear. Something like the ease and placidity in such matters, which now obtain under democratic government in Switzerland, may ensue. The same influences will cause claims of public employment, based on partisan service, to decline in importance, and the ordinary tests of competency, such as exist in the business world, will prevail in the public service also. The empirical influences which now pervade the sphere of government will also decline, and the management of public affairs will take on a more scientific character. At present, intellectual authority has no means of proper contact with legislation. Expert advice is regarded by the people with a distrust not unreasonable in view of the way in which authorities differ, and of the extent to which charlatanry assumes the air of wisdom. But trusted leadership may resort to any consultation that it finds advantageous, and thus the resources of special ability and information may be brought directly to bear upon the elucidation of any question of public policy.

Such a system of government would preserve everything of value in the parliamentary system of government, while avoiding its defects. There is an inherent weakness in the parliamentary type of government, suggesting the possibility that in the end it may turn out to have been after all a transitory phase of political development. Already signs multiply that parliamentary institutions are a melancholy failure on the continent of Europe; and in England, where the type was formed, they seem to be sustained by the force of traditions of behavior which are gradually weakening. Perhaps the most remarkable of the passages in "The Present Discontents," which surprise one by their miraculous prescience, is that in which Burke called attention to the fundamental requirement for the successful operation of the parliamentary system. He said : "The popular election of magistrates, and popular disposition of rewards and honors, is one of the first advantages of a free state. Without it, or something equivalent to it, perhaps the people cannot long enjoy the substance of freedom ; certainly none of the vivifying energy of good government. The frame of our commonwealth did not admit of such an actual election ; but it provided as well and (while the spirit of the constitution is preserved) better for all the effects of it than by the method of suffrage in any democratic state whatever."

What Burke prophesied was indeed accomplished to the letter, as Bagehot has shown in his commentary on the English constitution. The development of the cabinet system enabled the English people to elect their government, through the agency of Parliament as an electoral college, with the peculiar excellence that the college continued to preside over its work, and to test its worth, with power to undo it and refer the matter to the constituencies for a fresh declaration of public opinion. But the parliamentary type of government was the product of aristocratic control, and, with the increase of democratic forces, its adjustments are being disturbed, and processes of change are perceptible that may impair its efficiency. The conditions, which make parliamentary government a system of national choice, will have been destroyed if the constitution of the government becomes a composition of the forces of parliamentary factions, in which case the possibility is conceivable of ministries as poorly embodying the national will, and as unstable in their power, as those which flit across the stage of public affairs in France. It is to be hoped that the noble traditions of duty and responsibility which have been created in English public life will be a sufficient protection against degradation, and will safeguard every change ; but England has yet to make terms with democracy, while every advance which America achieves in the art of government is firmly based upon democratic foundations. Certainly, when the President shall have been converted into a Grand Elector, whose function is to constitute the government, every excellence which Bagehot claimed for the parliamentary system will have been gained for the presidential type of government, and both as the archetype of national unity, and as a practical institution of government, it will comprehend every element of majesty and strength.[1] Such a circumstance as that the actual

---

[1] This forecast of the ultimate type of American government, based upon direct inference from the actual tendencies of our politics, agrees with the conclusions reached by Mr. Herbert Spencer, upon philosophic grounds, as to the final outcome of political evolution. Mr. Spencer says, " Concerning the ultimate executive

constitution of the government will by no means
be confined to parliamentary circles, may eventually be counted as a special advantage. There
is no natural conjunction between parliamentary
talent and administrative ability, and it enlarges
the resources of government to have the ability of
the nation to choose from in forming an administration, free from any conditions of merely parliamentary distinction.

[But this implies that democratic progress will
omit a stage of political development, the most
brilliant that has yet illumined the history of the
human race. The course of political evolution is
marked by lustrous periods, when the expanding
energies of nations for a time achieve a type of
government exactly suited to the national life
and character.] Such a period is that of the era
of parliamentary government in England, the
splendid traditions of which cast a reflected light
upon our own national legislature, although the
only time when it shone by any light of its own,
or gave any souvenirs to popular tradition, was
during the age of Clay, Webster, and Calhoun.
That period is as near an approach to a brilliant
parliamentary era as the course of our political
development is ever likely to permit to us. All

agency, it appears to be an unavoidable inference that it must become in some way or other elective; . . . and that the functions
to be discharged by its occupant will become more and more auto-
matic." Political Institutions, section 578.

grand expressions of national character, whether in literature, art, or politics, are orchestral in their quality, every note of the national genius contributing to the result. To produce the Elizabethan drama required an epoch when a people, intelligent but unlearned, brave and free, yet reverential of authority, possessing a national consciousness vividly awake and throbbing from extraordinary excitements of world-wide battle and thrilling adventure, demanded satisfaction for their intellectual cravings in a noble form that they could see and hear. The fame which has attended the working of parliamentary institutions in England requires a theatre venerable in structure, august in renown, unique in political eminence, and surrounded by social esteem, so that the actors command both celebrity and appreciation. No such concurrence of favoring circumstances is possible under the conditions which, in this country, distribute public attention and detach political interests from the general interests of society. But it does not follow that we shall be losers thereby ; for the aim of democracy is not to develop a social order with which the duties and responsibilities of government may be safely deposited : its ideal is the creation of a perfect medium for all the activities of the social organism. All leadership is naturally aristocratic, and to aristocracy, and not to the mass, are due the gains of humanity ; but the democratic type of government will develop a natural aristocracy, authenticated solely by merit, and free from all the losses and offsets which are entailed by special provision for the maintenance of an aristocratic class. There will be great public administrators, just as there are now great engineers, great inventors, great manufacturers, great merchants, great captains of industry. The political career will select appropriate talent, but it will be more unobtrusive, less engaging of public notice, more subordinate and accessory in its functions. By so much as the activities of politics are perfected in their adaptation to the general needs of the social organism the less they will intrude upon the public consciousness. Nothing is more unscientific than the current notion that to have a good government it will be necessary to educate every citizen into being a good politician. To expect that political development should contravene the universal law of the specialization of functions as the concomitant of progressive development, is a singular idea. The perfection of the type implies that the spontaneous operation of social instincts will adequately sustain political activities, as it does all other activities of the social organism, by the unforced play of individual tastes and inclinations. People who do not have a taste for politics need not reproach themselves for their aversion : they may have a higher vocation ; which, as for women, is certainly the case.

The resultant economies of social force may be

grandly utilized, for this perfection of the type may be attended by an outburst of national genius of surpassing brilliancy. The reproach is made to America that it has a borrowed civilization, and that with all its material gains it has made no real contributions to culture. This varies the old complaint against democracy, which was that, although it produced an expansion of the intellectual energies of the people, with splendid results in art and literature, it was incompatible with social order, and was sure to end in moral exhaustion and political degradation. In concentrating the national energies upon material improvement, — an object naturally attended by extreme solicitude for the maintenance of order, — the republic provides for the stability of its political institutions, and thus escapes the traditional peril of democracy. That the character of its civilization is acquisitive rather than creative is a distinct advantage during the period in which it is engaged in laying, deep and strong, the foundations of social order, and at the same time it may be establishing a culture whose worth will be proportionate to the thoroughness of the preparation. The greatest advances in human destiny have been the work of nations which borrowed a civilization as a starting-point for the creation of a new type under the stimulus of free institutions. Time may have been when the artists and savants of Egypt regarded with patronizing disdain the crude, adaptive civilization of Greece ; but there came an outpouring of democratic genius which supplied all the materials of culture with which the world has worked ever since.   The Renaissance, which set in motion the processes of modern civilization, was also the product of democratic forces.   From such eras humanity derives the principle of progress, without which civic organization would be only a large exhibition of instincts of social agglomeration, such as communities of ants, bees, or wasps display on a smaller scale, but in greater perfection. [If mankind is ever going to ascend to a still higher plane of psychical activity, it is at least most likely to be the result of such an expansion of social energies as only a democratic order can evoke; and if it is the mission of America to adjust to democratic conditions all that civilization has now to offer, the accomplishment of that task will provide such opportunities for the free expression of the noblest capacities of humanity as may produce an epoch of incomparable grandeur.]

Such speculations may appear fantastic, but they are no more so than would have been a forecast of the Victorian age just before its dawn, when the state of English politics was darkest. It may be admitted that there is no warrant for confidence in any abstract law of human development.   The process of evolution is a statement of order, not an index of direction, and decay and dissolution are just as conformable to it as growth and development.   Mr. Charles Francis Adams, remarking upon some of the perils through which our government has passed, observed : " Much of the favorable working of a form of government, or the opposite, may be traced to circumstances having no necessary connection with its intrinsic excellence.   The Polish constitution of 1791 was immediately overthrown by the interference of neighboring powers interested to destroy it.   The constitution of the United States has survived till now, and bids fair to last much longer.   But if we could for a moment suppose the geographical position of the two countries to have been exactly changed, looking back at the nature of the politi-cal controversies which agitated America for many years, it is at least open to question whether as marked disorders would not have been developed under the Constitution of the United States as were ever found in the worst of times in Poland." [1] All this is very true ; and it is equally true that the insular position of England provided favorable circumstances, without which the peculiar excel-lences of her political development would have been impossible of attainment.   Local circum-stances are, after all, the most influential factor in determining governmental arrangements ; but the conditions were peculiarly fortunate for the development of a new and superior type of gov-

[1] Note on p. 374, Vol. IV., of his edition of John Adams' Works.

ernment, when English institutions were planted
in the New World and began an independent career. From a humanistic point of view, it was the
transmission of the intellectual estate of the Ro-
manized world, relieved from entail to privileged
classes, and intrusted to a people whose capacity
for government had been developed by the direct
succession of their institutions from their own
race origins, and whose political habits had been
made instinctive by the continuous discipline of
their own race experience. In this aspect, American politics may be regarded as at work upon the
denouement of a drama of liberty whose acts have
included the destinies of nations. Materials for
it were provided by obliterated empires, the remains of which science is disinterring. It was
begun by Greece and systematized by Rome; revived by Italy and enlarged by Europe. Its latest
episodes have been the Renaissance, the Reforma-
tion, and the Revolution, in their various national
phases, with widely different results. The world
now waits to see how it will come out in the hands
of America. Mr. Lecky has recorded the opinion
that "the future destinies and greatness of the
English race must necessarily rest mainly with
the mighty nation which has arisen beyond the
Atlantic."[1] De Tocqueville long ago foretold that
all the European states would follow the same law
of development as ourselves, and would end in the

[1] History of England, Vol. IV., p. 113.

democratic system which shall have been established here.[1]

When existing conditions are viewed with discernment, grounds of confidence as to the future are afforded by evidences of political virtue which, after the dust of present turmoil subsides, may cause these times of struggle and anxiety to be regarded as the heroic age of America.

The generation which endured the Civil War has witnessed the rehabilitation of the prostrated section, and has seen the ascendency of the race reëstablished in the face of tremendous odds. Extinction of the bitterness of conflict is so complete that late combatants hold fraternal reunions on fields over which once they fought, and both they and their children rally around the flag at their country's call; while distinctions between victors and vanquished in eligibility to public service are effaced. This period of our national existence has also seen the development of our material resources carried to a point which confers industrial primacy, with corresponding extensions of enterprise and business organization; implying resources of probity no less ample than of intelligence and skill. And, finally, the nation has shown the world that democratic institutions and an industrial type of society are compatible with the possession, in their highest degree, of all the heroic qualities which are the peculiar claim of

[1] *Democracy in America,* Vol. II., Chap. IX., p. 190.

militancy, while combining with them a deadly precision of attack which is the expression of an abounding mechanical skill, such as only industrialism can produce. Such manifestations show that the sources of national greatness are uncorrupted, so that amid the baleful confusion of our politics patriotism may cherish the hope that a purified and ennobled republic will emerge —

" Product of deathly fire and turbulent chaos,
Forth from its spasms of fury and its poisons,
Issuing at last in perfect power and beauty."

APPENDIX

DIRECT PARTICIPATION OF THE HEADS OF EXECU-
TIVE DEPARTMENTS IN THE PROCEEDINGS OF
CONGRESS

*Extract from Senate Report, No. 837, 46th Congress, 3d Session,
February 4, 1881*

THE power of both houses of Congress, either sepa-
rately or jointly, to admit persons not members to their
floors, with the privilege of addressing them, cannot be
questioned. " Each House may determine the Rules of
its Proceedings," is the provision of the Constitution.
Under this power each house admits a chaplain to open
the proceedings with. prayer. Under this power the
House of Representatives constantly admits contestants
to argue their title to membership, and sometimes admits
counsel to argue in the same behalf. No one would doubt
the power of the Senate to extend the same privilege to
a claimant, or his advisers.

By the act of 1817, it is prescribed that " every Territory shall have the right to send a Delegate to the House
of Representatives of the United States, to serve during
each Congress, who shall be elected by the voters in the
Territory qualified to elect members of the legislative
assembly thereof. . . . Every such Delegate shall have
a seat in the House of Representatives, with the right of

debating, but not of voting." And under this authority the Delegates of the eight Territories sit to-day in the House of Representatives, and participate in its debates. A precedent directly in point has stood unchallenged since the first year of the organization of the government. The act of 1789, organizing the Treasury Department, provided that "the Secretary of the Treasury shall, from time to time, digest and prepare plans for the improvement and management of the revenue and for the support of the public credit . . . shall make report and give information to either branch of the legislature, *in person* or *in writing*, as may be required, respecting all matters referred to him by the Senate or House of Representatives, or which shall appertain to his office."

When Hamilton made his great report on the public credit in 1790 he was, on motion, after discussion, required to make it in writing, because the details were so numerous that, delivered orally, they would not remain in the memory of his hearers; but the power and the propriety of requiring the personal presence of the Secretary were not then called in question, nor have they been questioned at any time since. This bill only permits and enjoins that to be done by all the Secretaries at convenient times which the law of 1789 required and permitted to be done at any time by the Secretary of the Treasury.

Your committee thinks it too plain for argument that Congress may enjoin upon the heads of departments the duty of giving information in the manner required by this bill. The constitutional provisions in relation to the executive departments are very simple. The President "may require the Opinion in writing of the Principal

Officer in each of the executive Departments upon any Subject relating to the Duties of their respective Offices ; " and " Congress may by Law vest the Appointment of such inferior Officers as they think proper in the President alone, in the Courts of Law, or in the Heads of Departments." These are all the provisions of the Constitution on this subject. Congress may, by inevitable implication, prescribe other duties and define other powers. Every act organizing every department has prescribed the duties of the principal officers, and has required the head of every department to report directly to Congress in reference to the discharge of the duties thus imposed upon his office.

If by a line of precedents since the organization of the government Congress has established its power to require the heads of departments to report to it directly, and also its power to admit persons to the floor of either house to address it, the argument would seem to be perfect that Congress may require the report to be made or the information to be given by the heads of departments on the floor of the houses, publicly and orally. The provision of the Constitution, that " no Person holding any Office under the United States shall be a Member of either House during his Continuance in Office," is in no wise violated. The head of a department, reporting in person and orally, or participating in debate, becomes no more a member of either House than does the chaplain, or the contestant or his counsel, or the Delegate. He has no official term ; he is neither elected nor appointed to either house ; he has no participation in the power of impeachment, either in the institution or trial ; he has no privilege from arrest ; he has no power to vote.

We are dealing with no new question. In the early

2 C

history of the government the communications were made by the President to Congress orally, and in the presence of both or either of the houses. Instances are not want-ing — nay, they are numerous — where the President of the United States, accompanied by one or more of his cabinet, attended the sessions of the Senate and House of Representatives in their separate sessions and laid before them papers which had been required and infor-mation which had been asked for.

" *Wednesday, July* 22, 1789. — The Secretary of Foreign Affairs (Mr. Jefferson) attended, agreeably to order, and made the necessary explanations." — *Annals of Congress, First Congress,* volume 1, page 51.

" *Saturday, August* 22, 1789. — The Senate again en-tered on executive business. The President of the United States came into the Senate Chamber, attended by Gen-eral Knox, Secretary of War, and laid before the Senate the following statement of facts, with the questions thereto annexed, for their advice and consent." — *Annals of Con-gress, First Congress,* volume 1, page 66.

And again on the Monday following the President and General Knox were before the Senate.

" *Friday, August* 7, 1789. — The following message was received from the President of the United States, by Gen-eral Knox, the Secretary of War, who delivered therewith sundry statements and papers relating to the same." — *Proceedings of House of Representatives, Annals of Con-gress,* volume 1, page 684.

" *Monday, August* 10, 1789. — The following message was received from the President, by General Knox [Sec-retary of War], who delivered in the same, together with statement of the troops in the service of the United

States." — *Proceedings of House of Representatives, Annals of Congress*, volume 1, page 689.

Instances of this kind might be almost indefinitely multiplied, but these serve sufficiently to exhibit the practice established at an early day by those who framed the Constitution. The committee refers to the Annals of Congress, at the pages cited, for very interesting details of the proceedings of those respective days. They are too long to be copied here in full.

This bill thus being clearly within the letter of the Constitution is, in the opinion of your committee, as clearly within its spirit.

Your committee is not unmindful of the maxim that in a constitutional government the great powers are divided into legislative, executive, and judicial, and that they should be conferred upon distinct departments. These departments should be defined and maintained, and it is a sufficiently accurate expression to say that they should be independent of each other. But this independence in no just or practical sense means an entire separation, either in their organization or their functions — isolation, either in the scope or the exercise of their powers. Such independence or isolation would produce either conflict or paralysis, either inevitable collision or inaction, and either the one or the other would be in derogation of the efficiency of the government. Such independence of coequal and coördinate departments has never existed in any civilized government, and never can exist.

.   .   .   .   .   .

If there is anything perfectly plain in the Constitution and organization of the Government of the United

States, it is that the great departments were not intended
to be independent and isolated in the strict meaning of
these terms; but that, although having a separate existence, they were to coöperate each with the other, as the
different members of the human body must coöperate
with each other in order to form the figure and perform
the duties of a perfect man.

The connection of the executive and the legislative
departments of the government illustrates this position
most strongly. Congress can pass no law without the
assent of the President. The President can establish no
office without the consent of Congress. Congress must
provide him with the means of executing the great trusts
confided to him. He must communicate to Congress
the information and make the suggestions of legislation
which his experience in administration teaches to be desirable. And so uniformly has Congress acted upon this
interdependence of the executive and the legislative departments, that, as has been before said, Congress requires the chief officers of every executive department to
report to it directly as to the performance of the duties
and the execution of the powers confided to it.

The result has been that the executive department,
comprising in this term the President and the chief
officers, has exercised necessarily and properly great influence on the legislation of Congress.

The principles enacted into laws are comparatively few
and simple. The machinery by which these few and
simple principles can be carried into actual administration is complex, and can be perfected by experience
only. The duties of administration necessarily compel
the heads of departments to become familiar, not only

with the best policy, but with the best methods of carrying policies into actual execution, and the consequence is that members of Congress, much less familiar, do in fact seek, either individually or through committees, the counsel and advice of these officers, and are, to a very great extent, influenced by them.

The influence is exerted by means of the annual reports, of private consultations, and of special reports made in answer to special resolutions of inquiry by either house, and the question really submitted to the consideration of Congress by this bill is, whether these means of communication will not be greatly improved by consultation between the members of Congress and these officers, face to face, on the floor of the houses. Your committee cannot doubt that the result would be most beneficial, and that no elaboration of reasons is necessary to bring Senators to the same conclusion.

It has been objected that the effect of this introduction of the heads of departments upon the floor would be largely to increase the influence of the executive on legislation. Your committee does not share this apprehension. The information given to Congress would doubtless be more pertinent and exact; the recommendations would, perhaps, be presented with greater effect, but on the other hand, the members of Congress would also be put on the alert to see that the influence is in proportion only to the value of the information and the suggestions; and the public would be enabled to determine whether the influence is exerted by persuasion or by argument. No one who has occupied a seat on the floor of either house, no one of those who, year after year, so industriously and faithfully and correctly report the proceedings of the houses, no frequenter of the lobby or the gallery, can have failed to discern the influence exerted upon legislation by the visits of the heads of departments to the floors of Congress, and the visits of the members of Congress to the offices in the departments. It is not necessary to say that the influence is dishonest or corrupt, but it is illegitimate; it is exercised in secret by means that are not public — by means which an honest public opinion cannot accurately discover, and over which it can therefore exercise no just control. The open information and argument provided by the bill may not supplant these secret methods, but they will enable a discriminating public judgment to determine whether they are sufficient to exercise the influence which is actually exerted, and thus disarm them.

It has been objected that the introduction of the heads of departments on the floor would impair the influence of the executive power; that it would bring them and Congress in closer relations and thus lessen their dependence on the President, and, to that extent, deprive him of his constitutional power and relieve him of his constitutional responsibility. It would be enough to say, in answer to this objection, that no power exists anywhere to diminish the duties or powers or responsibilities imposed by the Constitution upon the President. The committee ventures again to repeat that the effect of the bill does not seek to — and will not — aggrandize or impair the executive power as defined in the Constitution and vested in the President.

The President, and the President alone, is the constitutional executive; he and he alone is the coördinate executive branch of the government; he and he alone is the "Commander-in-Chief of the Army and Navy of the United States, and of the militia of the several States when called into the actual service of the United States." He and he alone " shall have power to grant reprieves and pardons for offences against the United States ; " to make treaties with the advice and consent of the Senate, provided two-thirds of the Senators present concur ; to nominate and by and with the advice and consent of the Senate to appoint embassadors and other public ministers and consuls, judges of the Supreme Court, and all other officers of the United States whose appointments are not otherwise provided for ; " to give to Congress information as to the state of the Union ; " on extraordinary occasions to convene and adjourn Congress ; " " to receive embassadors and other public ministers ; to take care that the laws be faithfully executed ; to commission all the officers of the United States ; " and to exercise the veto power. These are the functions of the executive power which is vested in the President by the Constitution. They can be performed neither in whole nor in part by another ; neither the President nor the Congress nor both can delegate them or abridge them. Both the President and the Congress are bound to maintain and protect them. The departments and their principal officers are in no sense sharers of this power. They are the creatures of the laws of Congress, exercising only such powers and performing only such duties as those laws prescribe.

The First Congress, after long debate, decided that the President should have the power of appointment and removal, unimpaired, except, as in all other cases, by impeachment ; and that the Secretaries should perform all the duties imposed upon them by law and by the constitutional power of the President to call for written opinions. The Secretaries were made heads of departments; they were charged by law with certain duties, and invested by law with certain powers to be used by them in the administration confided to them by the laws. They were in no sense ministers of the President, his hand, his arm, his irresponsible agent, in the execution of his will. There was no relation analogous to that of master and servant or principal and agent. The President cannot give them dispensation in the performance of duty, or relieve them from the penalty of non-performance. He cannot be impeached for their delinquency; he cannot be made to answer before any tribunal for their inefficiency or malversation in office; public opinion does not hold him to stricter responsibility for their official conduct than that of any officer. They are the creatures of law and bound to do the bidding of the law.

This bill will not change their legal relations, either to the President or to the Congress. It will not make their tenure of office in any wise dependent on the favor of Congressional majorities or on adverse votes of either or both of the houses. They cannot assume undue leadership in Congress, because success will not prolong, as defeat will not terminate, their tenure of office. They may be removed by the President at any moment, notwithstanding their success. They may be maintained in office by him during his whole term, notwithstanding their defeat. At the end of his term they will almost certainly leave office and probably soon have place in Congress. Their independence of Congress will prevent their succumbing to its will, and will rouse the natural jealousy of

Congress to resist their power becoming too great. The concurrence of opinion between the President and Congress is not essential, perhaps is not possible. Neither will be broken down by the assertion of the will of the other in its own department, because both will soon be called to judgment by the people, and the people will correct any antagonism which threatens the effective working of the government.

This system will require the selection of the strongest men to be heads of departments, and will require them to be well equipped with the knowledge of their offices. It will also require the strongest men to be the leaders of Congress and participate in debate. It will bring these strong men in contact, perhaps into conflict, to advance the public weal, and thus stimulate their abilities and their efforts, and will thus assuredly result to the good of the country.

If it should appear by actual experience that the heads of departments in fact have not time to perform the additional duty imposed on them by this bill, the force in their offices should be increased, or the duties devolving on them personally should be diminished. An under-secretary should be appointed to whom could be confided that routine of administration which requires only order and accuracy. The principal officers could then confine their attention to those duties which require wise discretion and intellectual activity. Thus they would have abundance of time for their duties under this bill. Indeed, your committee believes that the public interest would be subserved if the Secretaries were relieved of the harassing cares of distributing clerkships and closely supervising the mere machinery of the departments. Your committee believes that the adoption of this bill and the effective execution of its provisions will be the first step towards a sound civil-service reform, which will secure a larger wisdom in the adoption of policies, and a better system in their execution.

GEO. H. PENDLETON.
W. B. ALLISON.
D. W. VOORHEES.
J. G. BLAINE.
M. C. BUTLER.
JOHN J. INGALLS.
O. H. PLATT.
J. T. FARLEY.

———

Story on the Constitution, section 869 *et seq.* : —

The heads of the departments are, in fact, thus precluded from proposing or vindicating their own measures in the face of the nation in the course of debate, and are compelled to submit them to other men who are either imperfectly acquainted with the measures or are indifferent to their success or failure. Thus that open and public responsibility for measures which properly belongs to the executive in all governments, and especially in a republican government, as its greatest security and strength, is completely done away. The Executive is compelled to resort to secret and unseen influences, to private interviews, and private arrangements to accomplish its own appropriate purposes, instead of proposing and sustaining its own duties and measures by a bold and manly appeal to the nation in the face of its representatives. One consequence of this state of things is, that there

never can be traced home to the Executive any responsibility for the measures which are planned and carried at
its suggestion. Another consequence will be (if it has
not yet been) that measures will be adopted or defeated
by private intrigues, political combinations, irresponsible
recommendations, and all the blandishments of office, and
all the deadening weight of silent patronage. The Executive will never be compelled to avow or support any
opinions. His ministers may conceal or evade any expression of their opinions. He will seem to follow, when,
in fact, he directs the opinions of Congress. He will assume the air of a dependent, when, in fact, his spirit and
his wishes pervade the whole system of legislation. If
corruption ever eats its way silently into the vitals of this
republic it will be because the people are unable to bring
responsibility home to the Executive through his chosen
ministers. They will be betrayed when their suspicions
are most lulled by the Executive under the disguise of an
obedience to the will of Congress. If it would not have
been safe to trust the heads of departments, as representatives, to the choice of the people as their constituents,
it would have been at least some gain to have allowed
them seats, like territorial delegates in the House of
Representatives, where they might freely debate without
a title to vote.

In such an event their influence, whatever it would
be, would be seen and felt and understood, and on that
account would have involved little danger and more
searching jealousy and opposition; whereas it is now
secret and silent, and from that very cause may become
overwhelming. One other reason in favor of such a right
is that it would compel the Executive to make appoint-

ments for the high departments of government, not from personal or party favorites, but from statesmen of high public character, talent, experience, and elevated services ; from statesmen who had earned public favor and could command public confidence. At present gross incapacity may be concealed under official forms, and ignorance silently escape by shifting the labors upon more intelligent subordinates in office. The nation would be, on the other plan, better served, and the Executive sustained by more masculine eloquence as well as more liberal learning. . . . There can be no danger that a free people will not be sufficiently wakeful over their rulers and their acts and opinions when they are known and avowed, or that they will not find representatives in Congress ready to oppose improper measures or sound the alarm upon arbitrary encroachments. The real danger is when the influence of the rulers is at work in secret and assumes no definite shape ; when it guides with silent and irresistible sway, and yet covers itself under the forms of popular opinion or independent legislation ; when it does nothing, yet accomplishes everything.

INDEX

MUNICIPAL PROBLEMS.

BY

FRANK J. GOODNOW, LL.D.,

*Professor of Administrative Law, Columbia University
in the City of New York.*

Cloth. 16mo. $1.50, net.

COMMENTS.

"We question if any other book before has achieved quite the important service to what may be termed theoretic municipalism. . . . One that all those interested in municipal matters should read. . . . Moderate in tone, sound in argument, and impartial in its conclusions, it is a work that deserves to carry weight."— *London Liberal.*

"Here is without doubt one of the most trenchant and scholarly contributions to political science of recent writing, remarkable for analytical power and lucidity of statement."— *Chicago Evening Post.*

THE MACMILLAN COMPANY,
66 FIFTH AVENUE, NEW YORK.

MUNICIPAL HOME RULE.

A Study in Administration.

BY

FRANK J. GOODNOW, LL.D.,

Professor of Administrative Law, Columbia University
in the City of New York.

Cloth. 16mo. $1.50, net.

COMMENTS.

"Indeed, we doubt if any author has achieved such eminent success in the solution of the difficult problems of city government as the author of the present work." — *Times-Union*, Albany, N.Y.

"A scholarly, thoughtful, and independent criticism of municipal experiences and the plans now urged to better municipal conditions. . . . The volume is an exceptionally valuable one to close students of municipal affairs." — *Outlook*.

"Every one interested in municipal reform, and the possibility of securing honest and effective government for American cities, ought by all means to give studious attention to Professor Goodnow's philosophical presentation of the subject." — *Boston Beacon*.

"It is one of the finest studies in administration that has ever been offered to political students." — *Inter-Ocean*

THE MACMILLAN COMPANY,

66 FIFTH AVENUE, NEW YORK.

AN OUTLINE FOR THE STUDY

OF

CITY GOVERNMENT.

BY

DELOS H. WILCOX, Ph.D.,

of Columbia University.

12mo. Cloth. $1.50, net.

The author holds that the City problem is the key to the immediate future of social progress in this country, and he offers for the first time a systematic outline for the study of the whole municipal field, indicating the chief problems in order, with facts and illustrations sufficient as a basis for intelligent interest and a guide to the sources of further information. He discusses in turn problems of function, of control, and of organization, and his book will be very useful, not only to students in colleges and secondary schools, but even more to any class of citizens who are interested in the betterment of municipal conditions through the development of intelligence and the sense of civic responsibility.

THE MACMILLAN COMPANY,

66 FIFTH AVENUE, NEW YORK.

www.ingramcontent.com/pod-product-compliance
Lightning Source LLC
Chambersburg PA
CBHW032308280326
41932CB00009B/744